UNIVERSITY RELIGION SERIES

UNIVERSITY RELIGION SERIES

Theology for the Layman

The Christian Virtues
CHARLES E. SHEEDY, C.S.C.

Evidence for Our Faith
JOSEPH H. CAVANAUGH, C.S.C.

God and the World of Man
THEODORE M. HESBURGH, C.S.C.

Redemptive Incarnation
ALBERT L. SCHLITZER, C.S.C.

GOD AND THE WORLD OF MAN

GOD AND THE
WORLD OF MAN

by *Theodore M. Hesburgh, C.S.C., S.T.D.*

President, University of Notre Dame

UNIVERSITY OF NOTRE DAME PRESS

Notre Dame, Indiana

Imprimi Potest: Theodore J. Mehling, C.S.C., Provincial

Nihil Obstat: William H. Robinson, C.S.C., Censor Deputatus
Thomas O. Barrosse, C.S.C., Censor Deputatus

Imprimatur: ✠ Leo A. Pursley, D.D.,
Bishop of Fort Wayne — South Bend

April 3, 1961

———————

Second Edition 1960
Second Printing 1962
Library of Congress Catalog Card Number 60-8647

Preface to the Second Edition

THERE HAVE BEEN MANY scientific and some theological developments regarding the origin of the world and of man since this book was written ten years ago. In order to present these most recent developments to college and university students, I have asked one of our theology professors at Notre Dame, Father John Dunne, C.S.C., S.T.D., to revise completely Section III of Chapter V. This he has done, and I would like to thank him, both personally and on behalf of all the students who will have the opportunity to study his fascinating answers to questions which continue to excite both our scientific and theological curiosity.

Theodore M. Hesburgh, C.S.C.
President
University of Notre Dame

February 20, 1960

Preface to the First Edition

THIS BOOK HAS GROWN OUT of many classes in Dogma at the University of Notre Dame. Its object, then, coincides with the purpose of those classes: to impart a solid knowledge of some basic theological truths. It is hoped that this knowledge will not be sterile, but will become the groundwork of Christian wisdom in the lives of young Americans on the college level, who can find in these basic truths an underlying pattern of Christian thinking and Christian living.

Whatever merit may be in this book is due to the age-old efforts of many famous theologians whose thoughts and names reoccur in the pages that follow. Whatever is practical in the attempt of this book to bring the ancient wisdom of Theology to bear upon some of the problems of this modern day may be attributed to many classes of University students who raised the proper questions and impelled the writer to rephrase his answers until they attained some measure of clarity and cogency.

We might mention in passing that while the book is theological in intent, our selection of topics has always been weighted in favor of the laity who today have become increasingly mindful of their need for a deeper knowledge of the truths of Theology in order to participate more intelligently in the great lay movements of liturgical revival and Catholic Action that characterize our age.

It would not be Christian on my part to introduce this book without mention of the constant encouragement and help of many of my fellow Holy Cross priests, especially Fathers O'Toole, Kenna, and Robinson who read the text, and Fathers Simonitsch, Sheedy and Lochner of the Religion Department whose generous collaboration was of immeasurable assistance. To these and many others I am most grateful.

The following pages are humbly dedicated to the Gracious Lady whose name our University is proud to bear: Notre Dame. May she guide our efforts to the glory and service of Her Son.

THEODORE M. HESBURGH, C.S.C.

Contents

xi

xii   *Contents*   35 – 39

89(#1) –
104

CHAPTER I

Introduction

THE FIRST ESSENTIAL THING in beginning is to have some place to go. And because this book represents a stage in the systematic study of theology, we must first see where we are going in relation to where we have already gone. Also, because the course in Dogma is one of many courses in the university, we must see the relation of this course to all others you are studying. Education is not a series of patches sewed onto a crazy quilt, but an ordered assembling of many tight fitting parts.

This then is our first step:

1. The relationship of Theology to the other courses of the University.

2. The inner relationship of the various branches of Theology.

3. The Content and Structure of Dogmatic Theology.

You will notice that we start off with the broadest field and narrow it down. In this way we know exactly where we stand: how this course is related to everything else we are studying, how it is related to everything else we have studied thus far in other religion courses, and what exactly we aim to study this semester.

I. THE RELATIONSHIP OF THEOLOGY TO THE OTHER COURSES OF THE UNIVERSITY

The shortest cut to this relationship is to say that Catholic Dogma is the heart of theology. Dogma is related to the other courses in exactly the same way that theology is related to the other branches of knowledge studied here. That relationship has been very clearly outlined in a book which many of you have read, Cardinal Newman's "Idea of a University."

Newman shows that if you were to classify all the branches of knowledge which a university professes to teach, you would have to place theology at the peak of the pyramid. The basic reason is that all the other sciences, excepting philosophy, treat only of created things. Moreover, all the other sciences use only human means of knowledge. But theology treats first and foremost of God, and goes beyond the sources of human knowledge, since it uses knowledge given to man by God through divine revelation.

These then are the two great claims of theology to justify its top position among all the branches of knowledge taught at the university: 1) The object of theology is the highest of all seeking, God Himself. 2) The means of acquiring this knowledge of God are given us by God Himself too, through His revelation. These two points have been well explained by a modern writer, Walter Farrell, o.p., in his *Companion to the Summa* (a modern version of the greatest theological book of all time, the *Summa Theologica* of St. Thomas Aquinas). To give a brief summary:

A. Theology Treats of God

Theology is wisdom, old with the agelessness of eternity; but young with the youth of the eternal beginning. The wise man to be consulted for the answers of the new house that is going up is the architect, not the bricklayer; if he (the architect) does not know the reasons for things, there are not any. He may be stupid in other lines, but in this one, because he is the master of the *ultimate* purposes of the building, he is wise; in any line, *this knowledge of ultimate purposes brings wisdom.* When the knowledge is of the last of all purposes, it brings that wisdom that needs no qualification; by it a man is simply wise. This will be the man who knows the answers that really matter; these are the answers for which the theologians exist . . . for a theologian treats of nothing except in relation to the first being and the last end. He is in the intellectual order what the saint is in the practical order: a man wholly engaged with God. The saint knows the important answers by the quick intuition that has its deep roots in love; the theologian, by the reasoned argument that has its roots deep in study.[1]

---

1. Farrell, *Companion to the Summa*, Vol. I, p. 17, Sheed & Ward, New York, 1941.

B. Theology Has a Super-Human Source of Knowledge: God's Revelation

To be quite frank, there are many men who will never arrive at wisdom under their own power if they live to be a hundred, and have absolutely nothing to do but think. To be equally frank, it must be admitted that the wisest of men are going to make mistakes. . . . Man, even in those things that are not strictly above his human powers, must have help. He can assert his absolute independence only at the cost of compromising his knowledge of reality, and ultimately, at the cost of failure in the living of human life. He must accept truth from the source of truth; and be thankful that the truth is given to him (by God). There is nothing so completely useless as the illusion that we are self-sufficient, for there is nothing so completely false . . . we must have wisdom from the beginning of life. It cannot be our own; nor is it sufficient if it is some other human being's. *It must be divine, for only God is wise from the beginning.* To begin life with the wisdom lent us by divinity, and end it by possessing that wisdom, to meet the charges at each station of life with divinely-minted coin; to see the road that stretches before us through the far-seeing eyes of God—this is not an insult to human nature, it is an ennoblement of it.

In this atmosphere of nobility theology draws its first breath of life, for the deposit of divinely-revealed truth constitutes the life principle of all theological science. If philosophy, as the apex of natural intellectual effort has deserved the name of human wisdom, then theology is rightly called divine wisdom. All its varied fabric is given solid substance by the thread of divinity that is woven into it; if we unravel that complex fabric, that single thread will always lead back to God, the source of truth and the goal of it. . . . Drawing its life-blood from the source of all order, theology is vibrant with such significances as man would not have dared dream, with divine significance for creatures who hardly dare to face human life let alone dream of living divine life.[2]

Theology, then, treating of God, and using God's revelation to men as the deepest source of its knowledge, has the first place among all the varied branches of knowledge at a university. A man studies to become learned or wise, and theology is the ultimate wisdom, because it studies Wisdom Himself, and His own answers to the basic questions of life.

Newman lamented the fact that so many universities profess to teach all knowledge, and yet neglect theology. The following quo-

2. Farrell, *Ibid.*, pp. 12–14.

tations are two of the most important statements of Newman regarding the position of theology in relation to university education:

Is it, then, logically consistent in a seat of learning to call itself a University, and to exclude Theology from the number of its studies? And again, is it wonderful that Catholics, even in the view of reason, putting aside faith or religious duty, should be dissatisfied with existing institutions, which profess to be Universities, and refuse to teach Theology; and that they should in consequence desire to possess seats of learning, which are not only more Christian, but more philosophical in their construction, and larger and deeper in their province?

But this, of course, is to assume that Theology *is* a science, and an important one: so I will throw my argument into a more exact form. I say, then, that if a University be, from the nature of the case, a place of instruction, where universal knowledge is professed, and if in a certain University, so called, the subject of Religion is excluded, one of two conclusions is inevitable,—either, on the one hand, that the province of Religion is very barren of real knowledge, or, on the other hand, that in such a University one special and important branch of knowledge is omitted. I say, the advocate of such an institution must say *this,* or he must say *that;* he must own, either that little or nothing is known about the Supreme Being, or that his seat of learning calls itself what it is not.[3]

If then, in an Institution which professes all knowledge, nothing is professed, nothing is taught about the Supreme Being, it is fair to infer that every individual in the number of those who advocate the Institution, supposing him consistent, distinctly holds that nothing is known for certain about the Supreme Being; nothing such, as to have any claim to be regarded as a material addition to the stock of general knowledge existing in the world. If on the other hand it turns out that something considerable *is* known about the Supreme Being, whether from Reason or Revelation, then the Institution in question professes every science, and yet leaves out the foremost of them. In a word, strong as may appear the assertion, I do not see how I can avoid making it, and bear with me, Gentlemen, while I do, viz., such an Institution cannot be what it professes, if there be a God. I do not wish to declaim; but, by the very force of the terms, it is very plain, that a Divine Being and a University so circumstanced cannot co-exist.[4]

The situation has not changed much in the world today where much attention is paid to the physical sciences like physics, chemis-

3. Newman, *The Idea of a University,* p. 21, Longmans, Green & Co., New York.
4. Newman, *Ibid.,* pp. 24-25.

try, biology; great favor is lavished on the social sciences, the mathematical sciences, history, languages and the like; and yet not a word is mentioned, not a class scheduled in most secular universities regarding theology. Much also is made of philosophy, and rightly, for it is the highest of sciences in the order of human wisdom. Philosophy is the key to human wisdom, for it studies the ultimate answers to all things as far as human reason can probe. But in the right order of things, philosophy too is subordinated to theology as human wisdom is subordinated to divine wisdom, and man to God.

All of this has a very practical conclusion in the life of every university student. He may highly value his technical courses and merely put up with his religion course, but actually, he may thus thwart his whole university training. He may leave school technically perfect, an honor student in math or physics or engineering or business, yet completely illiterate in the wisdom that really matters, that teaches to live rather than merely to make a living. He may be armed with all the immediately practical answers, yet totally unfit to answer the ultimate questions that will face him throughout his life. Without the ultimate answers one simply cannot be cultured or truly intelligent. And there are no ultimate answers except in philosophy and theology.

To sum up: Theology must not only be theoretically the apex of all university learning. The ultimate answers it sees with the eyes of God must impregnate the whole field of university teaching and learning. That is the basic difference between Catholic education and other education. In Catholic education, the various truths are united in reference to the ultimate truths of theology. Economics does not exist for itself, any more than money exists for itself. All things are seen in relation to man's last end and first beginning which is God. Man's knowledge and man's scale of values are not centered in man but in God, do not rest on human reason alone, but on human reason aided by God's revelation. Thus we can arrange this hierarchy of sciences in order of importance:

a) THEOLOGY

Divine Wisdom (Knowledge of Ultimates by Faith and Reason.) (The study of God, *theou*—of God, plus *logos*—science, based on

God's revelation, as studied by human reason, giving man the last word on the basic questions of life.)

b) PHILOSOPHY

Human Wisdom (Knowledge of Ultimates by Reason alone.)
(The study of the ultimate answer of all things known by human reason—primarily the study of Being [the universal notion of all things] and of Thought [the way we know all things].)
The study of:
Metaphysics—being in general.
Logic—rules of thinking.
Epistemology—validity of human thought to attain truth, i.e., the being of things as they are.
Theodicy—being of God.
Psychology—being of soul and its powers of mind and will.
Cosmology—being of the physical universe.
Ethics—being of human acts as good or bad: morals.

c) ALL THE OTHER SOCIAL, PHYSICAL, MATHEMATICAL SCIENCES

Which fill out human wisdom by the proximate answers to immediate particular questions: things that can be seen, felt, measured, compiled. An amassing of facts in particular specialized fields, of themselves giving no ultimate answers to life or its final meaning.

This is the true hierarchy of learning in a university which professes to teach all knowledge. Without philosophy, and especially without theology, there is no true or complete human culture, no true Christian wisdom. It is possible to be a Ph.D. on the lower level of knowledge and still be unlearned and unprepared to live life and achieve its inherent purpose and meaning, because these are simply not within the competence of the sciences on the lower level. The truths on the theological level will still be important (and practical) 1,000,000 years hence.

Thus far we have seen the relationship of theology to the other courses of the university. We can conclude that theology is at the core of a Catholic education. The next step is to see the inner relationship of the various branches of theology, or in other words, how the various courses in religion are related one to another. We shall see that a deep or serious knowledge of religion involves a unified view of all its parts.

II. Relationship of the Branches of Theology to Each Other

The key to the unity of theology is Christ Our Lord. The Christian religion as we know it is Christocentric. Our deepest knowledge of it comes from Christ. A deep knowledge and living of it leads directly to Christ.

If you were to stop ten people on the street today and ask them what religion is, you would undoubtedly get many varied answers. Some would say: "Religion is what you believe." Others would say: "Religion is living right, doing good, and treating other people as you want to be treated." Still others would say: "Religion is going to Church, worshipping and serving God." There is something of truth in all of these statements, but religion considered in its totality, is not any one of these statements, but a complexus of all three of them. The Christian religion is centered in Christ, Our Way, Our Truth and Our Life. . . . Christianity, therefore, is not merely a set of truths to be learned, but a life to be lived . . . it is knowing and believing in Christ as our Truth, living His Way, worshipping Him and receiving Him as our Life.

Take the word 'religion' apart. It comes from the Latin: *religare,* meaning to bind back. Bind what back to what? Answer this question and you have the two important factors in religion: God and man. It is not merely the complexus of all things that bind man to God; ours is a redemptive religion. Man has fallen and must be bound *back* to God. And all the bonds that unite man and God in the Christian religion are centered in Christ, the one mediator between God and fallen mankind.

The problem is obvious enough. Religion was needed to reunite God and Man. A mediator was needed, and in the wisdom of God's plan he was not to have the defect common to human mediators. They are generally biased or prejudiced in favor of one or another side. God sent His only begotten Son, born of the Virgin Mary. Christ is the perfect mediator because He has divinity in common with God and humanity in common with man; He is both the son of God and the son of Mary. He perfectly united humanity to divinity in His Person. By His Redemptive work and the religion He founded to perpetuate it, He reunites God and all men. To do this He takes away the barrier of sin by His death on the Cross, and brings grace, a share in His divine life, as the vital means of uniting God and men. This is why, in the Christian world, three of the most celebrated days in the year are Christmas, the day when Christ was born, the day when men first saw the Word made flesh, and Easter, the day when He arose from the dead to bring new life and hope to a hitherto defeated mankind. The other important day is Pentecost, when He sent His Church into the world to perpetuate for all time the work of His Incarnation and Redemption . . . the promise of Christmas and Easter.

We are now in a position to show how all theology and religion for us are centered in Christ. When He came as the unique mediator between God and men, He stated his position very clearly. He said that He had come to take away the sins of the world, to bring us life, new life, and life more abundantly. But the precise way in which He binds men back to God in Himself is best expressed in these famous words of His: "I am the Truth, the Way and the Life." In outline form:

Christ—Church——Men———Religion————————Theology

Truth	Teaches	Mind	What we believe Creed	Dogma (Doctrine)
Way	Governs	Will	How we live Code	(Morals, Commandments and Christian Virtues)
Life	Sanctifies	Soul	How we worship Worship	The Mass and Sacra- ments (Liturgy)

The above outline shows how all religion and theology are centered in Christ. Christ continues His religion, His work of binding man back to God, through His Church, which He founded to do precisely what He came to do. The Church teaches Christ as our Truth, to be believed by our minds; the Church governs our wills according to the Way of Christ; the Church also sanctifies us, brings us the Christ-life of Sacraments and Prayer. Thus, Christ through His Church brings something to the whole man, soul, mind and will, bringing men completely back to God the Father in Himself, the Son. Those who possess Christ as their way, truth and life are truly sons of God, intimately reunited to the Father, in Christ and the Church, His Mystical Body.

In this pattern, theology may be defined as a study of Divine

Life, in God, in the angels, and in men. Its various parts are Dogma, the Sacraments, and Morals. You may wonder where apologetics fits into this picture. Strictly speaking, apologetics is not theology, but the vestibule of theology. Theology, as we have already seen, is based on revelation, and involves belief or faith in what God has told us about Himself and the religion He founded. But we must have a reason for believing, as St. Paul says, we must be able to give a reason for the faith that is in us. This is what apologetics does. It uses reason, human reason, philosophy, and the gospels as historical books to show that our faith is reasonable. It establishes the fact that there is a God, that He has revealed these divine mysteries, founded this church, and that thus it is reasonable for us to accept what He has told us, in other words, to have faith. Then theology steps in, and studies what God has revealed, classifies and systematizes all the data of revelation. That is why theology may be defined as the science of what is intelligible in what is believed. Theology studies what we know of these divine mysteries that we cannot fully understand.

As to the relationships between the three branches of theology that we have outlined, we can say that Dogmatic is the most fundamental. Moral theology seems more practical, but without dogmatic theology it simply would not be intelligible. There are many religious leaders today who are calling for a wiping out of dogma or creed, on the supposition that if all beliefs were scrapped, men would simply live together in peace and harmony (morals) without the differences of creed which today separate them. But religion without a creed is like a body without a skeleton, or a building without a foundation.

We live morally because we believe in very definite truths, such as the existence of a God who will reward the good and punish the wicked. We worship Christ in the Eucharist because we believe that He redeemed us on Calvary and re-enacts that sacrifice in the Mass. We are baptized because we believe that we are fallen from the Divine Life of grace and must be born again of water and the Holy Spirit, to regain that divine life and Sonship lost for us by Adam. Moreover, in the Mass we give perfect honor and glory to our Father, through Christ, with Christ and in Christ. The Son became Man to give us a pattern for our divine Sonship, and this great work of regeneration is accomplished in the unity of the Holy Spirit.

Obviously, all this would be meaningless without a belief in the Holy Trinity. We live as we do in a Christian way, we worship as we do in the Catholic Church, because of what we believe. Our dogma or creed is the foundation of our religion or Christian way of life. Take away the creed, and there is a body without a soul, left to disintegrate into many various parts.

Thus, while the subject matter of this book is primarily speculative—a study of divine truths, not of men's moral actions or forms of worship—yet it is basically practical in that it provides the broad outline of truth that underlies our way of life, without which our way of life would be meaningless. We shall emphasize throughout the work how it does touch life.

Up to this point we have seen how theology in general is related to the other courses in the university, and how the various branches of theology (or religion) are related to each other. Having settled these fundamental issues, we are now ready to analyze that particular section of theology that we are to study in this course: Christian Dogma. This is the last point in our introduction.

III. The Content and Structure of Dogmatic Theology

The word 'dogma' comes from a Greek word *dokein* meaning 'to think.' We have already seen that it is the segment of religion that pertains directly to the mind. Other words used for dogma are doctrine or creed. Therefore, Dogmatic Theology is the sum of all those theoretical truths about God and men that we believe and know by faith. These are summarized in the Apostles' Creed.

In the Prologue for his *Summa Theologica* (Book I, q. 2), St. Thomas outlines his work thus: "Because the chief aim of this sacred doctrine (of theology) is to teach the knowledge of God, not only as He is in Himself, but also as He is the beginning of all things, especially of rational creatures, and their last end, in our endeavor to expound this science we shall treat:

1) of God (Nature of God, Persons in God, Creation, etc.).
2) of man's advance towards God (moral theology mostly).
3) of Christ, who as man is our way to God."

Our order of procedure in this book is based on the same outline. The particular treatment of man's actions from a moral standpoint is presented elsewhere. Since theology is the science of God, we can outline it thus:

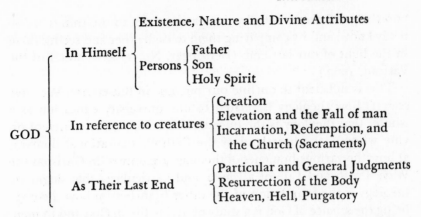

Obviously, this is covering a great deal of territory. It is particularly difficult in that it consists of the deepest mysteries of the Christian religion, things that we would never know about without the express revelation of God, and the gift of faith to accept it. The whole structure is based on God and revolves about the two most fundamental mysteries of the Christian religion: the *Trinity* and the *Incarnation*. All the creeds (the Apostles' Creed, the Nicene Creed, the Athanasian Creed) are built on this structural basis: "I believe in God, the Father Almighty . . . and in Jesus Christ, His only son, Our Lord (with this part covering the doctrine of the Incarnation built up at length), and in the Holy Spirit, etc." We shall see more of this point later when showing in reference to tradition, how the Creed developed in the early Church.

It might well be remarked here that since this is a university course, we will not be content with a mere catechetical knowledge of these mysteries. We shall use philosophy, the summit of human wisdom, to achieve a deeper and well ordered knowledge of these divine mysteries. We shall also draw practical conclusions from them to see how they are vital and fundamental to the Christian life. Much of what is treated will not be remembered, but this is not a mere memory course, but a development in thinking theologically, in the ability to see and judge the ordinary things of life in the light of the divine wisdom of theology. And while we cannot fully understand these mysteries this side of the beatific vision, the Church has declared in her official teaching that human reason illuminated by faith, when it carefully, piously and seriously seeks some knowledge of these mysteries can come to a most fruitful knowledge of them, both by comparing them to the things we already know, and by comparing them to each other and seeing them in the light of our last end. (Denzinger, No. 1796, Council of the Vatican, 1869.)

This is sufficient to outline our purpose in this course. We have seen 1) how theology is related to our university education as a whole: that theology is the queen of all sciences, the source of divine wisdom, the heartland of the Catholic educational domain; 2) how the various branches of theology are unified in Christ as the Way, Truth and Life of all men, and particularly that dogmatic theology is the foundation of the other branches; 3) how theology being the science of God is a study of divine life in God and in men, that dogmatic theology systematizes all these divine mysteries that comprise the creed, all that we believe on faith because God has revealed it. The next step after this introduction is to say a few words about faith, since everything we speak of in this course is accepted on faith.

CHAPTER II

Faith

THE IMPORTANCE OF FAITH in approaching theology is easily understood if we consider that theology is the science of faith. Although theology uses human reason and philosophy, the highest science of human reason, it begins with the truths known only by faith. Reason is used in theology only to classify the truths, to compare them, and to try to understand the terms of the mysteries, to see that the bare terms do not involve any contradiction. But the fundamental factor in theology is always faith, the acceptance of truths revealed by God Himself.

Our treatment of faith will cover four points:

1. The Nature of Faith
2. The Obligation of Faith
3. The Rule of Faith
4. The Subject Matter of Faith.

This concluded, we will be able to commence our study of the various truths of faith that make up the proper subject matter of Dogma, according to the outline given above.

I. THE NATURE OF FAITH

The word 'faith' has many different meanings in English, so it will be necessary first of all to differentiate the faith of which we are speaking from many other commonly accepted usages of the word.

Faith in general has reference to a special kind of knowledge.

There are two different ways of knowing something: 1) we know something by our own reasoning power, v.g., that two and three make five, or that Chicago is a large city because I have been there; 2) we know something from somebody else, v.g., we take the professor's word for the structural composition of uranium, or an historian's evidence for the fact that Napoleon was defeated in Russia. Another way of putting it would be to say that we know the truth of some things on their own internal evidence that we see for ourselves, and the truth of other things on external evidence which we accept from someone else.

Now while faith is a special way of knowing something, a knowledge we call belief as opposed to sight, it is nevertheless a real kind of knowledge. It is *not credulity*—accepting anything we are told —for in faith, we accept something as true on real evidence. *Neither is it blind emotion,* for once the evidence is conclusive, the will moves the mind to accept the truth of the proposition because of the evidence that supports it externally, even though its internal truth is not apparent.

So much regarding faith in general, as a special way of knowing. This natural faith is as common as rain and sunshine in daily life. We do not prove and test everything in life for ourselves. We are continually taking someone else's word, the druggist's, the doctor's, the mechanic's, the teacher's. We could hardly exist without accepting many things in life as true because this or that authority said so.

Now the faith we speak of as the foundation of theology is, of course, not natural faith, but supernatural faith. In *supernatural* faith, we accept something as true because God has said so. This procedure is *reasonable,* because we know from apologetics that there is a God, that He can and did reveal a body of religious truths, and that we can and do know for certain what He revealed. Moreover, we know that He set up His Church to officially teach and promulgate the truths that He came to teach. With all this evidence that God, the Supreme Truth, said something, we are evidently reasonable in accepting it on faith. Note, however, that such knowledge is *not rational,* for we do not figure it out with our own minds. As a matter of fact, the mysteries that we believe, are by definition truths that we cannot figure out by our own minds. God can tell us that the deepest mysteries are so, e.g., that there are three persons in God, but even then, our minds are powerless to comprehend completely how this truth is so.

Besides the evidence that God said so, our wills need the grace of God to embrace all the mysteries that God revealed, and to live by them. Supernatural faith is not only reasonable but *free*. However, it is a freedom under grace, for while God gives us grace to believe, He will not force us to believe. Our full acceptance of the faith must be voluntary. This is further demonstrated by the fact that faith can be lost.

One more point must be made regarding the nature of faith. Besides being reasonable and free, it is also *certain*, not merely giving us probable or conjectural knowledge. Although the things we believe are beyond full comprehension, their truth is more certain than those things which we do fully comprehend. This may seem incredible at first glance, but not if we examine our grounds for believing. We believe the things that we fully comprehend as true, because of the internal evidence we perceive for their truth. In other words, their truth rests upon the exercise of our human finite minds. But in regard to the truth of supernatural mysteries, known by supernatural faith, we know that they are true because God has testified to their truth. In this case, we are most certain of the truth, because it rests not upon the evidence seen by a finite mind, but upon the word of an infinite mind, on the evidence of Supreme Truth, and this gives the *greatest of certainty*.

A word should be said here regarding *doubt*. Many students in the course of studying dogma have objected: "Why worry ourselves by viewing these difficult mysteries? It just brings doubts into the mind. It would be much better merely to accept them blindly without going into them too deeply."

By way of answer, we must first make a distinction. It is true that a deeper study of the mysteries of our faith will give us a greater insight into their difficulties. But in the words of the great Cardinal Newman, "ten thousand difficulties do not make one doubt." *Doubt* has reference to the truth of the mysteries. Once we are convinced that God has revealed them, we need have no doubts about the fact that they are true, for He who is Truth Itself has testified to their truth, and His Church proclaims this word of His to the world. Now dogma helps in this department, for it studies the word of God and shows just where, and how God revealed each mystery, and in what words the Church has proposed His truths. As to *difficulties,* they are unavoidable in any matter that cannot be fully understood, and mysteries are by definition such matters. If mysteries were not difficult for us they would not be mysteries, and there would be no merit for us to accept them on faith in God's word. Even so, dogma does not start out to accentuate the difficulties. It does show that however difficult they are, they are not contradictory to reason, and moreover, by comparing them in the over-all pattern of Catholic belief, theology does lead to a deeper comprehension of these revealed mysteries. As to the difficulties it does point out, our faith is also deepened thereby, and our merit increased, for we realize more and more that we know them by God's word alone, and however difficult they may be, we still accept them as true because God has said that they are so.

Cardinal Newman has elaborated this point in the story of his own conversion, and in his attitude towards the Catholic Faith. We can well meditate on his words:

> From the time that I became a Catholic, of course, I have no further history of my religious opinions to narrate. In saying this, I do not mean to say that my mind has been idle, or that I have given up thinking on theological subjects; but that I have had no variations to record, and have had no anxiety of heart whatever. I have been in perfect peace and contentment; I have never had one doubt.
>
> I was not conscious to myself, on my conversion, of any change, intellectual or moral, wrought in my mind. I was not conscious of firmer faith in the fundamental truths of Revelation, or of more self-command; I had not more fervor; but it was like coming into port after a rough sea; and my happiness on that score remains to this day without interruption.
>
> Nor had I any trouble about receiving those additional articles which are not found in the Anglican Creed. Some of them I believed already, but not any one of them was a trial to me. I made a profession of them upon my reception (into the Church) with the greatest ease, and I have the same ease in believing them now. I am far of course from denying that every article of the Christian Creed, whether as held by Catholics or by Protestants, is beset with intellectual difficulties; and it is a simple fact, that, for myself, I cannot answer those difficulties. Many persons are very sensitive of the difficulties of Religion; I am as sensitive of them as any one; but I have never been able to see a connection between apprehending those difficulties, however keenly, and multiplying them to any extent, and on the other hand doubting the doctrines to which they

are attached. Ten thousand difficulties do not make one doubt, as I understand the subject; difficulty and doubt are incommensurate. There of course may be difficulties intrinsic to the doctrines themselves, or to their relations with each other. A man may be annoyed that he cannot work out a mathematical problem of which the answer is or is not given to him, without doubting that it admits of an answer, or that a certain particular answer is the true one. . . .

People say that the doctrine of the Transubstantiation is difficult to believe; I did not believe the doctrine till I was a Catholic. I had no difficulty in believing it as soon as I believed that the Catholic Roman Church was the oracle of God, and that she had declared this doctrine to be part of the original revelation. It is difficult, impossible to imagine, I grant . . . but how is it difficult to believe? . . . But for myself, I cannot indeed prove it, I cannot tell how it is; but I say, "Why should it not be? What's to hinder it? What do I know of substance and matter? just as much as the greatest philosophers, and that is nothing at all." And, in like manner, of that majestic article of the Anglican as well as of the Catholic Creed . . . the doctrine of the Trinity in Unity. What do I know of the Essence of the Divine Being? I know that my abstract idea of three is simply incompatible with my idea of one; but when I come to the question of the concrete fact, I have no means of proving that there is not a sense in which one and three can equally be predicated of the Incommunicable God.[1]

In summary: Supernatural Faith is:

Belief, on the word of God;

reasonable, since we have real evidence from reason that there is a God and that He has spoken on this matter believed;

Not rational, since the object of our supernatural faith is a mystery, a truth which we cannot fully know or understand by reason (we might suspect the existence of some lesser mysteries, e.g., the angels, and understand quite a bit about them once their existence is revealed);

Free, i.e., voluntary acceptance of the truth, under grace, however, as we need God's grace to fully accept and live according to the divine mysteries of His religion;

Certain, and not merely probable or conjectural knowledge, even more certain than natural truths we know ourselves, for the truth of the mysteries we believe is found in the Divine Mind, Truth Itself;

---

1. Newman, *Apologia pro Vita Sua,* pp. 238–240, Longmans, Green & Co., New York.

Open to difficulties, since we cannot fully understand the mysteries that have been revealed. However, there is no reason to confuse these difficulties with doubts. We accept the fact that these mysteries exist since God said so, even though we cannot fully understand or explain how they are so.

So much for the *nature* of faith.

II. THE OBLIGATION OF FAITH

It is enough here to insist that faith is necessary to salvation. This is true first of all because Christ Our Lord said so: "Going forth into the whole world teach all nations . . . those who believe and are baptized will be saved, those who do not believe will be condemned" (Matthew 16:16). The reasoning behind this is not difficult to comprehend. If Christ came as our Truth, and outlined for us the true way of salvation, we have to accept that way to be saved. Faith opens up to us all the vision of the way of life eternal, and a knowledge of all the means that Christ has ordained to help us along that way. Take away faith, and all of these things are non-existent for a man. This is why the solemn teaching of the Council of Trent declares that "Faith is the beginning of man's salvation, the foundation and root of all justification without which it is impossible to please God and to join the company of His children (Denz. 801)." The Council quotes St. Paul who says that a man is justified by faith (Romans 3:22).

Faith then is not only important but necessary for by it man renders unto God "the full homage of his intellect and will" (Council of Vatican, Denz. 1789). In return for this full subjection of mind and will to God, he receives the full knowledge from God of what he must do to be saved. Without it, he is missing this essential know-how of salvation.

We have already made the point that faith is a free act, and it requires the grace of God to make that first act of faith and to keep in possession of the virtue of faith. We can now add to this that it is possible to lose the faith also. This is only possible formally by an act of disbelief, a mortal sin against faith. However such acts do not merely happen; they are prepared by a number of other factors, such as not practicing the faith we have, by alienating ourselves from God in other ways, especially by continued habits of sin.

There are a number of difficult questions connected with the obligation of the faith for salvation, for example, what of the salvation of people who have had no contact with the faith. These questions will be answered later in connection with the universal will of God to save all men, the necessity of the Church, Redemption, and especially of Baptism. There are all facets of the same problem, and eventually receive the same answer that God condemns no one to hell except through his own fault.

A practical conclusion to this point on the necessity of faith for salvation is to be thankful for the faith that is ours, to be grateful for the efforts of so many people, past and present, who have brought it to us, to nurture and strengthen it by living it manfully and daily, to bring it to others by showing our lives as a living example of truth of the Catholic Faith. In the words of Christ we have the whole picture:

The Fact: "You are the light of the world."

The Command: "So let your light shine before men."

The Reasons: 1) "That they may see your good works—

2) "And glorify your Father, who is in heaven"
(Cf. Matthew 5:13–16).

III. THE MOTIVE (OR RULE) OF FAITH

The problem of this section is to answer the question: Why do we believe what we believe? If you were to challenge the ordinary Catholic to explain why he believes some point of doctrine he would probably say, "Because the Church teaches it." While this is not a completely untrue motive for believing, neither is it a completely true one. The Church does not manufacture divine mysteries, she teaches authoritatively the mysteries revealed by God. The ultimate motive for believing, then, is God's word, and the proximate motive is the Church teaching God's word.

It is important to understand this relationship, because many people in the world today rebel against what they call the 'dogmatism' or 'authoritarianism' of the Church. In reality, they are rebelling against God and His word, for the Church represents nothing else. For example, if someone asks a Catholic why he doesn't believe in divorces, he simply does not give an adequate answer if he says, "Because the Church is against them." The full answer is that God is against them, and the Church, representing

God in the world today, is against them. And when the Church inveighs against divorce it will quote the words of God: "What God has joined together, let no man put asunder," and "If a man puts away his wife and marries another, he commits adultery" (Cf. Mark 10:2–12; Matthew 19:1–12). Admittedly, those are strong words to say to a world that wants to make up its own rules for life. However, they are not the Church's words but Christ's, ultimately.

The world today may also resent the Church's speaking for God, but again that is not the Church's arrangement but God's. "Who hears you hears *Me,*" said Christ. "Go teach all nations . . . who believes will be saved, who does not believe will be condemned" (Cf. John 12:42–50; Mark 16:14–15). This is not the place to consider infallibility, but it will help to remember that Christ promised His Church that the gates of hell would not prevail against her. We can be grateful to have the Church's word to reassure us that Christ has really taught *this,* and not that. In summary, then, our motive for believing is that God said so, and the Church so teaches, in the name and on the authority of God.

We must note here that when we speak of the 'motive' for believing we are looking for the *reason why we accept on faith the mysteries of religion as true.* Do not confuse this with the 'purpose' of believing which is to get God's word on the truths necessary for salvation.

We are now in a position to understand the theological method. As the science of faith, theology does not merely seek a deeper knowledge of divine mysteries, but seeks out the source of these mysteries. It traces each mystery of faith back to the source of faith: the word of God and the teaching of the Church. This brings up the obvious question: "Where do we get the word of God on these mysteries of Faith?" Theology traces out the course of revelation from God to men. In outline it would look like this:

by word of Mouth — Tradition

God—Christ—Apostles—↕ —in and thru Church—to all men

by written word — Holy Scriptures

To state this in longer form, God sent His only begotten Son, Christ, who revealed these mysteries, especially to the apostles, the official teachers upon whom He founded His Church, under the visible leadership of St. Peter. The word of Christ was left permanently in the Church through the twin sources of divine revelation, the spoken word, or *Tradition* (the record of what was said and done in the early Church according to the word of Christ) and the written word or *Holy Scripture,* the divinely inspired writings of the Apostles or their scribes. Given this deposit of divine revelation, the Church is commissioned by Christ to guard, preserve, interpret and teach it unto all men, in the name of Christ and on the authority of Christ.

Holy Scripture and Tradition are then the two great sources of faith, for they give us God's word. Theology must make unceasing use of them in finding the mysteries it studies. Since they are going to be used very often, anyone studying theology should be well acquainted with Scripture and Tradition. We must remark here that we differ from the Protestants on this point, in that they hold Scripture as the sole source of divine revelation. They also hold that it is up to each individual Christian to interpret Scripture, whereas we hold that both Scripture and Tradition are officially interpreted by the Church.

The best we can do here is give a short résumé of these two sources and a comparison of them.

Holy Scripture is known to all as the Bible. This in turn is divided into the Old Testament and the New Testament. The *Old Testament* is by far the largest part, covering (in 45 books) the time from the beginning of the world to the Christian era. These books are of three kinds. 1) *Historical:* like the Pentateuch (the first five), and others like Ruth, Kings, Tobias, Judith, Esther, etc. These treat of the history of the chosen people or of certain personages. 2) *Didactic:* like Job, Psalms, Proverbs, Ecclesiastes, etc. These treat of ethical or moral instruction. 3) *Prophetic:* like Isaias, Jeremias, Ezechiel, Daniel, etc. The major and minor prophets have several functions, but mainly, they foretell the coming Messias and the Messianic Age.

The golden thread that runs through the Old Testament is the promise of a Redeemer to come. Many particulars of His Life are foretold; His universal reign is predicted. Someone has said that the New Testament is the fulfillment of the Old. Our use of the Old Testament will be mainly in reference to Creation. It is used also in Apologetics to show that Christ fulfilled all the prophecies regarding the Redeemer to come. Very few Catholics have read the entire Old Testament, and it is a shame, for this too is the word of God, a word that has had a deep influence on our culture, literature, art and liturgy.

The *New Testament* is the segment of Scripture which we shall use most. It comprises the four apostolic accounts of the life of Christ: Matthew and John were apostles, Mark wrote for St. Peter and Luke for St. Paul. Besides there is the account of early apostolic times, the Acts of the Apostles, the letters of the apostles, Paul, Peter, John, James, Jude, and one prophetic book, the *Apocalypse* of St. John. All these writings of the Old and New Testament are the inspired work of God. They were originally written in Hebrew, Aramaic, or Greek, and subsequently translated into Latin by St. Jerome when that language became the common tongue of the people. His translation is called the Vulgate. It was made in 382 at the command of Pope Damascus. The Catholic English version (generally distinguished from the King James Version) was made from the Vulgate by English scholars, exiled by the English Reformation, at Douay (Old Testament—1609) and at Rheims (New Testament—1582). For many years this has been the only available English version. Recently, however, American Biblical scholars have produced a new and more readable English version of the New Testament, as has also Monsignor Ronald Knox in England.

It is impossible to do justice to theology without referring continually to Holy Scripture. Those who wish to learn about God should read continually this great treasury of His inspired words. The Council of the Vatican had this to say about Holy Scripture: "These (books) the Church holds to be sacred and canonical; not because having been carefully composed by mere human industry they were afterwards approved by her authority; not because they contain revelation with no admixture of error; but because, having been written by the inspiration of the Holy Spirit, they have God for their Author and have been delivered to the Church as such" (Denz. 1787).

We think of Holy Scripture as the collection we now have in the Bible, but the books of the New Testament were not collected together and declared to be the only inspired books until the Council of Carthage, held in 397 (Denz. 92, Cf. Denz. 84, 162, 173). This declaration was the work of the teaching Church, drawing on the living tradition of what was accepted in the whole Church up to that time. This introduces us to the other source of revelation, Divine Tradition.

Tradition is generally distinguished from Scripture as the spoken word from the written word. Tradition comprises all that was said and done in the early Church. St. John says, as he finishes the last Gospel: "But there are many other things which Jesus did; which, if they were written every one, the world itself, I think, would not be able to contain the books that should be written" (John 21:25). We know that Christ gave the Apostles many instructions after His resurrection from the dead, during the forty days that preceded His ascension into heaven. And then the Church went on following His instructions. Thus, from what the Church did, we can learn what Christ said. After all, the Church was functioning for some decades before the first Gospel was written, and almost four hundred years before all the inspired books of the New Testament were collected into one Bible.

Tradition then is a correlative and important source of God's word, coming both before and after the New Testament. If we could draw a line of time to bring out this fact it would look like this:

Duration of Tradition

33 A.D.	50 A.D.	100 A.D.	397 A.D.	605 A.D.
Christ's Death, Beginning of the Church and Tradition	New Testament written		New Testament collected in one book by the Council of Carthage	Death of St. Gregory, End of Tradition

There must of course be some record of the doings in the Early Church that constitute Tradition. We find this record in the writings of the *Fathers*. The Fathers are all those ancient, holy, orthodox writers who have been approved by the Church, the guardian of both Scripture and Tradition. While their writings are not inspired, as is Scripture, still when they concur in relating a fact in the Early Church that comes from the teaching of Christ through the Apostles, we can find in this account an unmistakable record of Christ's word.

We must admit that there is considerable ignorance among Catholics regarding this important source of revelation called Tradition. Few indeed have read much, if any, of the magnificent Christian literature of the Early Church. And yet it is far-reaching. In the standard collection of the writings of the Fathers by Migne, we have 221 large volumes in Latin, and 165 volumes in Greek. These include magnificent sermons, letters, theological treatises and discussions by such great names as Augustine, Ingatius of Antioch, Cyril of Jerusalem, Cyril of Alexandria, Basil, Gregory the Great, Gregory of Nyssa, Ambrose, Hilary and many others. Many of these works are now appearing in English collections sponsored by American scholars.

To give a very brief example of the kind of thing that can be found in Tradition, rather than in Scripture, consider the following passage from the 'Didache,' a Greek document entitled the "Teaching (didache) of the Twelve Apostles," written shortly after St. John's Gospel, and only rediscovered a few decades ago. "Meet together on the Lord's Day (Sunday—as opposed to Jewish worship on the Sabbath) and break bread and celebrate the Eucharist (the Mass), having confessed your transgressions (Confession) so that your sacrifice may be pure. Let no one who is at variance with his neighbor join you until he is reconciled, that your sacrifice may not be defiled. For this is that sacrifice that was spoken of by the Lord, 'In every place and time offer Me a pure sacrifice' " (*Didache*, Chap. 14). Here is an open mention of common worship on Sunday, celebration of Mass and forgiveness of sins through confession, something which is in no part of Scripture so clearly proclaimed. The above statement of the earliest practice of the Church could have been written last week to describe a modern Catholic community.

We could repeat the same process to show how the Apostles' Creed, the brief summary of all the truths of the Church, was formed in connection with the baptismal ceremony, when the catechumens were asked to profess their faith in the basic Christian dogmas of the Trinity and the Incarnation. Around this profession was built up a summary of the Christian truths that has resulted in the Apostles' Creed. In early 200 A.D., a Roman named Hippolytus wrote a book on the Liturgy of the Church at that early period. In treating of Baptism, he reproduces the profession of faith demanded of the catechumen: "Do you believe in God, the Father Almighty? Do you believe in Jesus Christ, the son of God, who was born of the Holy Spirit from the Virgin Mary, who was crucified under Pontius Pilate, died, was buried, rose living from the dead on the third day, ascended into heaven whence he will come to judge the living and the dead? Do you believe in the Holy Ghost, the holy Church and the resurrection of the body?" Note how closely this approximates our Apostles' Creed, and how it is divided according to the three persons of the Trinity, with an elaborated section on the Incarnation of Christ. Here again, Tradition gives us a record of the teaching of Christ not so specifically contained in Holy Scripture. Theology thus uses Tradition as well as Scripture to trace the Christian mysteries back to the Word of God from which they are originally derived.

We noted before that Christ founded His Church to continue His teaching. For us, *the Church is the proximate rule of faith,* for it proposes to us here and now, all these teachings contained in Scripture and Tradition. Just as the constitution of the United States is not left open to each American's interpretation, but is interpreted for us authoritatively by the Supreme Court, so the whole deposit of revealed truth is interpreted for us by Christ's Church. "Go teach all nations, . . . who hears you, hears Me . . . As the Father sent me, I send you" (cf. Mark 16:13–19; Matthew 28:16–20; Luke 8:48; John 20:21).

Just as in the case of finding God's word in Scripture and Tradition, we must ask here too, where do we find the official teaching of the Church? Fortunately we do have a collection of the official teachings of the Church, especially those given through the Councils of the Church. But unfortunately it is only available in Latin, and we will have to translate those sections of it that we will use. This collection has been quoted already where we gave the abbreviation Denz. and a number. The *Denz.* refers to Denzinger who first edited this collection of Church documents. His book is called the 'Enchiridion Symbolorum' or 'Collection of the statements of the Creeds.' We shall have occasion to cite Denzinger many times in connection with the official teaching of the Church in such general councils as Nicaea, Constantinople, Ephesus and Chalcedon in the first four centuries, as well as Trent in the sixteenth and the Vatican Council in the nineteenth century. A glance through the index of Denzinger's collection is enough to impress one with the age and wisdom of the Church. It begins with St. Peter the Apostle and ends with John XXIII, 257 popes who form a visible link between Christ and His Church. We think of America as fairly old, and yet there have only been ten popes during the whole span of our history.

We must not return to the main trend of our thought. We have taken a brief glance at Holy Scripture and Apostolic Tradition because they are the sources from which theology draws its knowledge of the divine mysteries of faith revealed by God. We have also glanced briefly at the Church since she has been commissioned by God to interpret and teach in His name, the truths contained in these sources of revelation. We can now more fully understand the motive of faith. If asked why we believe, we say, *ultimately* because God has revealed these truths, and *proximately* we accept the revealed truths as the Church teaches them.

An interesting application of what we have here stated is found in an article of *Time* magazine (Feb. 6, 1946). It cites an approval of the Planned Parenthood program (birth control) by the Federal Council of Churches. In criticizing this statement on a moral matter by a religious body, *Time* goes right to the heart of the question. This is a matter of theology and faith, and therefore should be supported by the sources of faith. But of course, the statement does not mention them, so *Time* says very pointedly: "Neither Biblical nor patristic authority (i.e. Tradition from the Fathers) was cited in support of the argument. The approach had been sociological, not theological." That is as devastating a criticism as can be made of a theological statement by a religious body.

IV. The Subject Matter of Faith

This is the last point on faith and may be covered rather briefly. It answers the question: "What must be believed?" In view of what has already been seen, the answer is simple: "All that God has revealed, as the Church teaches it."

Now God has not revealed everything in exactly the same way. Some truths are directly and explicitly stated in revelation, such as the power to forgive sins: "Whose sins you shall forgive they are forgiven them" (John, 20–23). Such things we say are believed by divine faith. Other truths are contained in revelation in an indirect and implicit manner, such as for example, the Immaculate Conception. Now when the Church explicitly defines such a doctrine as contained in revelation, it too is held by *divine faith*. Moreover, when the Church officially designates any doctrine as contained in divine revelation, we add another word to designate our full motive for believing, we say it is held by *divine catholic faith:* 1) divine because revealed by God; 2) catholic because defined by the Church in the name of God. There is one more distinction that may be useful. Some truths are taught by the Church which are not in themselves revealed, but which have some connection with revealed truths. Our motive for believing these is the authority of the Church, God's official teacher on earth, and consequently we call our faith in such statements, *ecclesiastical faith* (from the Latin word 'ecclesia'—church).

In a word, though, the total subject matter of divine faith is what the Church teaches as revealed by God. Such truths are contained in summary in the Apostles' Creed.

There is one last word which must be said regarding the many truths which we hold by faith from God and which we shall study in dogma. Many have wondered how the gradual growth of the whole pattern came about. What we have already said above should help answer this question. The 'growth' is not by addition of elements from without. The Church started with the whole revelation from God and nothing has been added to this deposit of revelation since the death of the last of the apostles to whom it was committed. But men have thought deeply on these revealed truths, errors have arisen to misinterpret them, and always the infallible Church has separated truth from error, and stated ever more explicitly, many of the truths implicitly contained in God's word to men. The growth then has been, in the words of Newman, the growth of a vital idea, from the inside out, not from outside in, by addition.

Cardinal Newman has written some lucid lines regarding this question in his famous *Essay on the Development of Christian Doctrine*. We will quote a few of them here to illustrate what we have said. Newman emphasizes,

> . . . that the increase and expansion of the Christian Creed and Ritual, and the variations which have attended the process in the case of the individual writers and Churches, are the necessary at-

tendants on any philosophy or policy which takes possession of the intellect and heart, and has had any wide or extended dominion; that, from the nature of the human mind, time is necessary for the full comprehension and perfection of great ideas; and the highest and most wonderful truths though communicated to the world once for all by inspired teachers, could not be comprehended all at once by the recipients, but, as being received and transmitted by minds not inspired and through media which were human, have required only the longer time and deeper thought for their full elucidation.[1]

Newman shows that the Catholic Doctrine held today, though more fully developed, is both logically and historically the same as the ancient faith and states: "that modern Catholicism is nothing else but simply the legitimate growth and complement, that is, the natural and necessary development of the doctrine of the early church, and that its divine authority is included in the divinity of Christianity." [2]

In some of Newman's other works, we find the same idea clearly expressed:

> It is well known that, though the creed of the Church has been one and the same from the beginning, yet it has been so deeply lodged in her bosom as to be held by individuals more or less implicitly, instead of being delivered from the first in those special statements, or what are called definitions (statements of the Councils), under which it is now presented to us, and which preclude mistake or ignorance. These definitions, which are but the expressions of portions of the one dogma which has ever been received by the Church, are the work of time; they have grown to their present shape and number in the course of eighteen centuries, under the exigency of successive events, such as heresies and the like, and they may of course receive still further additions [by additions Newman means more explicit statement of what the Church has always implicitly held] as time goes on.[3]
>
> To the Apostles, the whole revelation was given, by the Church it is transmitted; no simply new truth has been given to us since St. John's death; the one office of the Church is to guard 'that noble deposit' of trust, as St. Paul speaks to Timothy, which the Apostles bequeathed to her, in its fullness and integrity.[4]

---

1. Newman, *Essay on the Development of Christian Doctrine*, pp. 29f, Longmans, Green & Co., New York.

2. *Ibid.*, p. 169.

3. Newman, *Difficulties of Anglicans*, I, pp. 349f; Longmans, Green & Co., New York.

4. *Ibid.*, p. 327.

Doctrines remain implicit till they are contravened; then they are stated in explicit form.[5]

We will see very often in considering the various dogmas studied in this book that the outcropping of heresies often occasions a more explicit statement of the true doctrine by the Church.

It is now easy to understand why the total subject matter of the faith is not merely what God revealed, but what God revealed as the Church teaches it. If it were not for the infallible guiding hand of the Church under the inspiration of the Holy Spirit, we would not have today the clear picture of all these revealed truths that we actually do have. But this is not surprising, for Christ told His Apostles in promising His Holy Spirit: "But the Paraclete, the Holy Spirit whom the Father will send in My name, he will teach you all things, and bring all things to your mind, whatsoever I shall have said to you" (John 14:26). "But when He, the Spirit of Truth, is come, He will teach you all truth" (John 15:13).

This concludes our study on faith. We saw in turn: 1) the *nature* of faith, its main qualities or characteristics, with an added word concerning doubt; 2) the *obligation* of faith as necessary to salvation; 3) the *motive* or rule of faith with special attention to the sources of God's word, Holy Scripture and Tradition, and the Church which God established to officially interpret and teach His word; 4) and lastly, the *subject matter* of faith, with the added notion of how this subject matter develops from within.

We should now be prepared to approach the study of the mysteries of faith themselves, since we have established our method of knowing them, and the means that theology, the science of faith, uses to study them.

The pattern for all of these mysteries has already been determined in the pages outlining the content and structure of dogma. We begin with the study of the divine mysteries relating to God in Himself, the fact that He exists, the Divine Nature and its attributes, the theological problems relating to those attributes in reference to man, the three Persons in God.

5. Newman, *The Via Media*, I, p. 223, note 4; Longmans, Green & Co., New York.

CHAPTER III

The One God

THE FIRST GREAT TRUTH that is studied in theology is God Himself. This first tract is called in theological manuals, *De Deo Uno,* the One God. It is the study of the existence, nature and attributes of God, preliminary to the consideration of the three Persons in God. The matter of this present tract is also studied philosophically in Natural Theology or Theodicy, since man can know something of the *nature* and attributes of God from reason alone, even though the Trinity of Persons in God can be known only by faith.

The order of our treatment will be as follows:

1. The Knowability of God: His Existence.
2. The Nature or Essence of God.
3. The Attributes of God.

First we must solve the fundamental question, "Is there a God and can we know Him?" The second question to be answered is: "What is God?" The complete answer to this question involves our third point, a consideration of the various attributes of God.

I. THE KNOWABILITY OF GOD'S EXISTENCE

One of the greatest questions of all time has been: "Can we know God?" It is not our problem here to give all the answers to that question. However, the teaching of the Church has given us a very solemn statement on the *possibility* of knowing God by human reason. We must study this briefly.

At the time of the Vatican Council, there were two opposing errors regarding the knowledge of God. Both agreed in this that

30

they made it impossible for human reason to know God. *Traditionalism* (De Lamennais, De Bonald, Bonnetty, Ventura) tried to oppose the rising tide of Rationalism by exalting faith at the expense of reason. These men taught that it was impossible to know God except from a primitive revelation which was handed down from generation to generation. The other error, for which there are many names, can be bracketed under the title of Atheism. *Negative Atheism* (Agnosticism or Scepticism) says that man cannot know God by reason because there simply are no convincing arguments for the existence of God. *Positive Atheism* (Materialism, Pantheism, etc.) directly denies God as a Supreme Being distinct from the world, and superior to it.

Against all of these errors, the Church vindicated the validity of the human reason in searching for God. "If anyone shall say that the one true God, our Creator and Lord, *cannot be certainly known by the natural light of human reason through created things,* let him be anathema" (Vatican Council, Denz. 1806).

Not long after this statement, a new heresy called Modernism (Loisy, Tyrrell, etc.) arose. The Modernists taught that while it was possible to know God, this knowledge comes from an inner feeling of need for God. Man, as it were, produces God to fill his need for God. This inner need and feeling is his evidence of God's existence, and therefore the Modernists would hold that while man can know God, he cannot scientifically demonstrate or prove His existence. This called for a second and more explicit statement from the Church. It includes what the Vatican Council previously taught, but adds some further data regarding the *demonstrability* of God's existence. This second statement is found in Pius X's *Oath against Modernism,* an oath which must be taken by all those who are ordained in the Catholic Church, also by those who receive pontifical degrees or teach for the Church.

"I profess that God, the beginning and the end of all things, can certainly be known *and demonstrated* by the natural light of reason 'by the things that are made (Romans 1:20),' that is, by the visible work of creation as from effect to cause" (Denz. 2145).

It would be well to analyze the content of these two statements, for they have deep significance for the rest of this study. The general subject is our knowledge of God, and regarding this the Church makes four points:

A. Object of This Knowledge

God is a unique and personal Creator of the world and separate from it. All of the elements of this first point are clarified in another statement of the Vatican Council (given in the next section) regarding the God we know. They may also be demonstrated philosophically by reason which can know God. This first point is in opposition to the Atheists, Polytheists, Pantheists, Materialists, etc.

B. Means of This Knowledge

God is thus known by the natural light of human reason. This is opposed to the Traditionalists, Agnostics, Atheists, etc.

C. Sources of This Knowledge

Human reason gains this knowledge by using the principle of *causality:* by proceeding from the visible things of this world to the God who made them, and alone explains their presence here. St. Thomas applies this principle in five famous ways:

1) *From motion* to the first Mover who Himself is unmoved and explains all other motion;

2) *From things caused* to the first Uncaused Cause who explains all the effects;

3) *From beings that need not be* (contingent being) to Being that must be (Necessary Being—He who *is*);

4) *From finite, limited perfections,* to Infinite Unlimited Perfection Who is the Source from which all perfections flow;

5) *From order in the universe* to the Personal God who conceived of this order, put the universe in order, and keeps it in order. Those opposed to the above point on the validity of reason are of course opposed to this point, too, on the process of this reasoning.

D. Mode of This Knowledge

By the above processes God can *certainly* be *known* (Pius IX, Vatican Council), and His existence can also be *demonstrated* (Pius X, Oath against Modernism). The Atheists and Agnostics are against both these statements; the Modernists are only against the latter statement.

There may be a question in someone's mind as to why the Church has gone to such lengths to defend the validity of man's reason in attaining a knowledge of God. The answer to this question should be clear to those who have studied Apologetics. The knowledge of God's existence from reason is one of the preambles of faith, since we show from reason that there is a God and that He has revealed something before we demand an act of faith in what He has revealed. Man begins with the natural equipment he has from God. One of the most important parts of man's natural endowment is his intelligence. The Church must defend this as well as any other element in human life.

However, note that in the above pronouncements of the Church, it is *not* stated that every man *does* know and demonstrate the existence of God by reason alone. It only teaches that man *can* know, but from that possibility, we cannot infer the fact. As a matter of fact, few people go through a strictly scientific demonstration of God's existence. It is significant that God has revealed reasonable arguments for His existence for such as these to read in the Bible. One of the most famous is the following from the *Book of Wisdom* (Chapter 13):

> But all men are vain in whom there is not the knowledge of God: and who by these good things that are seen, could not understand Him that is, neither by attending to the works have acknowledged who was the workman:
> But have imagined either the fire, or the wind, or the swift air, or the circle of the stars, or the great water, or the sun and moon, to be the gods that rule the world.
> With whose beauty, if they, being delighted, took them to be gods: let them know how much the Lord of them is more beautiful than they: for the first author of beauty made all these things.
> Or if they admired their power and their effects, let them understand by them that he that made them is mightier than they:
> For by the greatness of the beauty, and of the creature, the creator of them may be seen, so as to be known thereby.

St. Paul bears out this same point in his Epistle to the Romans when he claims that the pagans who live as though there were no God are inexcusable because God can be known 'by the things that are made' (The words quoted by Pius X).

"For the invisible things of Him (God) from the creation of the world are clearly seen, being understood by the things that are made; his eternal power also, and divinity; so that they are inexcusable" (Romans, 1:20).

St. Paul also said to the Athenians that God had made all mankind "that they should seek God, if happily they may feel after Him or find Him, although He be not far from every one of us, for in Him we live, and move and are" (Acts 17:27–28). And speaking to the pagans at Lycaonia he pointed out that although men had strayed from God's path, "Nevertheless He (God) left not Himself without testimony, doing good from heaven, giving rains and fruitful seasons, filling our hearts with food and gladness" (Acts 14:16).

Therefore, in regard to this first point on the knowability of God, we hold very definitely *that we can know and demonstrate that there is a God by human reason alone,* even while we admit that many people are tremendously helped by God's revelation concerning His existence.

The rest of our treatise on God will be an unfolding of all the implications bound up in that most pregnant of all facts: there is a God and we can know Him. Walter Farrell has stated a few of these implications in reference to what we know of God from the five proofs of St. Thomas. The following should be read in conjunction with the outline of those five proofs given.

1. "The fact of the existence of a *first unmoved mover* means that there is no movement, from the crushing force of a tidal wave to the rise and fall of a breast in sleep which does not depend every instant on God; there is no change, from the imperceptible coloring of a leaf in autumn to the upheaval of a social revolution in which God does not play a major part.

2. "The existence of a *first uncaused cause* means that in the swaying struggle of men's lives, the triumphs of their greatest thoughts and works, their masterpieces, their literature, their architecture, the soarings of the poet or the crisp command of the soldier, there is no instant from which God can be excluded. No walls are thick enough, no wastes lonely enough, no army powerful enough, no governmental edict sweeping enough, no hatred bitter enough to exclude the action of the first cause.

3. "The existence of an *absolutely necessary being* means there is a divine sustaining hand whose withdrawal means annihilation;

it means that we cannot contact anything of reality without confronting divinity; that God is closer to us than we are to ourselves, that every moment of life, every particle of dust, every stitch of a garment is permeated with divinity or it could not continue to be.

4. "That there is an *all perfect being* means that all the beauty, the love, the goodness that lift the heart of a man out of himself are but shadows of the infinite on the pool of life, vague hints of the ineffable that lies at the beginning and end of life.

5. "That a *supreme intelligence exists* makes it plain that the hairs of our head are indeed numbered; that there is no step, no breath, no success or failure that is without its meaning, without its place in a divine plan, a supreme order, that necessarily goes beyond the human mind's power of assimilation." [1]

II. THE NATURE OR ESSENCE OF GOD

Once we know *that* God is, the next obvious question is: "What is He?" This of course has reference to the essence of God, since the essence is *that which makes a thing what it is*. It is no simple question to ask what makes God what He is. The best we can really do is to go to Revelation and find there the names that have reference to God.

The classical text in this matter is found in the second book of the Old Testament. During the time that the Israelites were being detained in Egypt, God appeared to Moses in a burning bush that was not burnt. God told Moses that He was the God of Abraham, the God of Isaac and the God of Jacob. He then told Moses to go to the Pharaoh and to bring the chosen people out of Egypt.

Then, "Moses said to God: Lo, I shall go to the children of Israel, and say to them: the God of your fathers hath sent me to you. If they should say to me: What is His name? What shall I say to them?

"And God said to Moses: *I am who am.* He said, Thus shalt you say to the children of Israel: *He who is* hath sent me to you" (Exodus 3, 13–14).

The Hebrew word for *He who is* is 'Yahweh.' Because of their great respect for the ineffable name and nature of God, the Jews never pronounced this word, but read in its place 'Adonai,' the

1. Farrell, *Companion to the Summa*, Vol. I, pp. 45–46.

Lord. During the Middle Ages the vowels for Adonai were read into the consonants for Yahweh, and a corrupted form of the word for God, 'Jehovah,' came into being.

Yahweh is the best word we have to express the nature of God, because the best we can say of Him is that He simply *is*. Philosophers have expressed this by a term from technical metaphysics, 'aseity' which means that God is 'self-existence,' or 'subsistent Being' or 'Pure Act.' Every other being is derived from Him. Other famous Old Testament names for God are: *Shadai*, the Strong or Mighty One; *Kadosch*, the Holy one; *Elion*, the Sublime, the Most High. These express His intrinsic perfection of nature.

In the New Testament we have a text which recapitulates the deep meaning of the name Yahweh: "I am the Alpha and the Omega (first and last characters in the Greek alphabet), the first and the last, the beginning and the end" (Apocalypse 22:13). This indicates, like Yahweh, that God is simply the Supreme Being without past or future, who simply *is*, and always *is*, from Whom all other beings come and to Whom all go.

Pointing out this essential notion of Supreme Being or self-existence will hardly satisfy us in our search to know God. We must add to this essential notion, the many attributes or characteristics which we can apply to God alone, in an attempt to achieve a fuller idea of His Being. Actually in doing this, we are always studying the precise same reality, for while existence, essence and attributes are distinguished as different realities in man, in God they are all identified. His essence is simply 'to be' (existence), and His attributes are just helps for us to see the one simple reality that He *is*.

III. THE ATTRIBUTES OF GOD

If God is one simple reality, without limitation, parts, beginning or end, it may seem foolish to speak of His attributes. However, in doing this we are doing much the same as sending a beam of light through a prism. It is only one same beam of light, but the prism allows us to see the various colors that are inherent in it. God is one simple reality; all the characteristics we attribute to Him are identified in Him, but nevertheless it helps our knowledge of Him to see separately all these various perfections which are perfectly realized in Him. Always, however, we must remember this essential difference between God and men: we *have* attributes, e.g., Joe has a good mind, exceptional musical ability, etc., whereas God *is* His attributes, e.g., God is Truth, Life, All-Knowledge, etc. Keeping this in mind, we can still study the various attributes that give us a fuller concept of God. We are actually following the Church in this, for the Church in the Vatican Council gave us a résumé of God's attributes.

"The Holy, Catholic, Apostolic, Roman Church believes and confesses that there is one true and living God, the Creator and Lord of heaven and earth, omnipotent, eternal, immense, incomprehensible, infinite in understanding and will and every perfection, Who since He is one, single, altogether simple and incommunicable spiritual substance must be said to be really and essentially distinct from the world, in Himself above all things that are, or can be conceived outside Himself" (Denz. 1782).

Before discussing these individual attributes, we must first study the basic difficulty inherent in knowing or saying anything at all about God. All our basic, direct thoughts and words have reference to created, finite, limited things. How then can we know or say anything at all about God? The answer lies in the notion of *analogy*, which is a way of using the same word about two different beings, and applying it in a sense that is somewhat the same, but basically different. Thus we say that a piece of pie a la mode, a football game, a man's character, and God are *good*. Obviously the word 'good' is only perfectly realized in God, but we know what it means in reference to the created, finite things, and we know something about God when we apply the same word to Him by analogy. All our language about God is analogical, and while it is imperfect, indirect knowledge, it is knowledge, and it is definitely better than no knowledge. St. Paul put it this way: "At present we are looking at a confused reflection in a mirror; then, we shall see face to face (in the beatific vision); now, I have only glimpses of knowledge; then, I shall recognize God as he has recognized me" (I Corinthians 13:12).

Philosophers and theologians have outlined the following three ways of knowing about God and speaking of Him:

1) By affirmation: we can perceive many simple perfections in this world, which do not of themselves involve any imperfection. We apply them by affirmation to God, realizing that if there is any imperfection in the finite way they are realized on earth, that

imperfection is absent in the infinite way they are in God. For example, God is Good, God is Truth, God is Holiness.

2) By negation: we also perceive certain imperfections and limitations that go with our own finite world. We can deny these in God, saying for example that God is immutable (not changeable), infinite (not limited), and immense (not limited to one point in space at a time). Because our words are geared to created things, we must use this way of negation very often in speaking about God. This is why St. Thomas says that we know more what God is *not,* than what He is. However, this too is real knowledge, because when for example we say God is infinite (not limited) we imply something positive . . . that He has all perfections without any imperfections or limitation.

3) By supereminence: this involves affirmation, but adds to it that we apply perfections to God in the superlative degree. This is a very common way of speaking about God, pulling out all the stops on our language keyboard, so to speak: for example, God is All Good, God is All Powerful, God is All Knowing, the Most High.

These three ways of speaking about God are complementaries, that is, we must use them all in unison to get an adequate picture of God. One theologian has compared them to the three modes of artistic expression: painting, sculpture and poetry. The painter produces his picture *affirmatively* by brushing colors on the canvas. The sculptor proceeds *negatively* cutting an image into stone. And the poet, by use of metaphors, *images* and colorful expressions, treats his subject *superlatively.* Thus too, we speak of God affirmatively, negatively and superlatively. The result is certainly a more complete knowledge of Him "Who inhabits light inaccessible, Whom no man has seen, nor can see" (I Timothy 6:16).

In outlining the various attributes that we predicate of God, theologians generally classify them according to two broad divisions:

1) Quiescent: Those attributed to God considered in Himself, also called *entitative* (going with His essential Being, as opposed to operation, although both are one in God) or *absolute* (as opposed to relative attributes referring to God's activity as regards creatures).

2) Operative: Those attributed to God considered in His ac-

tivity as regards creatures (Creator, Provider, in His omnipotence and omniscience).

We shall study all the attributes of God under these two headings.

A. *Quiescent Attributes of God*

1. Infinity

This is a very fundamental perfection of God. It is a negative attribute, since it denies that which is evident in every other living being outside God, namely, limitation. Literally, infinity means limitless, or boundless (Latin, *finis*—limit boundary). It follows directly from what we have already seen, that God is the Supreme Being. If God is all being, it is impossible for Him to be limited in any way, for all limitation is a lack of being or reality. Every living being outside God receives existence which is limited by a nature into which, and according to which it is received. Even the being of an angel is limited by the boundaries of the angelic nature. But the nature of God is simply 'to be'—He is all reality, without any possible limitation of reality. He is first, for He receives nothing from anyone, and gives to all things everything they are.

It is no simple matter to imagine this absence of all limitation in God. As a matter of fact it cannot be imagined. It would be easier to conceive of infinity in God positively, not as the absence of all imperfection, but as the presence of all perfection. This is how the Vatican Council put it: "Infinite . . . in every perfection." This is a logical conclusion, for every perfection is some aspect of being or reality. And God is Supreme Being. Moreover, since all the reality of this world comes from God, all the perfections of this world also came from God, and must somehow be realized in Him. The cause must have what it causes. As the Psalmist puts it: "He that planted the ear, shall He not hear? Or He that formed the eye, shall He not see?" (Psalm 93:9).

The saint, like Francis of Assisi, finds it easy to stay in the presence of God, for he sees the fingerprints of God in all the beauties of this world. For the saint, all that is good, true or beautiful in this world is only a faint shadow of the goodness and truth and beauty of God. That is why all these things do not lead a saint away from God, but rather, make him desire all the more to be with

God, to possess God who made all these things and is immeasurably more good, true and beautiful than these reflections of Him. Now we can understand why St. Paul described heaven, which is the possession of God, in these words: "Eye has not seen and ear has not heard, nor has it entered into the heart of man to imagine the things that God has prepared for those who love Him" (I Corinthians 2:9; Isaias 64:4).

The Psalmist has expressed the infinity of God succinctly in his prayer: "Great is the Lord, and greatly to be praised; and of His greatness there is no end" (Psalm 144:3).

2. Immensity

This is another negative attribute, applying the infinity of God to space. God is not limited by any space, as we are. Neither can He be said to be contained by any place. He simply IS everywhere. Wherever there is anything, there He is, for He is the cause of that being and must sustain it in being. Immensity comes from the Latin word for 'measure' and thus indicates that God is not measured to any place whatever. Other more common words for this idea in English are ubiquity, or omnipresence.

Sometimes people ask: "Where was God before the world was created?" But this question has no meaning. 'Where' is a word concept that goes with material creation. Only matter has parts that can be in juxtaposition to one another, giving rise to the reality of 'being somewhere' in relation to something else. For example, we are now where we are because the parts of our body are in juxtaposition to other material things—walls, buildings, other people, etc. But there was nothing material before the creation of the world, so there was nowhere to be. At that time, as now, God simply IS. Now that there is some place to be, God IS everywhere totally, that is, He is not contained in any one place. Of course this is possible because He is a simple spirit with no parts to be in relation to other things. This is how we say that the soul, also a spiritual substance, is totally in every part of the body. A spirit is present where it operates, and this will give us the key to understanding how God is present everywhere at once.

God is present everywhere:

a) *By His Knowledge:* We speak of persons being 'miles away' when they are daydreaming. After Christmas vacation, the men in class are bodily present, but mentally still back home. Now since

God knows all things that are, He is present to all things by His knowledge. "Neither is there any creature invisible in His sight: but all things are naked and open to His eyes" (Hebrews 4:13).

b) *By His Power:* God does not simply make things as a human craftsman would, and let them lie. He must continue to sustain them in being. Humans only affect the becoming of a thing, from one thing to another, but God gives being to all things. Just as the electric light must have continual contact with the dynamo, the source of power, or it will go out, so all things must have continual contact with God, the source of all being, or they would sink back into the nothingness from which He drew them. "God . . . upholding all things by the word of His power" (Hebrews 1:3). This reminds us that God's presence in everything is not because of His need, but because of ours. Thus God is present to everything by His power. "Wisdom (God) reaches therefore from end to end mightily, and orders all things smoothly" (Wisdom 8:1).

c) *By His Substance:* This is a direct conclusion from the two ways of presence given above. If God is present to all things by His mind and will, by His knowledge and power, He is substantially present to all things, for there is no distinction of being or perfection in God. God *is* His mind and will; God *is* His knowledge and power. God is present by His knowledge and power, He is present in His whole being, substantially, for He simply IS His knowledge and power. "He is not far from every one of us: for in Him we live and move and are" (Acts 17:27–28).

The most famous scriptural passage for the omnipresence of God is Psalm 138:

Lord Thou hast proved me and known me
Thou hast known my sitting down and my rising up.
Thou hast understood my thoughts afar off
My path and my line Thou hast searched out.
And Thou hast foreseen all my ways . . .
Thy knowledge is become wonderful to me:
It is high, and I cannot reach to it.
Whither shall I go from Thy Spirit?
Or whither shall I flee from Thy face?
If I descend into hell, thou art present.
If I take my wings early in the morning,
And dwell in the uttermost parts of the sea:
Even there also shall Thy hand lead me

And Thy right hand shall hold me.
And I said: Perhaps darkness shall cover me;
And night shall be my light in my pleasure.
But darkness shall not be dark to Thee,
And night shall be light as the day;
The darkness thereof, and the light thereof,
Are alike to Thee. (Psalm 138:1–12)

Thus, even though it is a negative attribute, we can know something of God's perfection by applying His infinity to space as we
know it, and realizing that God is immense, omnipresent, ubiqui-
tous, everywhere, not limited to any place or contained in any
space. No matter how broadly we conceive the universe in terms
of billions upon billions of light years, its almost inconceivable
expanse cannot limit or contain God. He is everywhere within it,
and overflows it, because everything in it comes from Him, and if
He were not present to everything, nothing would exist.

A modern author has applied this concept to human life with
unforgettable words:

> The ubiquity of God, in common with all the divine perfections, is
> not a cold, abstract thing, meaningless to men. Its significance for
> human living is inexhaustible. In the concrete, it means, for instance,
> that God is in the surge of the sea, the quiet peace of hills and valleys,
> the cool refreshment of rain, the hard drive of wind-driven snow. In
> the cities He is in the bustling of crowds, the roar of traffic, the strug-
> gle for pleasure, for life, for happiness, in the majesty of towering
> buildings.
>
> In homes He is not to be excluded from the tired, drowsy hours of
> night, the hurried activity of morning, from the love and quarrels,
> the secret worries and unquestioning devotion, the sacrifice and
> peace that saturate a home.
>
> In every individual one of us, God is more intimately present than
> we are to ourselves. Every existing thing within us demands not
> only the existence of God but also His constant presence, from
> every rush of blood from our hearts, to every wish, every thought,
> every act. In other words, everything that is real must have God
> there as the explanation, the foundation, the cause of every moment
> of its reality.[2]

3. Eternity

This attribute is a further application of the infinity of God, now
applying it to time. We saw in considering the immensity of God
that He is not limited to any space. The eternity of God means

---

2. Farrell, *Companion to the Summa*, Vol. I, p. 64.

negatively that He is not limited to any time. He transcends time as He does space; He is outside and beyond it.

Again, we will have trouble imagining this, but by purifying what we know of time, we can conceive something of what eternity means. Philosophers say that time is the measurement of the changes of things in this world. To illustrate this, think of how slowly time seems to pass when there is little change in the place, or action or situation, as for example, how time drags for a lone survivor on a life raft, floating under a hot sun, all day long, upon a motionless sea. Or remember how we completely lose our sense of time while asleep. We might have been asleep an hour or ten hours. It is all the same for there is no change to record. Time then is a quality of things that change. It is seen in terms of past, present, and future, recording successive changes that take place. If we purify this notion, we can have some idea of the eternity of God.

First of all, there is no past, present or future with God. His is an *eternal now.* We can have some idea of the concept, 'no end,' for we will have no end since our souls are immortal. But the idea of 'no beginning' stumps us. Go back as far as you can in your mind, and then remember that eternity is beyond that. The inspired word of God uses this method of teaching us the eternity of God. "Before the mountains were made, or the earth and the world was formed; from eternity to eternity thou art God" (Psalm 89:2).

There is no need to measure duration in God, for God is always totally what He is. There is no change whatever to record in Him. "They shall perish but Thou remainest: and all of them shall grow old like a garment, and as a vesture Thou shalt change them and they shalt be changed. But Thou art always the *Selfsame* and Thy years shall not fail" (Psalm 101:26–28). For Him, past, present and future are all the same. "I am the Alpha and the Omega, the beginning and the end, saith the Lord God, who is, and who was, and who is to come, the Almighty" (Apocalypse 1:8).

Philosophers compare time and eternity by saying that time is an 'ever-flowing now.' The 'now' that was when we wrote the last sentence, is already past, therefore the 'now' is ever-flowing. But eternity is an 'eternal now,' as Boethius defined it. "Eternity is the possession, perfect and *all at once,* of life without beginning or end" (*De Consolatione Philosophiae,* V, 6). Eternity might best be compared to time as the dot in the center of a circle is compared to the circumference. Individual points all around the circumference of time are past, present or future in reference to each other. But the dot in the center is equally present to every point of the circumference. God is equally present in His eternal now to Alexander the Great, Julius Caesar, Napoleon, and Eisenhower. Around the circumference, minutes, hours, days, months and years are important to record the changes that successively take place, but in our changeless God, equally present to every moment of time, "One day is as a thousand years and a thousand years as one day" (II Peter 3:8). There can only be one reaction to the reality of this Eternal God who IS, totally and at all times, all perfection without beginning or end or change. In the words of the Divine Office, "To the King of ages, the immortal, invisible, the only God be honor and glory for ever and ever" (Capitulum of Prime, cf. 1 Timothy 1:17).

4. Immutability

This is another negative attribute, built up from the Latin verb for change (*mutare*). That God is immutable means that He is changeless, or unchanging. This is, of course, closely allied with what we have already seen. If God is infinite He has all perfection, if He is eternal He has all perfection all at once, hence there is no need for change. The difficulty here is that on earth change can be a sign of perfection. One must change to improve. But more accurately, change is a sign of perfectibility—the possibility of improvement. This, of course, must be denied of God. He has nothing to gain by change. He is all perfect as He is. As the philosophers say, He is Pure Act without any shade of potentiality. He is the Prime Mover who moves everything else and is Himself unmoved by anyone else. Being all perfect, there is nothing He can conceivably change to.

Some modern philosophers who think of everything in terms of evolution have tried to conceive of a changing God. In the words of Farrell: "(this) group takes a further step towards madness in advocating a kind of fluid, undeveloped god. God is the perfect in process, the principle of all struggling towards perfection through matter; yet this principle is fluid, for everything real is a process of becoming. Others within the group insist that god is the next higher step, the empirical quality just above the highest we know

. . . Maybe this undeveloped god is the finite world with its nisus towards deity, maybe this god is evolution; maybe it is the spirit of the rational order. Make it anything you like; but do not dare make it divine!" [3]

The ancient Stoics and the more recent philosophers, Hegel and Renan, are typical of the above attitude that calls for a changing God, or an evolving deity. Some modern philosophers make everything else evolve, man, the soul, the mind, morals. An evolving God is just the last step in the process.

Bishop Sheen has given us a concrete case of this attitude in his Introduction to a recent book. "This doctrine held by many today was a favorite subject of one of the recent Gifford lecturers (in England). His particular theory was that God was infinitely perfect though evolving. According to this theory, when there was only matter in the universe, God was a plant; and when there were only plants, God was an animal; and when there were only animals, God was at the mind-stage. Presently, he argued, we are at the mind stage and God is an angel. Some day we will be angels and God will move up a peg in the cosmic scale." The writer (Bishop Sheen) in a friendly discussion with that philosopher argued that an infinitely perfect being is one who possesses at each and every moment of His existence the plenitude of perfection. But his evolving deity in a million years from now would possess a perfection which he does not possess at this moment, and therefore is not and cannot be infinitely perfect. The professor naively answered: "I never thought of that." [4]

Holy Scripture also stresses this unchangeableness of God. He is called: "The Father of lights, with whom there is no change, nor shadow of alteration" (James 1:17). "I am the Lord, and I change not" (Malachias 3:6).

5. Simplicity

This is an attribute that requires some preliminary explanation. The word simple has taken on some connotations in English that are not at all allied with its philosophical meaning. For many people today, it would not seem like much of a compliment to tell them they are simple. Yet this is one of the key words used by the

3. Farrell, *Companion to the Summa*, Vol. I, p. 68.
4. Reys, *God and His Attributes*, Introduction pp. v–vi.

Vatican Council in its statement on God: "One . . . absolutely simple and immutable spiritual substance."

Taken philosophically, simplicity means not having composition of parts. To be composed involves imperfection. Our bodies, for example, are corruptible because they are composed of parts which can fall apart and decompose. There are no parts whatever in God. He is one simple reality, enclosing all perfection in one being. That is why we remarked above that none of these attributes we have spoken about are really distinct in God. He does not have these attributes. He *is*, in one simple being, all the perfection implied by these attributes.

We can say this in the concrete by remarking that God is a Spirit, without the slightest receptivity. Nothing is ever added to God. An angel is a spirit but is composed in this sense, that its angelic nature received existence from God. But God is His existence. Man's mind is spiritual, but we can distinguish man's mind from his thoughts, God *is* His mind and His Thoughts. God simply is what He is, or as Christ Our Lord said, "God is a Spirit" (John 4:24). Men learn the truth, follow the way, receive life, God *is* the Way, the Truth and the Life.

There have been those in the Church who thought of God in an anthropomorphic sense. There are those today who picture God as an old gentleman with a long white beard. But God can have no body, any more than He can have His existence identified with the world as the Pantheists would give us to believe. God is altogether apart, a unique and totally independent Being from whom all others receive their being and all that they are.

We get a glimpse of the perfection of simplicity in some works of art which are perfect in their simplicity. In them, the complexity of the subject is unified in one simple theme. The same may be said of a machine which can perform many functions with one simple mechanism. These are only faint traces of the simplicity of God, wherein all the varied perfections imaginable are united and realized in one altogether simple and uncomposed being.

6. Unity

This is a good note on which to end our consideration of the quiescent attributes of God. As we have seen, all these attributes are one in God, and God is by His very nature *One*. "Hear O Israel, the Lord Thy God is One God" (Deuteronomy 6:4). "I am the First and the Last and there is no God besides Me" (Isaias 44:6).

Monotheism was the constant stress of the Old Testament because most of the pagans were polytheists who believed in many gods. Some like Zoroaster in Persia were Dualists who spoke of two supreme beings, Ormuzd, the principle of all good, and Ahriman, the principle of all evil. This was somewhat revived along mitigated lines in Christian times by the Manichaeans, and the Albigenses. While this duality of gods, one good and one evil, is a facile way of explaining the evil in the world, it is philosophically untenable and against the Christian Faith which begins with these words: "I believe in One God" (Nicene Creed).

St. Athanasius says that "to speak of several equally powerful gods, is to speak of several equally powerless gods" (*Oratio contra Gentes*). There cannot be two all-perfect beings. And if they were two distinct beings, there would have to be some means of distinguishing them; one would have to have something that the other did not have as a point of distinction. If one had something that the other did not have, both would not be all perfect, one would be lacking something. Thus the Vatican Council defines that God is "One absolutely simple spiritual substance."

It used to be thought by some scholars that men were originally polytheistic, and that gradually the notion of God was purified to a monotheistic form. This has been thoroughly discredited by recent studies. The further back you go in a study of the history of religions, the most basic idea is the notion of one God. Polytheism is a corruption of this primitive notion of the one God.

Our whole idea of God is so coherent and unified that if God is not one in nature and being, He simply could not be. In his *Summa Contra Gentes* (I, 42), St. Thomas produces seventeen arguments to prove that God as we know Him is one God. We conclude our study of the quiescent attributes of God on this notion of the unity of God, for while we have distinguished many various attributes to help our minds understand the infinitely rich being of God, we must remind ourselves at the end that all these attributes are one in God, all identified in his rich oneness of nature. In His complete unity of Being we find realized all the perfection of infinity, immensity, eternity, immutability, simplicity.

B. Operative Attributes of God

Now that we have seen the quiescent or absolute attributes of
God, those things that pertain to God alone as considered in Himself, we must next study those attributes which we consider to describe His operation. When we spoke of God as infinite and changeless perfection, that may have seemed to connote inactivity. But
ours is a living God, and life is manifested by activity. Moreover,
He is a personal God, so that His life will be the height of intelligent activity. Like everything else in God, this activity too will
be infinite, limitless.

A person is someone who knows and loves. That is the difference
between someone and something. Since therefore God is an intelligent being, His life will be characterized by infinite knowledge and infinite love. In other words, His is the perfection of
mind and will raised to a superlative degree. We express this by
saying that God is omniscient and omnipotent, or more simply,
all-knowing and all-powerful.

1. Omniscience

This attribute simply means that God knows all things. To attain a clearer idea of all that this concept implies, we must specify
just exactly *what* God does know in knowing all things, and secondly, *how* God knows what He knows.

The first and foremost object of God's knowledge is *Himself*. It
could not be anyone else, for He is the highest object of all knowledge. Moreover, He alone comprehends Himself fully. If anyone
else fully comprehended Him, he would be God. "So the things
also that are of God, no man knoweth, but the Spirit of God"
(I Corinthians 2:10ff.)."Neither does anyone know the Father, but
the Son" (Matthew 11:27). Farrell has put this very well:

> Obviously we cannot deny God knowledge of Himself without
> making Him less divine. A man who knows nothing about himself
> needs medical attention and rest; plainly he is sick, a victim of
> amnesia. A man who gets himself mixed up with someone else, who
> imagines for instance that he is Napoleon or the archangel Gabriel,
> is evidently insane. If God is not sick or insane, He knows Himself;
> if, as has been shown, He is completely perfect, then He knows Him-
> self perfectly, for ignorance of self is certainly an imperfection.[5]

---

5. Farrell, *Companion to the Summa*, Vol. I, pp. 76–77.

God also knows *all other things that exist.* This is a direct result of His knowing Himself comprehensively, for in so doing, He knows everything else that actually derives from Him and depends upon Him for being. Moreover He knows all existing things in Himself, as in their Source, and Foundation, and First Cause. This is not a hazy or indirect knowledge, for the totality of all reality depends wholly upon Him and He knows it as such. When we know something, we must find something to know, but God's knowledge is creative. He does not have to look for things to know; they exist because He knows them and wills that they be. We must recognize truth, but He is Truth, the foundation of all we recognize as true.

Moreover, God's act of knowing is infinitely perfect, because it proceeds from an infinite mind, from Himself. He does not have to know things one at a time as we do, but knows all things perfectly in one perfect act of knowledge which also is Himself. God is His Knowledge. All-Knowledge is just another aspect of His simple, all-perfect Being.

Fully knowing Himself, God obviously knows *all possible beings,* besides all existing beings. He knows all the possible ways that His infinite being can be participated in, or imitated or shared by created beings. He even knows the free future actions of men, for these too are real and depend upon Him for being. He knows them as they are.

We find all these notions repeated many times in Divine Revelation. To give a few citations: "For the Lord knoweth all things . . . He declareth the things that are past and the things that are to come" (Ecclesiasticus 42:19). "For the Lord searches all hearts and understands all the thoughts of minds" (I Paralipomenon 28:9). "Thou hast forseen all my ways" (Psalm 138:4). The Vatican Council has recapitulated this doctrine in one terse yet solemn statement: "All things are naked and open to His eyes, even those which are yet to be by the free action of creatures" (Denz. 1784).

We have seen, in regard to the eternity of God, that all things are present to Him. This applies to His knowledge also. All that He knows, He knows in its proper sequence of time; even though it happened two thousand years ago, or will happen two thousand years hence, it is all present to Him in His eternal now. St. Augustine states it thus: "God knows all things in such wise that neither what we call things past are past therein (in His knowledge) nor what we call things future are therein waited for as coming, as though they were absent, but both past and future with things present are all present" (*De Trinitate,* 15, 7, 13).

Some object that if God sees future free actions of men these actions are no longer free. "If God sees them, they are present to Him. They will infallibly happen, and hence they are not free," so they say. This is mixing up our way of knowledge and God's, beclouding, rather than clarifying the issue. To answer this objection we must first assert the two fundamental truths. 1) God knows all things, even future free actions, before they happen. But, 2) man is free, and does act freely, according to the nature that God gave him. Otherwise, we should dismiss all our policemen and empty all our jails, for we cannot enforce the law if man is not free to obey or disobey it, nor can we punish a man for disobeying it unless he does so freely.

Now then, if God sees an action before it happens, how is it free? The answer is that God sees it in His eternal now, and He sees it according to its full reality, therefore as a free act. We can see actions happening right now, actions that depend upon the free will of men, such as men attending school. We can remember some of our free actions of the past. But these actions, present or past, do not cease to be free because we see them. Moreover, if we stood at the corner window high up in a skyscraper and saw two autos heading for a collision down both sides of the building below us, their collision would not cease to be free because we saw it before it happened. Neither does man's future free action cease to be free because God sees it as present. True, it will infallibly happen, but also, it will happen freely because that is the way God sees it, not necessarily happening, but coming from the free will of man in the future.

This co-existence of our freedom with God's foreknowledge is still a mystery, but not a contradiction. Bossuet says it is like holding two ends of a chain in the dark without seeing how the links are connected between the two ends. We admit that God's knowledge is creative, that He is the first cause of all the reality in world, but as St. Thomas has explained, God moves all beings according to their natures—the physical world according to strictly necessary physical laws, but man according to his free will, because that is a perfection with which God has endowed man.

We also know that God has His providential plan for this world, but this does not make us fatalists, because fatalists deny free will. They say, "Whatever you do or wish, this will necessarily happen." We say, "Pray as if all depended upon God, and then work as if all depended upon you." The exact truth is that our actions depend upon both God and man, but each in his own order of causality.

This is perhaps best illustrated by a story. It seems that one of the early Pilgrim fathers was going from his log cabin into town for some provisions. He had been gone only a few minutes when he returned. "What's the matter?" asked his wife. "Oh, I just forgot my gun, and you know how the Indians have been around lately." "That's silly of you to come back," she replied, "if it's foreordained that the Indians are going to kill you, it's just going to happen and that's that!" "Maybe that's the way you look at it," answered the settler, "but what if it's ordained that the Indians will kill me if they find me without my gun!"

If everyone had a fatalistic and pessimistic attitude on life, nothing constructive would ever get done. God has His blueprint but we are builders too, and He has endowed us with the power to work freely. In the inspired word of God, used in the epistle of the Mass for a Confessor Saint, the just man is praised "because he was able to have sinned, and did not do so" (Ecclesiasticus 31:8–11).

Such then is the knowledge or omniscience of God. He knows infinitely all things that are, or were, or will be, or can be, no matter how. He is the Truth in which all other truth participates. It is a wonderful truth of Faith that one day we too are destined to see this Truth, not haltingly as now, but face-to-face in the Beatific Vision of God.

We can readily see how beautifully the vision (of God) harmonizes, perfects, completes our nature. For here is the ultimate quenching of our thirst to get at the cause of things, here is the ultimate answer to our perpetual "why," here is the ultimate peace for that intellectual restlessness that refuses to be satisfied with anything the world of nature has to offer. Here is a fulfillment of our potentialities for all truth, a fulfillment so great that its abundance can be accommodated only by the gift of still greater potentialities within us. In this vision is the goal of our searching, the home for our wandering feet, the quiet for our clamoring heart; only God can offer us these things, and only by this vision can we directly, immediately come home to God.

> By this vision we see the unveiled beauty of God; not just a shining part of it, not an unending succession of its splendours, but all of it at once. It can be no other way, for God is simple; you must see all of Him or see Him not at all. The magnificence of that beauty is eternity's secret; the eye has not seen, nor has the ear heard, nor has it entered the mind of man to conceive it. . . . There it will not be the image, but the original; we shall see all of it, though our finite minds, even with divine help, will never be able to exhaust, to comprehend the infinitude of that divine perfection. As a matter of fact, we shall see a great deal we missed on earth for in heaven our insight into the perfections of creatures will not be limited to territory of a few squares in a city, of a few miles in a country or of a few years of life. God has in Himself all the perfections of creatures, the full story of the thoughts, hopes and struggles of those closest to our heart, a detailed account of the complicated laws of the universe. All these we shall see: not exhaustively, for that would be to comprehend the plans of God; not equally, but in proportion to the degree of that supernatural help which is the light of glory; not by images or concepts, but as God sees them, in His very essence. And we shall see them, not bit by bit, day by day, year by year, but all at once.[6]

In heaven, then, we shall partake of the true and most sublime Wisdom, which is the crowning characteristic of the Divine Mind. Here on earth, through our study of theology, we are approaching this eternal Wisdom as best we can. The secret of life is to let this Divine Wisdom pervade our minds and our attitudes and our days. "How deep is the mind of God's Wisdom, of His Knowledge, how inscrutable are His judgments, how undiscoverable His way . . . All things find in Him their origin, their impulse, the center of their being; to Him be glory throughout all ages, Amen" (Romans 11:33–36).

2. Omnipotence

Just as we said that God's mind is all-knowing, here we affirm that His will is all-powerful. Just as the primary object of His mind is Himself, Supreme Truth, so the primary object of His will is Himself, Supreme Goodness. God can no more not will Himself, or love Himself, than we cannot will our own happiness. We can

---

6. Farrell, *Companion to the Summa*, I, pp. 86–87.

be mistaken about what is the best means for us to achieve happiness, because of our faulty minds, but there is no room for error in God, He perfectly knows Himself and perfectly loves Himself. However, this is not the whole story, for as He knows other beings in Himself, so too does He love all other beings as participations in His own supreme Goodness and Beauty. "Thou lovest all the things that are, and Thou didst not make anything hating it" (Wisdom 11:24).

This may seem a little selfish to us, that God loves Himself first and foremost. But again, we are thinking of God in a purely human way. The ultimate goal of our life is outside ourselves, therefore it is selfish of a man, and the height of pride, to make himself the center of his life. But not so with God. He is the beginning and end of all things and He knows it. And we have just seen: "All things find in Him their origin, their impulse, the center of their being" (Romans 11:36). Yet God has not stopped with Himself, although He could have been perfectly happy in doing so. As we shall study subsequently, in His Mercy (and there is no other word to express it adequately), He has freely willed to create other beings to partake in His Being, yes even in His life and eternal happiness. And He freely loves them. And as if this were not enough, when His creatures spurned His gift, we have Bethlehem and Calvary as additional proofs of the depth of His Divine Love. His love like His knowledge is creative. He did not seek for us to love us. He made us to love us. The only adequate expression we can have for love such as this is to say with St. John, "God *is* Love" (I John 4:8). Like the other perfections of His Being it is identified with Himself and is therefore infinite.

The Vatican Council has also defined that God Who is "infinite in intellect and will" (Denz. 1782), "by His Goodness and almighty Power most freely created both material and spiritual creatures out of nothing, not to acquire or increase His own happiness but to manifest His perfections by the good things which He gives to creatures" (Denz. 1783).

As we have noted regarding God's knowledge, here too in His other operative attribute of omnipotence we find some human difficulties. We say, for example, that God can do all things, or anything. Then someone asks, "Can God make a square circle?" If not, they claim He is not omnipotent. Again, we must repeat,

God can do anything. But a square circle is nothing, a contradiction in terms. It would be talking nonsense to say that God can do or make nothing, and a square circle is exactly that, nothing. It still holds that God can do anything, but anything must be something.

3. Omnipotence and the Problem of Pain

We should not close this section with the discussion of the problem of evil. This is a negative aspect of life, brought on by a misuse of man's will. We do much better to regard God in His Providence, that disposition of His will which plans for each one of us, all the helps we will need to save our souls. That is the all-important consideration for God, as well as for us. There is no real evil except that which is incurred by the eternal loss of God. Leon Bloy put it positively when he remarked in the closing lines of his novel, *La Femme Pauvre,* that the only tragedy in life is not to be a saint. Consequently, since God made all men for a share in His eternal happiness, He arranges for all men to have all the necessary means to attain that end. This arrangement we call the Providence of God. That is why we truly call Him "Our Father." The essential duty of a father is to provide for his children. God provides for us eternally.

Conclusion and Summary

This third section on the One God should have made one point amply clear, that God is truly the beginning and the end of all things, that while we can know something of Him by reason alone, the perfection of His Nature is shrouded in the mystery of the Infinite. However, we can see that everything else is meaningless without Him for all things depend upon Him for whatever of being or perfection they have.

To better understand ourselves and the world we live in, we have successively (we shall not presume to say successfully) studied the fact that we can know the existence of God from reason, that we are as sure of His existence as we are of our own. We then saw His essence which is simply *to be.* This is summed up in His name, Yahveh: He who is, the name that can only apply to the Supreme Being without beginning, end or limitation. As to His perfections, we saw that they are Himself; *God* does not acquire or have perfections, as man does, God is His perfections. Moreover, they are not really distinct realities in Him as in us. They are just our imperfect way of visualizing the full import of that mysterious reality: Supreme Being.

From a view of His quiescent attributes of infinity, immensity, eternity, immutability, simplicity and unity, we see that the nature of God is truly unlike the nature of man. To every perfection in man, we find the absolutely perfect exemplar in God. The only human reaction adequate to this discovery is adoration.

The operative attributes of God gave an inkling of what it is to be a person in the fullest sense of the word: to know and to love perfectly, unendingly. That again is the reality of God. A share in this perfect happiness of possessing and enjoying all things in God is heaven's goal. But we saw that here on earth, where the infinite action of God's mind and will touches the finite action of man's mind and will, deep and mysterious problems arise. However, we saw that man is capable of the greatest good which is attainment of heaven, and consequently the emphasis in life should be placed on positive living to attain the good with the ever-present help of God's providence. The Christian Humanist must be optimistic, under God.

The next step in our study is a deeper glance at the life of God. Here we completely leave the realm of rational knowledge to study a mystery attainable only by faith in what God has revealed: that while He is a personal God, there is not only one Person in God. The One God is Father, Son, and Holy Spirit.

CHAPTER IV

The Holy Trinity

Now THAT WE HAVE SEEN the broad lines of what man can know by reason and faith about the nature and attributes of God, we proceed to the deepest and most fundamental of all Christian mysteries, the inner life of God, the Holy Trinity. This is the deepest of all mysteries for it concerns something we could never know by ourselves. Even after God has told us that He is Father, Son, and Holy Spirit we cannot understand how it is that there are three distinct and equal persons existing in the one divine nature.

Some may question why we even want to study so deep a mystery. Yet, if it is the most fundamental of all Christian mysteries, if God has deigned to reveal it to us, why should we not try to grasp what it is that He has revealed, how it is related to the other mysteries that He has revealed? How can we begin to study the other most fundamental mystery, the Incarnation of the Son, if we have not first studied the relationship of the Son to the Father, the relationship of both of them to the Holy Spirit?

In a recent book, F. Sheed has discussed this attitude of some Catholics in shunning a discussion of the Trinity. He says that the attitude of some is one of

> . . . intellectual unconcern—God has revealed certain things about Himself, we accept the fact that He has done so, but find in ourselves no particular inclination to follow it up. God has told us that He is three persons in one Divine Nature, and we say 'Quite so,' and proceed to think of other matters—last week's Retreat, or next week's Confession or Lent or Lourdes or the Church's social

teaching or foreign missions. All these are vital things, but compared with God Himself, they are as nothing: and the Trinity is
God Himself. These other things must be thought about, but to think
about them exclusively and about the Trinity not at all is plain
folly. And not only folly, but a kind of insensitiveness, almost a
callousness, to the love of God. For the doctrine of the Trinity is
the inner, the innermost, life of God, His profoundest secret.

He did not have to reveal it to us. We could have been saved
without knowing that ultimate truth. In the strictest sense it is His
business, not ours. He revealed it to us because He loves men and
wants not only to be served by them but truly known by them. It
is the surest mark of love to want to be known. The revelation of
the Trinity was in one sense a more certain proof even than Calvary that God loves men. To accept it politely and think no more
of it is an insensitiveness beyond comprehension in men who quite
certainly love God.[1]

We do then want to know what we can know about this deepest
mystery, for in knowing about it, we are knowing more about God,
we are penetrating His deepest secret. Our study will proceed as
follows:

1. The Statement of the Doctrine
2. Historical Errors regarding the Trinity
3. Sources of the Trinity in Revelation
4. Philosophical Discussion of the Doctrine
5. Theological Questions regarding the Trinity
6. Application of the Doctrine to the Christian Life

I. THE STATEMENT OF THE DOCTRINE OF THE HOLY TRINITY

From the outset, it is well to state precisely what we believe about
this doctrine. Many Catholics are fuzzy in their concept of the
Holy Trinity and involve themselves in impossible contradictions.
We can summarize the doctrine in two brief phrases:

> Three Persons, really distinct and equal
> Exist in One Divine Nature.

That there is One Divine Nature we have already seen in the
preceding section. That there are three distinct Persons, really
distinct and equal, subsisting in this one divine nature is the new
element.

One of the most authoritative and explicit statements of this

1. Sheed, *Theology and Sanity*, pp. 65–66, Sheed & Ward, New York, 1946.

doctrine is that of the Athanasian Creed, named after St. Athanasius but probably composed by St. Fulgentius (468–533), after the main lines of this doctrine had been defined by the Church in the course of the great trinitarian heresies. The following is a translation of part of this great creed which priests recite in their Divine Office for Sundays:

> The Catholic Faith is this, that we worship one God in Trinity and Trinity in Unity, neither confusing the Persons, nor dividing the substance. For there is one Person of the Father, another of the Son, and another of the Holy Spirit. But the Godhead (nature) of the Father, of the Son and of the Holy Spirit is all one, the glory equal, the majesty co-eternal. . . . The Father is made by none, neither created, nor begotten. The Holy Spirit is of the Father and of the Son: neither made, nor created, nor begotten, but proceeding (Denz. 40).

Obviously, our problem here is not mathematical. We are not saying that there are three gods and still One God. We say there are three Persons in One Nature (of God). Hence, we cannot even begin to know what we are talking about until we know something about the words 'Person' and 'Nature.' God is not three and and one at the same time in the same way because person and nature are not the same thing. He is three Persons but one Nature.

While we will come back to this point later in the philosophical discussion of the doctrine, for the time being we must at least have an elementary notion of what we mean by person and nature so we can speak about the mystery.

Person answers the question: "Who is it?" The person is the subject, the agent, the one who acts, as the philosophers say: 'the subject of attribution.'

Nature, on the other hand, answers the question, "What is it?" Nature makes a thing what it is. It is that by which a subject acts in a certain way. A dog acts like a dog because he has canine nature; an angel acts like an angel because it has an angelic nature; God acts infinitely because He has the Divine nature.

Even among human beings we note the difference of person and nature. There is one common nature, human nature, possessed by everyone in the classroom. And yet there are as many persons as there are individuals possessing this intelligent nature. If you ask *"who* is writing this?" I answer, "I am" signifying a person. And you persons are reading it. But if you ask *"what* I am" I answer, "a human being," signifying my human nature. The agent in both cases, writing or reading, is the person. And that *by which* we act, that which makes us capable of writing or reading, is our intelligent nature. So person and nature are not the same thing even in us. Person is *who* we are, and nature is *what* we are.

Now if we apply this to God, asking first *what* God is, we get the answer we have studied in the last section: One simple infinitely perfect being. But when we ask *Who* God is, we are told by divine revelation that He is Father, Son and Holy Spirit. The mystery is, how can three distinct persons equally exist in one nature? With us, one nature and one person always go together. But this is no reason why there can not be three persons in the one *divine* nature. We would never surmise it or guess it if left to our own rational powers, but such is the mystery of the Holy Trinity as revealed to us by God.

So difficult is this concept of three persons, really distinct and equal, in one divine nature, that innumerable errors have been made by men in attempting to express it. We are going to discuss these errors now, so that by seeing what the Trinity is *not,* we may come to a more precise idea of what it *is.*

II. HISTORICAL ERRORS REGARDING THE HOLY TRINITY

The doctrine of the Trinity is so fundamental to Christianity that before many centuries had passed, practically all of the possible errors had arisen and been refuted by the Church. Of course there are many errors regarding the Trinity today, but they are just old heresies with new labels. Once we study the basic, typical heresies, we can always diagnose and answer the modern versions of them.

First we must note that the Trinity is a doctrine absolutely special to Christianity. There have been many pagan religions with variations of many gods, but never a religion with three distinct and equal Persons in One God. Even within the Church, the points to be reconciled in this doctrine, namely the distinction and equality of the persons, have been historically overstressed at times, and this has led to heresy. We can summarize the type heresies under two general headings: 1) Those that overstress the *equality* of the persons in one divine nature to such an extent that they lose the real distinction between the persons; and 2) those that make the persons so *distinct* that they become subordinate to one another, and no longer equally possess the one divine nature. The truth of the mystery lies in preserving both elements: real distinction and equality.

A. Heresies That Lose the Distinction of Persons in God

1. Rationalists (Monarchians)

This heresy is easy to comprehend historically. For ages, the stress had been on the unity of God in the face of rampant polytheism. If one thing was certain to the chosen people at the time of Christ it was that God is One God. Now at first blush, mention of three persons in one God seems to offend the unity of God's nature—especially if the notions of person and nature are not too well understood. We recall how Christ was accused of blasphemy because He made Himself equal to God. This is today the position of the Jewish religion. They believe that God is personal, but hold that there is but one person in God. The same can be said of the Mohammedans. While the Monarchian heresy can be understood from this point of view, overstressing the unity of God to such an extent that the distinction of persons in God is lost, the *Rationalist* position is more unreasonable. They argue thus: We know by reason that there is on earth but one person with each single individual nature. They also can determine by reason that there is one nature in God. Now because they will only believe what they can understand and demonstrate by reason, the Rationalists openly reject the revelation of God regarding the Trinity of Persons and argue: if there is one nature in God there is only one person, because that is the only way we can understand it by reason. Like all rationalist positions, they make their little minds, not God's infinite mind, the measure of truth, and thus lose all comprehension of divine mysteries. This is the modern position of the Unitarians. Of course it also involves a denial of the divinity of Christ, for if there is no Trinity, the second person is not divine.

2. Modalism (Sabellians)

This heresy accepts the names Father, Son and Holy Spirit from revelation but so overstresses their unity in the divine nature that they become merely names for one person who manifests himself according to several modes, hence the name, modalism. There are various versions of this heresy; some say that God manifests himself now as creator, now as redeemer, now as sanctifier; some declare this to have happened historically in succession, beginning with God as creator in the Old Testament, as redeemer in the New Testament during the time of Christ, and as sanctifier since then. But always, it is a matter of one person manifesting himself in various modes, not of three distinct persons as we believe. Just as we have seen one person impersonate others, for the modalist, Father, Son and Holy Spirit are just the various impersonations of one same person, God. This is the belief of some modern Protestant sects who speak of Father, Son and Holy Spirit as different manifestations of one person, God. We might also add that some Catholics can easily fall into this error by taking some examples or illustrations of the Trinity too literally. There is no exact created illustration of the Blessed Trinity. This reality is unique in God. We can use an illustration of water as liquid, steam or solid to illustrate the unity of nature in God, but water is not fluid, steam and ice at the same time, whereas God is distinctly Father, Son and Holy Spirit simultaneously and eternally. Modalism finds an easy refutation in the Scriptural passages showing Father, Son and Holy Spirit acting as distinct personal agents at the same time (Cf. *infra* Baptism of Jesus).

B. Heresies That Lose the Unity of Nature in God

These errors originally stem from a Greek philosophy called Gnosticism. As errors against the Trinity, they may be bracketed under the term *Subordinationism* since they make the Son subordinate to the Father, or the Holy Spirit subordinate to Father and Son. These are the two common versions of this type-heresy.

1. Arianism

This heresy is named after Arius, the person who originated the doctrine that the Son is the highest of creatures but not God. This error is totally destructive of the Trinity and the Incarnation, for if the second Person is not God equal to the Father, then Christ is not the God-man, and there is no redemption for our sins. This heresy was very widespread in the early centuries of the

Church, and flourished under the patronage of the Emperors Constantine, Constantius, Valens and Julian the Apostate. It finally collapsed under the Catholic Emperor, Theodosius the Great, when Arianism ceased to be the Court-Religion. Dogmatically, Arianism was outlawed much earlier when orthodoxy triumphed at the Council of Nicaea, in 325 . . . This was the first General Council of the Church, famed for its Nicene Creed. The whole battle between Arianism and Catholicism hinged upon the one letter "i" (the Greek word *homo* meaning 'same' as opposed to *homoi* meaning 'similar'). The Arians claimed that the Son was 'similar' in nature to the Father, expressing this by the Greek word, *homoi* (similar) *ousios* (nature or essence). And the Council of Nicaea defined that the Son was of one *identical* nature with the Father, adding in parentheses (as the Greeks say) *homoousios*. This was a time when the Greeks had two words for it, and the Church would not add an iota (the Greek letter "i") because it meant the difference between Christ being God or a creature. The great personage who upheld the true doctrine throughout this period was St. Athanasius of Alexandria, who was a young deacon at the Council of Nicaea, later primate of Egypt. He was five times exiled from his Episcopal See at Alexandria during his forty-five years in that office, narrowly escaped death many times at the hands of the heretics, and finally in his eighties saw the truth conquer under Theodosius.

2. Macedonianism

This is but a variation of Arianism, sometimes called Semi-Arianism, which is applied to the Holy Spirit. Named for the region in which it flourished, Macedonianism taught that the Holy Spirit is also a creature, subordinate to the Father and the Son, and not God. The Second General Council of the Church at Constantinople was occasioned mainly by this heresy. This council repeated what was contained in the Nicene Creed on the Father and the Son, but added a few new lines regarding the divinity of the Holy Spirit against the Macedonians. With this heresy we are finished with the main type-heresies regarding the Trinity. While modern heresies do not parade under these ancient names, Arianism and Macedonianism are very much alive in the world today. The Liberal Protestants, and such Christian sects as do not believe in the divinity of Christ, such as Christian Scientists, are formally

Arians. The Holy Spirit has often been called the forgotten God, so much so that many who do not believe in His divinity do not even bother to state their case.

No matter what the version of modern trinitarian heresies, they generally fall into one of the above types or categories. Either they overstress the equality of persons so much that they make the three persons mere variations of one person, not three really distinct persons; or they overstress the distinction of Father, Son and Holy Spirit so much that they are no longer equal to each other but subordinate. But whatever the heresy, the answers that were given to these heresies in their ancient form, these same answers fit the new versions today, for they are eternal answers based upon God's word revealed in Scripture or Tradition. We shall now study this data of revelation to see how the correct notion of the Trinity, that of three distinct and equal persons existing in one divine nature, is the notion found in the word of God.

III. Sources of the Trinitarian Doctrine in Revelation

This is the best occasion we have had thus far to demonstrate how the sources of revelation can be used to discover a divine truth that could never be found by reason alone. In our general introduction we saw that there are two sources of divine revelation, Holy Scripture and Tradition. We shall make use of both of these sources in the present matter, for the Trinity, as one of the most basic Christian Mysteries, is revealed in both of them.

A. Holy Scripture

1. The Old Testament

There is a danger to be encountered here. In reading the Old Testament today, we must be careful not to read into it things we now know from the New Testament message. It is true that the New Testament is the fulfillment of the Old, but it seems that the best we can say of the doctrine of the Trinity here, is that it is only foreshadowed in the Old Testament and fully revealed in the New. Some scholars point to the use of the plural in speaking of God, for example in Genesis, "Let *us* make man to our image and likeness" (Genesis 1:26). This can however be explained as the plural of majesty, as is the usage today in our plural use of 'you' in most languages, to avoid undue familiarity. Though the Hebrew language uses the plural 'Elohim' for 'God' it is nevertheless followed by a singular verb.

There are other vague indications too, such as the triple "Holy, Holy, Holy, Lord God of Hosts" in Isaias 6:3. A better indication is the personification of Divine Wisdom in the sapiental books: "I came out of the mouth of the Most High, the firstborn before all creatures" (Ecclesiasticus 24:5). This is a foreshadowing of the usage of St. John in the New Testament, calling the second person of the Holy Trinity, the Word. However, for all these indications the Jews did not know of the Trinity, nor was there any indication of the precise names in any one text. The best approach to this is in the messianic prophecy of the psalms: "Thou art my son, this day have I begotten thee" (Psalm 2:7). The Church uses this text in the Introit of the Mass for Christmas.

One of the best and most authoritative statements of the point we have been making is that of J. Lebreton in his classical book on the origins of the Trinity:

> This does not mean that the passages of the Old Testament that seemed so full of meaning to the Fathers must now be considered as meaningless as far as the plurality of persons is concerned. We only wish to point out that they could not provide a sufficient revelation for the Jews, and that we ourselves, who believe the doctrine of the Trinity, cannot find there a certain proof of the mystery. On the other hand, the mystery of the Trinity provides the best explanation of these texts of the Old Testament.
>
> This interpretation seems to conform best with the thought of the Fathers; and although several of them quoted the Old Testament against the Jews to prove the distinction between the Father and Son, their thesis is not in itself a complete statement of the doctrine of the Trinity. St. Epiphanius, famed for his unwavering doctrine, says: 'The divine unity was first and foremost proclaimed by Moses, the duality (the distinction between Father and Son) was heavily stressed by the prophets, and the Trinity was clearly shown forth in the Gospel.' [2]

We shall therefore go to the Gospels for our clearest insight into this deepest of God's mysteries.

2. The New Testament

There are two basic ways of demonstrating the doctrine of the Trinity from the New Testament. We have already seen the unity

---

2. J. Lebreton, *History of the Dogma of the Trinity*, Vol. I, The Origins, p. 416.

of nature in God throughout our study of the One God in the last section. It remains to show that there are three persons who are 1) really distinct; and 2) equal as God, that is, equally possessing the divine nature. To find this we could study each person separately showing that the New Testament speaks in turn of the Father, and the Son and the Holy Spirit, speaking of them each, moreover, as God. This would require the study of a great many texts. We can take a shortcut by studying a few classical texts in the Synoptics, St. John, and St. Paul in which all three persons are mentioned together. The indications of distinction and equality will not be equally present in each text; some are better than others. But we must remember that the Church does not argue from any one of these texts alone, but rather from the combined impact of all the texts taken as a composite whole.

a. THE SYNOPTICS

The Annunciation: The angel Gabriel appeared to the Blessed Virgin and greeted her with the famous words of the 'Hail Mary.' He then announced: "Behold thou shalt conceive in thy womb and shalt bring forth a son; and thou shalt call His name Jesus. He shall be great, and shall be called the *Son of the Most High . . .* and of His Kingdom there shall be no end." But Mary said to the angel, "How shall this happen since I do not know man?" And the angel answered and said to her, "The *Holy Spirit* shall come upon thee, and the *power of the Most High* shall overshadow thee; and therefore the *Holy One* to be born shall be called the *Son of God*" (Luke 1:31–35). Surely here there is mention of the three persons as distinct from each other, particularly the Son of God (the Father), the Most High, and the Holy Spirit. And the Holy Spirit is specified as performing the miraculous work, the virginal conception of Jesus in the womb of Mary. The Son is clearly the Divine Son of God the Most High. While we do not use this text by itself to prove the complete doctrine of the Trinity, it is the first clear manifestation of the mystery in the New Testament.

The Baptism of Jesus: Jesus came from Galilee to John at the Jordan. At first unwilling, at last John baptized him. "And when *Jesus* had been baptized, he immediately came up from the water. And behold, the heavens were opened, and he saw the *Spirit of God* descending as a dove and coming upon him. And behold a voice from the heavens saying: 'This is my beloved *Son* in whom

I am well pleased' " (Matthew 3:16–17). This is a good text to use against the Modalists, for all three persons appear at once and all doing different personal acts. In the light of this there can be no successive impersonation of three persons by one person. This scene is a fitting prelude to Our Lord's public ministry.

The Baptismal Formula: After the resurrection of Jesus, and immediately before the ascension, the disciples went to the mountain of Galilee where Jesus had directed them to go. "And Jesus drew near and spoke to them saying, All power in heaven and on earth has been given to Me. Go, therefore, and make disciples of all nations, *baptizing them in the name of the Father, and of the Son, and of the Holy Spirit,* teaching them to observe all things that I have commanded you; and behold I am with you all days, even unto the consummation of the world" (Matthew 28:19–20). This is *the* classic text used by all theologians in demonstrating the revelation of the trinitarian doctrine. The foregoing two texts are particularly good in showing distinction of persons, but this shows both distinction and equality of persons in a concise and cogent way.

We can show how theologians argue from this text very well as the English translation follows the oldest Greek text word for word.

Baptizones	autous	eis	to	onoma	tou	patros
Baptizing	them	in	the	name	of the	Father

kai	tou	huiou	kai	tou	hagiou	pneumatos.
and	of the	Son	and	of the	Holy	Spirit.

The argument follows three steps: 1) "Baptizing"—this designates a divine action, conferring upon the one who is baptized a participation of the divine life, and a consequent remission of his sins. Now since only God can grant a share in His life, baptism is effected in His name. Note the singular 'name': the name of God is Father, Son and Holy Spirit. As St. Augustine says regarding this: "This is one God, for it is not in the *names* of the Father, and of the Son, and of the Holy Ghost, but in the *name* . . . you hear one name, there is one God" (*Tract in Joannem,* 6, 9). 2) The three persons are set off in Greek usage by the triple use of the definite article 'the' (*tou* patros . . . *tou* huiou . . . *tou* hagiou pneumatos). When the Greek speaks in a general *impersonal* sense, as we would say, the 'spirit' of Notre Dame, the article 'the' is not used. The article *tou* is used to indicate a *person*. The triple use here designates definitely three distinct persons. 3) These three persons are equal in performing this divine action of baptism for they are linked by the correlative conjunction 'and' (kai . . . kai). Hence they are equally God. To see how meaningful this is, note how meaningless it would be to add another name linked by an 'and,' for example, in the name of the Father and of the Son and of the Holy Spirit and the Pope. When the Corinthians in the Early Church made too much of St. Paul, he asked indignantly, "Were you baptized in the name of Paul?" Only these three Persons, distinct as Persons, yet all equally possessing the divine nature, can effect the divine action of Baptism. Leave one of the names out and the baptism is simply invalid.

Thus in the Synoptic Gospels, in the most solemn moments of Christ's annunciation, the beginning of His public life, and in His farewell commission of His apostles to go out and conquer the world to His Kingdom, the basic Christian mystery of the Trinity is revealed. We can treat of the other scriptural texts quite briefly, to show the continuity of the doctrine in St. Paul and St. John.

b. ST. JOHN

When Our Lord was having his Last Supper with the Apostles He spoke to them very feelingly of His Father and the Holy Spirit to give them a clearer insight into the life of God. Chapters 14 to 16 should be read in their entirety. Perhaps the outstanding verses are these: "And *I* will ask the *Father* and *He* will send you *another Paraclete* (the invisible divine counsellor, consoler, comforter, advocate, guide, friend, to take the place of the Son who fulfilled these functions visibly in His humanity), the Spirit of Truth whom the world cannot receive because it neither sees Him nor knows Him. But you know Him, because He will dwell with you and be with you" (John 14:16-17). This obviously has reference to three distinct persons and the divinity of each is implied throughout the context. A little later on He repeats: "These things I have spoken to you while yet dwelling with you. But the Advocate, the *Holy Spirit*, Whom the *Father* will send *in My name*, He will teach you all things, and bring to your mind whatever I have said to you" (John 14:25-26).

C. ST. PAUL

For a complete coverage of the texts in St. Paul on the Most
Holy Trinity, it would be well to peruse the classic work of F.
Prat, *The Theology of St. Paul*. In the second volume of this work,
Prat has a chapter entirely devoted to the Trinity in St. Paul. In
the final verse of his second epistle to the Corinthians, St. Paul
makes direct reference to all three persons: "the grace of Our Lord
Jesus Christ, and the charity of *God* (the Father), and the fellow-
ship of the *Holy Spirit* be with you all, Amen."

St. Peter begins his first epistle in as clear a reference to the
Trinity: "Peter an apostle of *Jesus Christ* . . . chosen unto the
sanctification of the *Spirit,* according to the foreknowledge of *God
the Father* . . ." (I Peter 1:1–2).

It should be fairly obvious by now that the New Testament gives
clear indication of the Holy Trinity, The Father, The Son, and
The Holy Spirit, One God. Of course, it was to take time before
this widespread data of revelation (we have only scratched the surface of it) was precisely expressed in the terms 'person' and 'nature'
which we use today, but the reality of the truth was there, and
under the light of the Holy Spirit, the clearest expression of it
would be accomplished technically against the technical errors
of the heretics.

Our next step is to show that the correlative source of revelation,
tradition, also gives clear evidence of the belief of the early Christians in this fundamental Christian mystery. Before these texts in
the New Testament were written, men had for decades shown their
belief in their prayers. As time went on, the Tradition became
more widespread, for the advent of heresies regarding the Trinity
brought many writings on the subject to light.

B. Tradition

Our problem here is to see what was said and done in the Early
Church to give evidence of their belief in the Trinity on the word
of Christ in apostolic times. We shall consider 1) the Fathers, the
great witnesses of Tradition; 2) the Councils of the Church, in
which the universal belief of the whole Church was solemnly declared and defined infallibly; 3) Church practices, which represent
belief in the Trinity put into practice.

1. Fathers

It is no small task to read all the Fathers in the early centuries of the Church, even on one point such as the Trinity. Since it is so fundamental a doctrine, it appears constantly. The best we can do here is to record the conclusions from a great scholar who has done this necessary reading, and has stated clearly and definitely, just what he has found in the Fathers on this subject. Our guide once more is Cardinal Newman whose conversion is due in great measure to his intensive study of the Fathers and his consequent realization that the Catholic Church alone teaches today the same complete doctrine that was professed in the apostolic Church. Newman has several treatments of this subject. We shall merely study one of them:

> Such being the chain of testimonies in the early centuries concerning the Divine Triad (Trinity), so far is clear at once, and has to be noted first of all, *that it is impossible to view historical Christianity apart from the doctrine of the Trinity.*
> . . . I have been referring to the principal historical witnesses summoned from every part of Christendom—from Rome, Lyons, Carthage, Alexandria, Samaria, Antioch, Smyrna. Faithful to the baptismal form, which indeed by itself is conclusive of the point I am insisting on, they all speak of a Trinity, and under the same three names used in that form, as their broad view, from first to last, they speak of the special theistic teaching which the Gospel substituted for the polytheism of the Empire. Three and only three, nor is there any string of testimonies producible from those early centuries in a contrary sense, though there were individuals, such as Theoditus, Noetus, Sabellius and Paulus, who, differing from each other, differed from the main tradition. The three Persons are absolutely separated off, as unapproachable, incommunicable, in reference to the created universe, distinct from it in the ideas which They suggest, as the Object of exclusive veneration which is equivalent to divine worship.
> . . . These passages (from the Fathers) coalesce and form one whole, and a whole in agreement with the subsequent teaching on the subject in the fourth and fifth centuries; and their doctrine, thus taken as a whole, will be found to contain these four main points:
> 1) Each of the Three Divine Persons is distinct from each
> 2) Each is God; (equality of the Persons)
> 3) One proceeds from Another in succession;
> 4) Each is in the Other Two.

. . . Looking then at the literature of Christianity from the time of St. John to the time of St. Athanasius, as a whole . . . in which what one writer says may be fairly interpreted, explained and supplemented by what others say, we may reasonably pronounce that there was during the second and third centuries, a profession and teaching concerning the Holy Trinity, not vague and cloudy, but of a certain determinate character:—moreover, that this teaching was to the effect that God was to be worshipped in three distinct persons (that is that there was a divine Triad, of whom severally the personal pronoun (He) could be used), Each of Whom was the One Indivisible God, Each dwelt in Each, Each was really distinct from Each, Each was united to Each by definite correlations— moreover that such a teaching was contradictory to and destructive of the Arian hypothesis, which considered the Son of God and a fortiori the Holy Ghost to be simply and absolutely creatures of God, who once did not exist, however exalted it might assert them to be in nature and grace.[3]

2. The Councils

The great General Councils of the Church were generally occasioned by some widespread heresy or schism. The first two General Councils had reference to the basic Christian Mysteries, the Trinity and the Incarnation. We can use these councils to determine what was believed generally in the Early Church for they not only give us a statement drawn up by Bishops and Theologians of the Universal Church, but their statement is very precisely worded, aimed to scotch a definite heresy generally, and approved by the Holy Father as the infallible teaching of the Church.

a. THE COUNCIL OF NICAEA, A.D. 325

This is the first General Council of the Church held in a city near Constantinople. In Denzinger it is entitled "Against the Arians," whose error we studied above. The Arians taught that there was a time when the Son did not exist, that he was therefore created, a creature of the highest order, but not God. They summed up their doctrine in the word we mentioned above, *homoiousios*—similar in nature (not *homoousios*—of the same identical nature as the Father). The famous Nicene Creed, which is the classic statement of the Council, expresses the Catholic belief "in one Lord, Jesus Christ, the only-begotten Son of God, Born

---

3. Newman, *Tracts Theological and Ecclesiastical*, pp. 158–162. Longmans, Green & Co., New York.

of the Father before all ages (i.e. eternally). God of God, Light of Light, *true God of True God*. Begotten, not made, *of one substance* (or nature) *with the Father*" (and here, in the Latin translation of the Greek original, just so that the Arians who wrote in Greek mainly would not be able to pervert the terms, the Fathers add: "Quod graece dicunt, homoousion—As is said in Greek, homoousion"—i.e. of the same, identical nature as the Father). In the next general council which we shall immediately study, this kernel of the whole controversy is translated by the one Latin word which we now translate into English: "Consubstantialis"—"Consubstantial with the Father." This settled once and for all, that the Son is not only distinct from the Father, but also equally possesses the Divine Nature, is equally God, and not a creature as the Arians taught. The original version of the Nicene Creed is found in Denzinger in Greek and Latin, No. 54.

b. THE COUNCIL OF CONSTANTINOPLE, A.D. 381

We saw above that no sooner had the Arians been condemned for their doctrine regarding the Son, than the Semi-Arians or Macedonians emphasized their same doctrine making the Holy Spirit a creature. All the Nicene Creed had stated regarding the Holy Spirit was belief in Him as a separate Person of the Trinity: "And we believe in the Holy Spirit" (Denz. 54). Hence the Second General Council of the Church was called at Constantinople fifty-six years later to clarify the doctrine on the divinity of the Holy Spirit against the Macedonians. The council adopted the Nicene Creed with very few changes in wording (like 'Consubstantial'). But when they came to the part, "And we believe in the Holy Spirit," they defined further: "The Lord and Giver of Life, Who proceeds from the Father (and the Son), Who, together with the Father and Son is adored and glorified, Who spoke by the Prophets" (Denz. 86). If the Holy Spirit is equally adored and glorified with the Father and the Son, it follows that He is equally God with Them.

These two councils give us the most basic and infallible teaching of the Church on the Most Blessed Trinity. As intelligent Catholics, we need not merely say that the 'Church teaches the doctrine'; now we know *where* and *when* the Church officially and solemnly proclaimed it. We can quote the original source. This final, completed version of the Creed is so important that the

Church has made it a part of the Mass on Sundays and great feast days. It is interesting to note that during High Mass, when the priest is sitting at the side of the sanctuary during the singing of the creed, he removes his biretta at the words *simul adoratur* proclaiming the divinity of the Holy Spirit. We often hear of the Creed in the Mass referred to as the Nicene Creed, written at the Council of Nicaea in 325. We know now that it is rather the Nicene-Constantinople Creed, completed, as to the doctrine on the Holy Spirit, in Constantinople in 381. Thus through the Councils, the Church made a definite and precise statement of the trinitarian doctrine revealed by Christ, proclaimed by the Apostles and Fathers, and believed by the whole Church for the years preceding the Councils, and the specific heresies that occasioned them.

3. Practices of the Church

Many practices in the Early Church, especially forms of prayer, show that the ordinary people, as well as the theologians, expressed their belief in the Trinity. This gives rise to an ancient formula: "Lex orandi, lex credendi est," the "Law of Belief is the Law of Prayer" or more broadly, "We pray the way we do, because we believe the way we do." For example, the Preface we use in the Mass for Sundays, which is always dedicated to the Holy Trinity, has for centuries expressed our belief in the Holy Trinity: "It is truly —meet and just, right and availing unto salvation, that we should always and in all places give thanks unto Thee, Holy Lord, Father Almighty, Eternal God, Who together with Thine Only-Begotten Son and the Holy Spirit, are One God, One Lord, not in the singleness of One Person, but in the Trinity of one substance (nature). For that which, according to Thy revelation, we believe of Thy (i.e. the Father's) glory, the same we believe of Thy Son, the same of the Holy Spirit (for all three have the same nature) without difference or distinction; so that in the confession of one true and eternal Godhead, we adore distinctness in persons, oneness in essence (nature), and equality in majesty."

In the ancient apostolic Church we have many such examples:

a. THE APOSTLES CREED

We have already seen how this creed grew out of the profession of faith required for Baptism. The basis of this faith is belief in the Trinity: "I believe in *God*, The Father, Almighty . . . and in Jesus Christ, His only Son . . . and in the Holy Spirit." Moreover, the Baptism itself was, according to the words of Christ, conferred in the name of the Holy Trinity. We find this order in the *Didache* (7, 1), written around the end of the first century: "Baptize in the name of the Father, and of the Son, and of the Holy Spirit."

b. ANCIENT DOXOLOGIES

One of the most ancient hymns of praise, still current in the Church today, is the "Glory be to God the Father, and to the Son, and to the Holy Spirit (or as is sometimes given: together with the Holy Spirit)."

c. CONFESSIONS OF THE MARTYRS

Many martyrs who began their Christian lives by Baptism in the name of the Holy Trinity, ended them in the same name of God. For example, in the Acts of St. Polycarp, Bishop of Smyrna who was martyred for the Faith in A.D. 156, we find this final profession of his belief: "O truthful God . . . I glorify Thee, though through the Eternal and Heavenly High Priest, Jesus Christ, Thy beloved Son, through Whom be glory to Thee, with Him in the Holy Spirit, both now and in the ages to come." (*Acta Martyris Polycarpii*, 14, 3). St. Epipodius of Lyons who died for the Faith a few years later, A.D. 178, confesses his faith in the same strain: "I confess Christ to be God, with the Father and the Holy Spirit and it is fitting that I should give back my soul to Him Who is my Creator and Redeemer" (Ruinart, *Acta Martyrum*, p. 65). Such examples could be multiplied, but from these very early examples, it is clear that the possession of the faith in the Trinity was held by the Christian people. The expression of this truth grew even more striking as time went on, as in the case of St. Euplus of Catania, martyred in 304: "I adore the Father and the Son and the Holy Spirit; I adore the Holy Trinity, besides which there is no God . . . I sacrifice and immolate myself to the Father, and to the Son and to the Holy Spirit" (Ruinart, *Acta Martyrum*, p. 325).

This is sufficient data for our study of the Holy Trinity as revealed by God in Holy Scripture and Tradition. Certainly the evidence is ample, whether we consider the Synoptics, St. John or

St. Paul. Tradition is equally clear in the Fathers, the first two General Councils at Nicaea and Constantinople, and the many Church practices indicating a belief in the Holy Trinity. Up to this point then, we have determined just what we believe, the various historical errors regarding this belief, and the sources of our belief in Divine Revelation. The rest of our treatment deals with a deeper understanding of the mystery insofar as that is possible, and an application of this basic Christian mystery to the Christian life.

IV. PHILOSOPHICAL DISCUSSION OF THE MYSTERY OF THE HOLY TRINITY

A mystery is a truth which we cannot fully understand. Ordinarily, the separate elements of the mystery are understandable, but the mystery is in *how* these seemingly opposing elements exist in the same truth. For example, we can understand the notion, three persons, and the notion, one nature, but put them together in the same truth and you have a mystery.

It is well to understand from the beginning that a mystery does not involve any contradiction. We could not believe in a contradiction for a contradiction simply cannot exist, it is nothing, like a square circle. If we apply the principle of contradiction (namely, a thing cannot be and not be something at the same time, and in the same way) to the Trinity, we see at once that it is not a contradiction. It is true that God is three and one at the same time, but not in the same way. He is three persons and one nature.

Person and Nature then are the key to the mystery. Since they are the terms of the mystery we do have to know something about them: at least that they are not the same thing. This has been sufficiently treated above in showing that person is *who* we are, the agent, the "I"; and nature is *what* we are, the principle of operation, that which makes us what we are, that by which we act. Now there are three persons who act in God, but only one nature of God through which they act. To put our knowledge of the mystery briefly, we do understand "what we believe"—the terms of the mystery, but we do not understand "how it is possible" to have three distinct and equal persons existing in one nature. But in any case, since person and nature are different things, we know that the mystery is not a contradiction.

In a recent book, *Beyond Personality*, C. S. Lewis has a good analogy to explain our predicament in the face of mysteries. He says, take a two dimensional figure, say a rectangle, and give it intelligence. "Now look, friend," we say to the rectangle, "you only know about two dimensions, because you only have experience of what you are, length and width. But there is another dimension, depth, that you know nothing about. However, by taking what you do know and rearranging these two dimensions of length and width we can show you something about depth. We take six rectangles, make a box or cube out of them, and there you have it, depth." Well, the rectangle can still answer, "I don't quite get it; I just know length and width." "Well, all right," we say, "we don't expect you to *understand* it fully, or see it, because after all, you are just a square. But take our word for it that you get depth from that arrangement of length and width." We might make the same experiment with ourselves in regard to a fourth dimension if there were some way of rearranging length and width and depth to get it. And we certainly can make the same experiment in regard to the Trinity: God reveals that two things we can know of ourselves, person and nature, are realized in a different way in the mysteries of the Trinity and Incarnation. Graphically,

	MAN	TRINITY	CHRIST INCARNATE
Person	1	3	1
	(no mystery)	....real mystery....	
Nature	1	1	2 (human and divine)

The mystery then is not in what we believe, because the terms taken singly are intelligible. How it is possible to have them all together in one truth is where the mystery lies. While it is beyond our finite intellect, it is not against our intellect to accept the Trinity if we have the authority of God to tell us that it is so. So much we can say by philosophy, but theology goes beyond this in its efforts to understand more of what we believe.

V. THEOLOGICAL QUESTIONS REGARDING THE HOLY TRINITY

When a theologian delves deeper into the inner life of God, he must always begin with what God said, for God's revelation is the beginning of wisdom in this matter. God has said that He is the Father, the Son, and the Holy Spirit, and there is certainly something to be gained from investigating just what God meant when he used those precise words and no others. To understand more about them is certainly to understand more about the life of God.

Theologians have speculated long and wisely upon the life of God as revealed in the Holy Trinity. There is no deeper or more difficult subject. St. Augustine and St. Thomas are the leaders here, as in most theological matters. Augustine has a celebrated analogy which is an approach at least to some kind of understanding of this mystery. Remember however that it is an illustration, not properly an explanation, for as one Dogma professor said after teaching five hours a week for three months on the Trinity: "If I've explained it fully, I'm a failure, for it cannot be fully explained."

To quote St. Augustine:

> And so there is a kind of image of the Trinity in the mind itself, and in the knowledge of the mind, which is the offspring and its word concerning itself, and love as a third, and these three are one and the same substance. Neither is the offspring less, since the mind knows itself according to the measure of its own being; nor is the love less, since it loves itself according to the measure both of its own knowledge and its own being (St. Augustine, *De Trinitate*, 9, 12).

Now the above statement has to be slightly enlarged upon. It is a question of the life of God. Life is shown in activity. As we have seen, the only activity in God is that of mind and will, knowledge and love. Now God knows Himself, perfectly, from all eternity, and that perfect knowledge, or perfect expression (word) of that knowledge is compared to the Son as the *Word:* "In the beginning was the Word and the Word was with God and the Word was God" (John 1:1). Just as a human father is said to generate a son *physically, in time,* so God the Father is said to *eternally* generate the Son *intellectually.* They are co-equal for the Son is the perfect *Image* of the Father as St. Paul says. Also, "God has spoken to us by His Son . . . ," Who is "the brightness of His glory and the figure of His substance . . ." (Hebrews 1:1-3).

The other possible activity of life in God is that of the will, to love. Now just as the Son is likened to the personified Knowledge or Wisdom of the Father, so the Holy Spirit is likened by St. Augustine to the Eternal and personified Love of the Father for the Son and the Son for the Father. The Holy Spirit is called the Spirit of Love, or the Gift, as it is the movement of love to give or be given.

A. Processions

Theologically, all of this is expressed by the word *Procession*. We say that the Son proceeds from the Father eternally, and that the Holy Spirit proceeds from the Father and Son eternally. There is no question of one being before the other, rather it concerns the order of life in God, from the Father to the Son and from both of them to the Holy Spirit. And this is not something that happened once upon a time, it happens eternally, is happening therefore, right now. We must beware of diagrams in this matter generally, but just to have something to point to, we illustrate God's life thus:

The arrows represent the procession of life from Father to Son, and from both to the Holy Spirit.

These processions are important in speaking of the distinction of Persons in God, for they set up, to our way of thinking, the relationships of Father, Son and Holy Spirit; Father being He from whom the Son comes, Son being He who comes from the Father, and Holy Spirit, He who comes from the Father and the Son. The most important theological axiom in this matter is that *apart from these relations, everything else is identical in God.*

Moreover we learn from metaphysics that relation is the only kind of reality that can distinguish the three persons without putting anything in the nature. For example, if you are watching a parade go by, you stand in a certain relationship of bystander to those passing, but when the parade has passed, the relationship of bystander no longer exists. Your status is different than before, and still your nature was identical throughout. Your relationship of bystander distinguished you from the people in the parade, but did not change your nature or theirs. Any other distinguishing

mark, like your weight, the color of your hair or skin, etc., puts
something in your makeup. Relation does not. Hence we say that
the three relationships of Father, Son and Holy Spirit distinguish
the three Persons in God without affecting the simplicity of the
Divine Nature which is identically one for all three of them.

If we might go back to our illustration with the arrows denoting
the procession of the Son and the Holy Spirit, we can show how
important is this sole mark of differentiation in the Trinity. In
the thirteenth century, some of the Christian Churches in the East
rejected that particular arrow between the Son and the Holy Spirit,
which designates that the Holy Spirit proceeds from the Son
(*Filioque*), as well as from the Father. Now if we reject the procession of the Holy Spirit from the Son as well as from the Father,
we no longer have a way of differentiating the Son from the Holy
Spirit. In the diagram, both would be designated by an arrow indicating procession from the Father alone. Hence the Son and the
Holy Spirit would be identical in procession, and therefore, identical persons, since only the difference of procession differentiates
the Persons. This would leave us only two persons in God. The
diagram, on the other hand, indicates the opposition of relation by
which we differentiate the Son from the Holy Spirit. "Everything is
identical in God apart from the opposition of relation" (Council
of Toledo, Cf. Denz. 278 and 280; Council of Florence, Cf. Denz.
703).

There are two false notions we must avoid in this theological discussion of the Trinity. 1) When we say that the Son proceeds from
the Father, and the Holy Spirit from the Father and the Son we are
speaking of the order of life in the Trinity, but we are not subor-
dinating the Son to the Father, or the Holy Spirit to Father and
Son. They are all equally God and they equally possess the Divine
Nature. 2) When we speak of the various relations such as Father
and Son, we cannot introduce the notions of time that such relations of origin involve on earth. The Father did not exist before
the Son. Here we speak of an eternal relationship. As a matter of
fact, relation as such does not involve priority of time. Your father
was not your father before you were his son; the relationships of
fatherhood and sonship arose simultaneously. So too, eternally,
God is the Father and the Son, and the same can be said for the
Holy Spirit.

The Athanasian Creed which we quoted at the beginning of this section gives the Church's teaching on this matter in very precise terms:

> The Father is made by none; nor created, nor begotten. The Son is of the Father alone; not made nor created but begotten. The Holy Spirit is of the Father and the Son; not made, nor created nor begotten, but proceeding.
> Therefore there is One Father, not Three Fathers, One Son, not Three Sons; One Holy Spirit, not Three Holy Spirits. And in the Trinity there is none before or after, none greater or less; but all Three Persons are co-eternal and co-equal. So that, in all respects, as is aforesaid, we must worship both the Unity in Trinity and the Trinity in Unity (Denz. 40).

B. Divine Missions

The doctrine of the Church on the procession of the Persons in the Holy Trinity is clearly illustrated in the Divine Missions. Mission involves being sent (*missus*—Latin for sent) to do a task. The Holy Scriptures speak several times of the Son who proceeds from the Father and is sent into this world for our salvation. "When the fulness of time had come God *sent* His Son into the world" (Galatians 4:4-6). "As the Father hath *sent* Me, I also send you." While this sending of the Son by the Father illustrates the eternal procession of the Son from the Father, again we must not read subordination into it, for in another place, Christ says: "I went out from the Father and came into the world" (John 16:28).

The Holy Spirit, proceeding from the Father and the Son, is also said to be sent by them. "The Holy Spirit, whom the Father will *send* in my name, He will teach you all things and bring to your mind whatever I have said to you" (John 14-26). This visible mission of the Holy Spirit takes place on Pentecost.

As the Father proceeds from no one, He is never said to be *sent*, but merely to *come:* "If anyone loves Me, he will keep my word, and my Father will love him, and we will come and make our abode with Him" (John 14-24).

Thus the visible mission of the Son and the Holy Spirit portray their eternal procession in the eternal life of the Trinity.

C. Appropriation

This is the last of our theological questions regarding the Holy Trinity. Appropriation regards particularly our way of thinking about the three Persons in the Trinity. As we have seen, there is only one distinction in the Trinity, that of the opposed relations of Father, Son and Holy Spirit. Outside of this, everything is one in God. Thus we conclude that all else in the actions of God proceed from all three Persons acting together through the Divine Nature which they all possess fully. But if all act together, we are left without any distinction of Father, Son and Holy Spirit in the actions of God in our world. However, both the Scriptures and the documents of the Church do *appropriate* (ad-propriare: Latin, to make proper to) certain actions to the Father, Son and Holy Spirit. This is not done meaninglessly. Just as we distinguish certain attributes in God, although they are all identified in the one simple Divine Nature, so too, based upon the processions in the life of God, we appropriate works of origin and power to the Father, works of wisdom and knowledge to the Son, and works of love and sanctification to the Holy Spirit. Human beings have to speak in a human way.

This appropriation gives us a basis of giving special honor to the three distinct Persons, without forgetting that they act as one. Thus we say in our creed, "I believe in God, the Father Almighty, *Creator* of heaven and earth, . . . I believe in the Holy Spirit, the Lord and Life-giver, or *Sanctifier.*" While we thus honor the Father and the Holy Spirit in a special way, we know that all three perfect the work of creation and sanctification. We can, however, say that the Son is the Redeemer in a proper and special way, for He alone of the three Persons became incarnate and died in His human nature for mankind on the cross. Even here, though, the divine element that made His death infinitely efficacious for all men must be attributed to the action of all three Persons through the one divine nature. Moreover, it was all three Persons who effected the Incarnation.

While the Church encourages this special honor given to each Person through appropriation, she is very careful to guard against any excess that would prejudice the basic truth that all three Persons act as one in this world. For example, the Church has never permitted a special feast day in the Liturgy to honor separately the Father, as God, or the Son or Holy Spirit separately as God. There is a great feast day for the Most Holy Trinity, and every Sunday of the year is specially dedicated to the Trinity. However, the only special feast days for the Son are regarding His coming into this world *as man,* and the various occurrences in His human life here such as His circumcision, transfiguration, death, resurrection and ascension into heaven. The same for the Holy Spirit. Pentecost is not a feast day of the Holy Spirit *as God,* but to commemorate His temporal mission to guide the Church, His coming to the Apostles that first Pentecost.

So much for the theological questions regarding the Trinity. Since the doctrine was revealed, this has been the most difficult ground of theology, the deepest point of our metaphysics. As Mr. Frank Sheed, a layman who has written luminously on this subject, concludes:

> What we must realize is that success in finding answers to this and like questions has a bearing upon our *understanding* of the doctrine of the Blessed Trinity, but none at all upon our acceptance of it. If we were trying to arrive at the doctrine by the effort of our own minds working upon the concept of the Infinite, then a problem en route to which we could not see the answer, would effectually bar our progress; till it was solved, we should never arrive at the Trinity. But we have received the doctrine from God Himself. Therefore we make this examination (of theological questions regarding the Trinity) not to *discover* the doctrine (for God revealed it); still less to *verify* it (for no effort of our mind could make it more certain than God's word); *but to understand it better,* to get more light on it from it, to know more of God as a result of it.[4]

VI. APPLICATION OF THE DOCTRINE TO THE CHRISTIAN LIFE

If the doctrine of the Holy Trinity is as important and fundamental to Christianity as we have shown it to be, then certainly it must have its important place in the Christian life. And indeed it does, first of all in the over-all pattern of this life, secondly, in the prayers by which we as Christians address ourselves to God, and finally through our relation to God through Grace and Holy Communion. While this treatment is not exhaustive, it should be provocative of a more conscious appreciation of the place of the Holy Trinity in our lives as Christians.

A. The Trinitarian Plan of the Christian Life

The doctrine of the Trinity sheds great light upon the over-all plan of the Christian life. Our fundamental attitude to God has

---

4. Sheed, *Theology and Sanity,* p. 88. Sheed & Ward, New York, 1946.

been expressed for us in the prayer of Our Lord, addressed to God as "Our Father." It was not fortuitous that Christ chose this word to reveal the first person of the Blessed Trinity to us. While the meaning of the word 'father' means infinitely more when applied to God, it does imply One from whom we came, upon whom we depend for life, and food and drink and all the things that sustain life, to whom we go with our difficulties, whom we consult in our trials. One who makes our final destiny, a home. If an earthly father evokes such thoughts, is it not easier to love God who fulfills all these fatherly functions to an infinite degree? Certainly, there is no comparison between the concept of God as an Infinite Being, and as Our Father.

But God is also the *Son.* Again, we can understand now in the light of what we have seen about the Trinity, why it was that the Second Person, the Son, and not the First or Third Persons of the Trinity, was sent to be Our Way, Truth and Life. The Son came to be the Saviour, because our pattern for salvation is to be by adoption, precisely what He is by nature, sons of God. "As many as received Him, He gave them power to be the sons of God" (John 1:12). According to St. Paul, Christ is the First Born of many brethren. From viewing His Life, His attitude toward His Father, "I come to do the will of Him who sent me . . . I do His will in all things," we learn the fundamental duty of the Christian life. Christians are other Christs, for they reproduce in their lives, the life of the true Son of God. And God the Father most truly loves His creatures when He sees in them the pattern of His Son's Life. Even more than this, we share the divine life of the Son through grace, so that as St. John teaches us:

And the Life was made known and we have seen, and now testify and announce to you, the Life Eternal which was with the Father and has appeared to us. What we have seen and have heard we announce to you, in order that you also may have fellowship with us, and that our fellowship may be with the Father and with His Son Jesus Christ (1 John 1:2-3).

Behold what manner of love the Father has bestowed upon us, that we should be called children of God, and such we are. This is why the world does not know us, because it did not know Him. Beloved, now we are the children of God, and it has not yet appeared what we shall be. We know that, when He appears, we shall be like to Him, for we shall see Him just as He is (in the

Beatific Vision). And everyone who has this hope in him makes himself holy, just as He also is holy (1 John 3:1–3).

And this is the testimony, that God has given us eternal life; and this life is in His Son. He who has the Son has the life. He who has not the Son has not the life (1 John 5:11–12).

How much more the Christian life means when we realize that it is patterned after that of the Son of God, and involves participation in His eternal life. How much easier to live this life when a Divine Person comes to earth to be our Truth, Way and Life.

Finally, though we have a harder time speaking of the invisible *Spirit of God,* we do know something of His place in the Christian life from what the Son has told us. At His last supper with His apostles, Our Lord told them that He was not going to leave them orphans, but was to send them another Paraclete, that is, another guide and consoler as He had been. While we cannot see the Holy Spirit, we can certainly appreciate the effect of His coming at Pentecost, when the Apostles were changed from fearful ordinary men to great Apostles who went forth fearlessly to preach the salvation of Christ in the face of death. The Church in her liturgy realizes her dependency upon the Holy Spirit to guide and strengthen the Christian people, and traditionally the Church has depended upon the Holy Spirit for the light and strength to live the Christian life in the face of ignorance and adversity. Moreover, from what we know of the Trinity, what more fitting Guide could we have than the Spirit of Love? If anything can reunite men to God, it is divine love, "The charity of God is poured forth into our hearts by the Holy Spirit who is given to us" (Romans 5:5). As St. Augustine said, "Love God and do what you will." Love of God, inspired by the Spirit of Love, is at the heart of Christian life.

B. The Blessed Trinity in Christian Prayer

The belief of Christians in the Holy Trinity should certainly find utterance in Christian prayer by which Christians speak to God. Here we find the truth of the ancient adage mentioned above: "We pray the way we do because we believe the way we do."

Christians traditionally have begun their prayers and work with the Sign of the Cross, incorporating the belief in the Trinity and in Christ's redemption. They end prayer often enough with the doxology: "Glory be to the Father and to the Son and to the Holy

Spirit." The official prayers of the Church end generally: "Through the same Lord Jesus Christ, Thy Son, Who liveth and reigneth with Thee in the unity of the Holy Spirit, world without end, Amen." There are several versions of this ending, but they all include the Trinity by name.

The formal mention of the Trinity in prayer is best shown in the prayers of the Mass. It begins with the Sign of the Cross; there is the Kyrie eleison in sets of threes; the Gloria which ends, "Thou alone, O Jesus Christ, are most high, together with the Holy Spirit in the glory of God the Father, Amen." Then come the prayers with a special invocation of the Trinity at the conclusion of them. The Creed as we have seen is built on the structure of the Holy Trinity and expresses our total belief in the Three Persons. The Offertory prayers are addressed in order to Father (Receive O Holy Father), Son (Grant that we may partake of His divinity Who did partake of our humanity, Jesus Christ, Thy Son Our Lord), and the Holy Spirit (Come Thou Sanctifier), with the final offertory prayer beginning, "Receive O Holy Trinity . . ." The Secret prayers are concluded in the name of the Trinity. The Preface that follows on Sundays is, as we have seen above, a marvelous synopsis of the doctrine of the Three Persons in One Nature. This is followed by the triple "Holy, Holy, Holy." The prayers of the Canon are concluded with the little elevation in these words: Through Him (Christ), and with Him, and in Him, is to Thee, God the Father Almighty, in the unity of the Holy Spirit, all honor and glory world without end. Then follows the prayer to "Our Father." One of the pre-communion prayers begins: "Lord Jesus Christ, Son of the Living God, Who according to the will of the Father, through the cooperation of the Holy Spirit, has by Thy Death given Life to the world . . ." The final prayer of the Mass is addressed to the Holy Trinity: "May the lowly homage of my service be pleasing to Thee, O most Holy Trinity . . ." The concluding blessing in the name of God is as follows: "May Almighty God, Father, Son and Holy Spirit bless you, Amen." The last Gospel is about the Word, who is with God, and yet God, too. Surely, in this greatest of all Catholic prayers, the Mass, we have ample evidence of our belief in the Trinity.

The blessings in the Church are given in the name of the Trinity, exorcisms are in the name of the Trinity, and the Sacraments which are the carriers of God's grace operate in the name of the Trinity. For example, in Baptism, the water is poured in the form of a cross three times during the invocation of the Trinity. In confession, the priest concludes the form of absolution: "Therefore, I absolve you of your sins in the name of the Father and of the Son and of the Holy Spirit." As soon as the spouses have exchanged their consent in marriage the priest says, "I join you in holy matrimony in the name of the Father and of the Son and of the Holy Spirit."

C. Divine Indwelling of the Trinity in the Soul by Grace

In his second epistle St. Peter tells us: "For indeed His divine power has granted us all things pertaining to life and piety through the knowledge of Him who has called us by His own glory and power—through which He has granted us the very great and precious promises, so that through them you may become *partakers of the divine nature*" (II Peter 1:3-4). St. Paul adds: "You are the temple of the living God" (I Corinthians 6:16). This is but an echo of what Christ promised: "If anyone love Me, my Father will love him and we shall come and take up our abode with Him" (John 14:23).

This sharing in the divine life by grace implies a sharing of what we have now learned the divine life to be: the life of the Three Persons. "Let us recall that God is not one Person, but Three Persons, hence all Three Persons, Father, Son and Holy Spirit, thus dwell within us. Since each Person is infinitely distinct from the Others, they dwell within us such as in fact they are: The Father, the source and well-spring of the Godhead; the Son, eternally begotten from the Father, the Splendour of His Glory, the Word eternally uttered; the Holy Ghost proceeding from Father and Son and their subsistent Love . . . Three Persons dwell in us, Each as He is in fact in the Divine Drama of Their eternal relationship, this relationship of each One to the Others is a reality *within* us. Each Person by ineffable intimacy touches our soul and is in contact with it" (J. P. Arendzen, *The Holy Trinity*, p. 130).

All therefore that we have seen of the inner life of God is not an abstract truth, but a divine reality that takes place in our souls, where, through grace, the Son is present as proceeding from the Father, and the Holy Spirit as proceeding from the Father and the

Son. One of the early Church Fathers, Origen, used to pray at the
crib of his infant child. When asked why he did so, Origen replied,
"because God is specially present here. My child is baptized, is in
the state of grace, and therefore the Holy Trinity is dwelling in
His soul, and the child is yet incapable of losing this divine presence through sin. So, if God is present, surely and specially in the
soul of this child, where better could I pray when I cannot go to
church?"

This truth is missed by many Christians who conceive of heaven
as a place where they are given something. Rather, we are carrying
heaven in our souls already. When a person dies in the state of
grace, he is not given a harp and a pair of wings and a long white
nightgown, rather, we are given the light of glory to see and enjoy
the God we already possess by grace.

D. The Holy Eucharist and the Trinity

Rarely enough do Christians think of Holy Communion in
terms of the Trinity, yet here too is a most intimate contact with
the Triune God. We do realize that in receiving Holy Communion, we are receiving within ourselves the Sacred Humanity of
Christ, and the Divinity of the Word which is hypostatically united
to the Sacred Humanity. But we cannot separate the Three Persons
in God, receiving the Son, without receiving at the same time the
other Two Persons. As Christ said: "Do you not believe that I am
in the Father and the Father in Me?" (John 41:10). And He adds
later on in the chapter, "I will not leave you orphans; I will come
to you . . . In that day you will know that I am in My Father
and you in Me and I in you" (John 14:19-20).

Now this intimate connection of the Father and the Son and our
union with them in sharing the life of God is especially promised
in relation to Holy Communion. "As the living Father has sent
me, and as I live because of the Father, so he who eats Me, he also
shall live because of Me" (John 6:58). One of the greatest theologians of our day concludes from this text:

> And so the Eucharist, in uniting us to Christ, divinises us. The
> grace which it gives is divinisation, adoption, union to the entire
> Trinity; its sacramental action attaches itself in Christ, and in His
> mission as Son, to the processions of the Trinity.[5]

5. E. Mersch, *La Théologie du Corps Mystique,* Vol. 2, p. 329.

Thus when we receive Holy Communion we receive the Glorified Christ as He is present in heaven, and with Him we receive the whole Trinity within us. The Trinity is present in us for it is present in Christ, and we possess Our Lord in Holy Communion.

Conclusion and Summary

With the completion of this fourth section on the Holy Trinity we have finished our study of the life of God in Himself. This is life at its fullest. Because it is infinite, divine and eternal life, we found it difficult to fathom. But we have learned something about God which we would never have known without His telling us about Himself. And if He has taken the trouble to tell us, it was certainly worth our meager attempts to learn as much as we could of what He had to say.

We tried first of all to sharpen our notion of just what this mystery means, and found it best defined in terms of Three Persons in one Divine Nature. From seeing the historical errors that resulted from overstressing the distinction of Persons or the unity of Nature, we came to correct balance between these two elements of the mystery. Then we traced its gradual revelation and unfolding through the Word of God in the Old and New Testaments, as well as through the widespread statement and practice of what God has revealed in Tradition. A philosophical study of the mystery assured us that there is no contradiction of reason involved in it. The theological questions of procession, divine missions and appropriation led us into the deepest channels of theology, but yielded some fruits in a deeper understanding of the mystery. Finally we applied this most fundamental of all Christian mysteries to the Christian life, and there found that at every turn we come face to face with God the Father, the Son, and the Holy Spirit, from Whom we came and to Whom we hope to go for that actual face to face vision in heaven.

Difficult though it be, God for us is these Three Divine Persons. This is the Divine Life now seen by faith, but enjoyed later by the vision of what we now possess by faith. After seeing what we can of God in Himself, we shall now study Him in His creation of the world and man.

CHAPTER V

The Creation of the World
and of Man

THEOLOGY BEGINS BY STUDYING the life of God in Himself. We have already done this by considering the One Divine Nature and the Three Divine Persons. The next great step is to study the procession of creatures from God, or in more specific terms, the Divine Life as shared by man. But before we can speak of men sharing the life of God, we must get men on the scene, and the scene is this world. Obviously we are faced with some very important questions that men have been attempting to answer for centuries. In this section we shall try to get a true vision of God as Creator, of the origin of creatures as coming from God. The order of procedure includes three long steps:

1. Why God created.
2. What creation is.
3. How actually did God create.

The first question begins with God Himself. We will first establish the *reason why* God wished things to exist outside Himself, all sharing His being, and some even sharing His life. The second question involves the *nature of this creative process* which is no small mystery. And lastly, once we have seen the various classes of beings that began to be in creation, we study the *manner,* insofar as it can be determined theologically, of this creation of the world and of man. This last point outlines the area in which most modern

88

questions regarding creation and evolution are found. When these three steps have been taken, the scene will be laid for an even greater mystery: the sharing of divine life by men.

I. WHY GOD CREATED

The question 'why' obviously seeks the purpose of creation, the end God had in view when He created. But here again, we must note that our words have to be qualified and taken in a special sense when applied to God. Purpose for us generally denotes something distinct from ourselves, which we do not have at present, but wish to acquire. This wish to attain something we do not have is our purpose, that which moves us to act.

A. God's Purpose in Creating

Now there is nothing outside God which could have moved Him to create. Before creation nothing existed but God. Being supreme perfection, he lacked nothing and could hope to acquire nothing by creation. Speaking then of God's purpose in creation, we merely mean the reason God had in mind when He freely determined to create the world and man. Since God is an intelligent being, He does have reasons for His actions. However, unlike us, He is always His own reason.

Father Farrell expresses this thought very well:

> From what we know of the nature of God, it should be clear that there is only one goal, one end, possible to Him: if He acts at all, He must act for Himself. God created the universe for Himself; His goal was God; the end of the universe is the same as its beginning, God. Anything else is simply unthinkable. If God were working to a goal other than Himself, divine independence would be a myth as would the primacy of the first cause; God would, through the long life of the universe, be creeping up on something He lacked, mapping out a campaign for the capture of something outside Himself.
>
> There simply cannot be anything outside of God that does not come from Him, He cannot lack anything and still be God. Aside from the divine nature, the divine action cannot tolerate any other end than God: God, the absolutely perfect agent, must act in a perfect manner, not in the imperfect manner of an imperfect agent striving to perfect himself. The perfect agent, having all perfection, can act only for himself.[1]

1. Farrell, *Companion to the Summa*, Vol. I, p. 179. Sheed & Ward, New York, 1941.

The last general council of the Church, The Vatican Council (1869–1870), gives a terse statement of the Catholic Doctrine on this point. This dogmatic statement of a solemn teaching body of the Church will be the basis of our discussion.

"The One True God, of His Goodness, Omnipotent Power, and Most Free Will, from the beginning of time created from nothing both kinds of creatures: spiritual and corporeal, that is to say, angelic and worldly, and then also humans, as a composite being constituted of both spirit and body. (God did this) not to acquire happiness, or to increase His happiness, but to manifest His perfection by the good things which He bestowed on His creatures" (Denz. 1783).

At this point in our discussion, we are mainly interested in the latter part of this statement, which answers the question: Why God created. God freely created to manifest His Goodness and Power outside Himself. God is glorified by the fact that the great variety of creatures manifest, even though in a limited and faltering way, the unspeakable Goodness and Power of God.

1. Glory of God

At first glance, it may seem selfish to us that God created to attain His own glory. But again, this is thinking of God in a too human way. It is we who profit by this manifestation of His glory. His glory is our perfection. As we have seen, since He is the beginning and end of all things, there cannot possibly be any ultimate purpose in His activity, but Himself. True, it would be selfish for us to act only for ourselves, but that is because we are not the ultimate Good. However, when God acts for Himself, goodness is bestowed upon us.

As the philosophical axiom goes: "The good tends to diffuse itself." God, Who is Goodness Itself, diffuses His goodness upon all creation. Everything originates in Him, manifests His perfection, and glorifies Him. Still, we are the ones who profit by His thus acting for Himself, for His action is only to give of Himself.

2. Good of Man

The key to understanding this is to realize that these two aspects of creation, God's glorification and our good, coincide. We have an indication of this in the angels' song the night of the first Christmas. "Glory to God in the highest, and on earth, peace to men of *good will.*" Peace or happiness for us depends upon good will, that is, glorifying God. Again to understand this fully, we must digress for a moment on the two different kinds of glory that God obtains through creation.

If we consider, first, all the visible works of creation except man, we find that all these creatures fundamentally and necessarily glorify God by their very natures and being, since all reflect something of His perfections. There is nothing conscious about their glorification of God; it is necessarily connected with their being what they are.

Science studies all these visible things and finds a wonderful order in their make-up. All that science does is to recognize the great order that exists in the world, and to correlate the various laws that are apparent in the workings of visible things. Thus astronomy observes and classifies order in the heavens, biology states the unchanging laws of life, chemistry notes the unchanging reactions of inorganic being, and so forth. These sciences do not create the order, they merely recognize and tabulate it. But by the very fact of its existence, it glorifies the perfection of its maker.

But there is one being in the world who does not necessarily glorify God. You might say that everything but man is a slave of God, necessarily glorifying God. But God wanted a free and conscious glory from one creature on earth who was to be His adopted son. So God gave man free will and a mind, a mind to recognize intelligently the glory of God in creatures, and a free will to use creatures consciously in such a way that they will glorify God.

B. God Glorified Two Ways

Thus we can distinguish, as theologians do, two different kinds of glory that God obtains from creatures: 1) *fundamental* glory inherent in the natures of irrational creatures, a glory necessarily given to God; and 2) *formal* or conscious glory, freely given to God by rational creatures. A beautiful sunset in some far-off spot in the Pacific gives fundamental glory to God by the very fact that it reflects His beauty. But only if a man happens to see it and glorify God because of it, is God given formal or conscious glory.

This brings us to some important conclusions: 1) Man is the only creature in the visible world who can consciously and lovingly glorify and honor God. 2) By the same token, man is the only one of the visible creatures who can dishonor God and sin against his order of creation. Science can tell us what the other creatures *will do,* according to their laws, to glorify God, but the science of human actions, Ethics, can only tell us what man *ought* to do, to give God glory.

The whole of visible creation depends in a very definite way upon man, if it is to render through man's use of it, a formal glory to God. We read in Genesis that all the things that God made are good. However, while all created things, as for example, food and drink, time, sex and wealth, are good in God's order, and give a *fundamental* glory to God, it is up to man to use them according to God's plan if they are to give *formal* glory to God. Man can vitiate each of these things by abusing them, can misuse them to dishonor God.

C. Man's Higher Destiny

Since so much does depend upon the good will of man, man alone by his good use of things in the world can merit through grace an eventual participation of God's happiness in heaven. But because they cannot freely honor and glorify God, there is no heaven for stars, nor for mountains, nor for the other glorious things of God's creation. They might be called the slaves of God, while man is God's child through grace, the heir to His heavenly Kingdom.

Moreover, it is obvious how much higher is the type of formal glory that man renders God. Pascal has a famous passage in his *Pensées* in which he notes that God is given more glory by a child kneeling by his bedside saying his night prayers, than by all the marvelous precision of the far-flung heavenly planets and stars. The reason? Because they glorify God by necessity, and the child glorifies and honors God as a Father, lovingly and freely and consciously.

The consequences of these facts are far reaching in human life. God *will* be glorified by the world He made to glorify His Name. But there is a special reward and eternal glory for the man who recognizes His plan in creation, and has the *good will* to glorify Him through using all the creatures in the world according to the divine plan. The man who glorifies God attains his own perfection and happiness. Indeed, so closely are the glory of God and the happiness of man connected, that one always involves the other. If a man could dishonor God through sin and still be happy, there would be no God, for His plan for creation would be vain and inoperative.

Hence, the key to human happiness, perfection and peace of soul is well summed up in the Angel's song: Glory to God in the highest, and on earth peace to men of *good will.* Men who glorify God through the good use of their free will in life, live in peace, grow in perfection as men, since they mirror more completely the perfection and order of God, and consequently are more happy. Moreover, their very peace, perfection and happiness give glory to God. Indeed all other creatures praise God and give Him glory through the way that such a man uses these created things in life. As St. Paul puts it: "Whether you eat or drink, or whatever else you do, do all for the glory of God" (I Corinthians 10:31).

D. God Creates Freely

There are two more points of doctrine that may be briefly made here. First, it follows from what we have said of the way 'purpose' is spoken of in connection with God, that He created *freely,* out of His own Goodness and Power. He did not have to create. Creation is entirely of His own free choice.

This point has been defined by the Vatican Council in the document quoted above. It has been reiterated over and over again in Holy Scripture. The Psalmist sings: ". . . all things, whatsoever He wished, He made" (Psalm 113:3). St. Paul reaffirms: ". . . He who works all things according to the counsel of His will" (Esphesians 1:3). There is obviously in this point of doctrine an incentive for gratitude on the part of intelligent beings who can realize that without God's creative love for the world, they might not have existed. Also, there is the incentive to make the most of a good gift.

E. Creation Adds Nothing to God

The second point we wish to make arises from a common objection. Many say, "If God created for His own glory, then that glory must add something to His nature." The answer to this should be clear by now. Nothing can be added to God, or He would

not be God, all perfect in Himself. It is we who profit by glorifying Him. More *being* did not exist after creation, only more *beings,*
participating in and reflecting God's perfect being.

An illustration may clarify the matter. Suppose you have a window box of flowers outside your window. On a certain day the sun
is shining brightly. Now you may or may not raise the awning. If
you do, the flowers begin to profit by the beneficent sunlight, getting the warmth and light they need for growth. But remark this,
whether you pull up the awning or not, the perfection of the sun
is not affected. It is not changed by the number of beings that come
under its healthful rays. It is only the things that are shone upon
that are perfected by the sun, not the sun by them.

So, too, our existence and our manifestation of God's perfection
do not affect the nature of God. Only *we* are changed and bet-
tered by His creative action. Naturally God wants men to glorify
Him on earth and to enjoy His happiness in heaven. But if they refuse to glorify His love in heaven, they will still glorify His justice
in hell.

II. WHAT CREATION IS

It is not too difficult to realize what the nature of creation is if
we differentiate it from every other kind of production existing
in the world. Creation is properly divine production. When we
make something, we always need something to start with. Actually
all we do is merely to change the external appearance or inner
form of what we work with. But creation is very different from all
such alterations.

A. Nature of Creation

Creation begins with nothing and ends with something. It is
the production of the whole substance, the total being, of what is
created. Nothing is presupposed in creation. Possibly an easy way
to visualize this is to realize that before God's omnipotent act of
creation, nothing existed but God. Everything that exists today
must look back to God for the ultimate explanation of its being.
God alone exists by His very nature as we saw previously. Everything else is caused, and ultimately finds an explanation of its
existence in the First Cause, without Whose creative action there
would be nothing but Himself in existence today.

Naturally this divine action of creation is a mystery. We can assert that it *did happen,* but are still at a loss to explain exactly *how* it happened. Finite minds cannot fathom this infinite action of God any more than they can fathom His infinite being, for these are the same thing in God. He is His action.

Many think that the great Greek philosophers, Aristotle and Plato, had an implicit, though somewhat confused knowledge of creation. However, this is a debated point. Many thinkers since the time of Christ have openly denied creation and have given false explanations of the origin of the world.

1. False Theories of Creation

Some, like the *Pantheists,* call for the emanation of the world from a single principle as we do, but they identify the creature with the creator. This making the whole universe divine is obviously against the nature of God as we have seen Him in our earlier treatise on His nature. Yet such was the basic theory of Fichte, Schelling and Hegel, the philosophic godparents of Marx's Communistic theories, and also of the modern Italian philosophers, Gentile and Croce.

There is another version of this theory in the tenets of *atheistic and materialistic evolution* which we shall study more at length in our next section. Basically this theory calls for the blind evolution of the world as we see it today, from some primal matter, without any adequate cause to explain where the matter came from or what accounts for the ordered development of the world and of life as we see it today.

A third and even more fantastic theory calls for a dual principle of creation. Haunted by the many evils and imperfections existing in the world, the *Dualists* postulate a good creative principle which accounts for the good in the world, and a bad creative principle which accounts for the evil. Obviously again, there cannot be two supreme principles. There can only be on supreme being, and only He can create; only He can give being. In Christian times this sort of thing that calls for dual principles in creation is a deification of the devil. We find the residue of such theories in the Manichaeans and Albigenses, who despise the body and material things as evil, the work of the devil. They have been thoroughly condemned by the Church when and where they appeared.

2. Creation in Holy Scripture

The Catholic notion of creation then calls for God as the Creator of all things, and recognizes that all creation is distinct from God and completely dependent upon Him for its being and direction. This fact is well documented in Divine Revelation.

The first words of the Old Testament are a testimony of God's creation of all things. "In the beginning, God created heaven and earth" (Genesis 1:1). In scriptural language, heaven and earth signify all things that are. All these were created in the absolute beginning, before which there was nothing.

The New Testament Gospel of St. John also begins by testifying of God's Word: "All things were made through Him, and without Him was made nothing that has been made" (John 1:3).

3. Creation in Church Teaching

We are all accustomed to profess our belief in the Apostles' Creed, that God, the Father Almighty, is "the Creator of heaven and earth . . ." The famous Nicene Creed professes it more explicitly: "the Maker of all things visible and invisible."

As various errors arose to contest the traditional Catholic doctrine on creation, a more explicit statement of Catholic belief was defined in the General Councils against the heretics. For example, in 1215, against the Albigenses, the Fourth Council of the Lateran professed a belief in the creation of all things by all three persons of the Trinity: "Consubstantial and co-equal and co-omnipotent and co-eternal, one principle of all things, creator of everything visible and invisible, spiritual and corporeal, Who in the beginning of time, by His omnipotent power created from nothing both kinds of creatures, that is to say, spiritual and corporeal, angelic and worldly, and then made human creatures, as it were a being common to both other kinds, constituted of both spirit and body. The devil and the other demons were of a good nature as created by God, but became evil by their own will" (Denz. 428). This statement was meant to oppose the contention that matter was evil in itself, and came from an evil principle, not from God.

In 1870, this doctrine of the Lateran Council was reiterated solemnly in the Vatican Council, as we have already seen in the statement from this council at the beginning of this chapter. More-

over, there were additional statements against more specific heresies. For example, the Vatican Council condemned Pantheism
which identifies the world and God: "If anyone says that the being
of God and the substance or essence of all things are one identical
reality, let him be condemned" (Denz. 1803). Against materialism,
which is one of the philosophical bases of godless Communism,
the Council declared, indirectly vindicating the creation of spiritual being: "If anyone is not ashamed to affirm that there is no
reality beyond matter, let him be condemned" (Denz. 1802). Finally, we are given a brief summation of the core of Catholic doctrine on creation, especially directed against both the materialists
and the pantheists of all colors: "If anyone will not confess that the
world and everything in it, both material and spiritual, were produced out of nothing by God according to their total reality, let
him be condemned" (Denz. 1805).

4. Creation Common to All Three Persons

All the testimonies of divine revelation coupled with the infallible teaching authority of the Church give us a rather complete
idea of what we mean when we say that God is the Creator of all
things. Of course, the intimate nature of creation, this divine action totally within God, yet producing an effect outside of Him
and distinct from Him is still a profound mystery.

We can say, however, from what we have already seen regarding
the Holy Trinity, that the action of creation is common to all three
divine Persons, even though we appropriate it to the Father. The
theological reason for this is that Creation is a divine operation,
and God's actions are identified with His essence which is common
to all three Persons.

Moreover, Holy Scripture speaks of creation in connection with
each of the three Persons:

1) "I confess to Thee, Father, Lord of heaven and earth" (Matthew
11:25; Luke 10:21);
2) "Through Him (the Word) all things were made" (John 1:2);
3) "The Spirit of God hovered over the waters (at creation)"
(Genesis 1:2).

This doctrine is succinctly declared by the Council of Florence:
"The One True God, Father, Son and Holy Spirit is the Creator

of all things visible and invisible" (Denz. 706). A practical conclusion to this point is that a study of the world can lead us to a knowledge of the First Cause, the God Who is One in Nature, but it tells
us nothing of the Three Persons in God for they act in unison
when creating.

5. Creation a Divine Action

There are several other points of doctrine that must be mentioned at this time. The first point should be fairly obvious by
now, namely, not only did God alone create all things, but only
God *could* create. The fundamental reason for saying this is that
creation gives being, and only the First Cause, He Who Is, can
effect being. Instrumental causes are useful once there is a subject
to work upon, but in creation there is no subject to begin with,
the thing created simply begins to be. God alone is the giver of
being. As we read in Isaias: "I am the Lord who makes all things
. . . and no one with me" (Isaias 44:24).

F. Sheed has a good summary of this point in the book we have
already cited:

> We have seen why God exists: He exists because what He is
> demands existence, cannot not-exist. But this created universe does
> not thus demand existence. How then does it exist? It can exist only
> because God Who alone possesses existence as of right, confers ex-
> istence upon it. God made it. And he made it of nothing. What
> else was there for Him to make it of? He could not make it of
> Himself, for He is utterly simple and changeless: there are no
> parts in Him which could be subtracted from Him and set going as
> a universe that was not He. In one sense, then, the act of creation
> can be stated quite simply. God willed that things which had not
> been should be. 'He spoke and they were made; He commanded
> and they were created' (Psalm 148:5). To create is to make a thing
> in its totality, that is to make the whole of it. A carpenter does
> not make the whole of a chair—the wood is not of his making.
> A poet does not make the whole of a poem, the words already existed.
> But God does make the whole universe, there is nothing in it that
> is not of His making, nothing that already existed.[2]

B. Scope of Creation

Once we have established that God made all things, and that
only God could create, it is relatively simple to show the actual

2. Sheed, *Theology and Sanity*, pp. 101–102, Sheed & Ward, New York, 1946.

scope or extent of the created universe. While God is a simple Being, He is all perfect, and therefore it is not difficult to imagine that it will take a great multiplicity of created beings to express the infinite, uncreated perfection of God.

If we wish to put all creation into definite categories, it is perhaps easiest to arrange it under the basic elements of matter and spirit, visible and invisible, as the teachings of the Councils express it. Thus all the visible creation can be categorized as material things, and all the invisible creation as spiritual beings. And while there is a great gap between these two types of beings, this gap is bridged by man who is partially spiritual and partially material being. Man is made up of body and soul.

1. Hierarchy of Creation

To go into the matter more deeply, and to arrange all of created being into a hierarchy of perfection, since some beings are more perfect than others, we must introduce the additional notion of life. Of course all spiritual being is alive, that is, it has within itself the power of moving and acting. Moreover, spiritual being has a very specific kind of life, rational life, which gives it powers akin to God, namely, the powers of knowing and loving. That is why beings endowed with spirit, like angels and men, bear the likeness of God as well as his image. Material beings do not all possess life, and even those below man who do possess life to some extent, have a very limited kind of life that ends with the disintegration of the material being, the animal or vegetable. But in any case, using these basic elements we can summarize the whole scope or extent of God's creation in order of perfection.

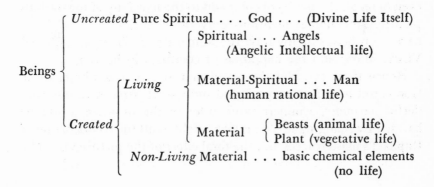

Beings
- *Uncreated* Pure Spiritual . . . God . . . (Divine Life Itself)
- *Created*
  - *Living*
    - Spiritual . . . Angels (Angelic Intellectual life)
    - Material-Spiritual . . . Man (human rational life)
    - Material { Beasts (animal life) / Plant (vegetative life)
  - *Non-Living* Material . . . basic chemical elements (no life)

Glancing up this scale of being, it is easy to deduce that the higher being a creature possesses, the more closely it mirrors God, the Highest of all Beings, He Who Is, Being Itself. In every work we can find some trace or vestige of the workman. In human works of craft or art, we come to know the excellence of the craftsman or artist. And the higher the art, the more excellent the masterpiece, the easier we are able to deduce the genius or the artist. Now God has left his fingerprints, so to speak, on all of creation. But the higher we ascend the scale of created beings, the more closely we are brought to a knowledge of God. We can learn something of the beauty of God from the dazzling panorama of the Swiss Alps against an azure sky. We can glimpse the power of God from the bridge of an ocean liner tossed like a chip of wood on the towering waves of the North Atlantic. But when we come to creatures like man, endowed with a soul that can know and love, the image of God is sharpened for us. For God said when making man: "Let us make man to our image and likeness" (Genesis 1:26). This is even more true of the angels, though we cannot see them.

2. Model for Creation

There can be no model for created beings but God Himself, for He alone existed before creation. Nor can there be any limit to the vast extent of beings who participate in the perfections of God, for His Perfection is limitless and inexhaustible. Sometimes, a person asks: "Could God have made a better world?" Of course, individual beings could be better. It would be better to be an angel than a worm. But if all the world were angels, we would lack the widespread picture of the limitless perfections of God. You might say that this particular being could have had better qualities, but even here, all the shades of color add to the harmony of the over-all picture. St. Thomas mentions only three things that could not have been better in any way: the humanity of Christ; the Blessed Virgin Mary; and the happiness of creatures in heaven.

Hence if we consider the world or universe as a whole, while God could have further perfected individual parts of it, the wonderful harmony, symmetry and order of the universe would be harmed by changing it. You might brighten all the colors in one of Raphael's masterpieces, but the total effect of the picture would be spoiled, for the total harmony of color is achieved by light and shadow, by the contrast of bright and dull colors.

The end or purpose of creation was to communicate the divine goodness so on every side of us we see something of the family likeness of God. The staggering variety of the universe is the result of divine ingenuity's struggle to paint, in the stiff medium of creatures, a likeness of the gracious beauty of God. Of course, even the divine artist failed. No creature is capable of receiving all of divine goodness, no one creature is capable of perfectly mirroring that divine perfection. It is more perfectly mirrored through the multiplication of different species of creatures; but even indefinite multiplication through all of an eternity fails to give back an adequate likeness of the face of God.[3]

C. Time of Creation

We cannot finish our discussion of the nature of creation without saying a few words about the time of creation. Men have wondered for centuries about the answer to the question: "When was the world created?" If we were to restrict ourselves to reason alone, the answer would not be found too easily. Aristotle, for example, thought that the world was eternal. Christian philosophers and theologians, among them great men like St. Augustine, St. Thomas and Suarez, say that it is not possible by reason alone to demonstrate that creation could not have taken place from all eternity.

They reason thus: If we have to demonstrate that the world had a beginning at a definite time, we would have to argue from the world or from God who made it. In studying the world, the nature of things tells us *that* they had to be caused, but the nature of a thing as such, does not say *when* it *had* to be caused. It merely shows essential dependence upon a cause without reference to time. On the other hand, if we argue from what we know of God, we know that God creates freely, and that He has existed from all eternity. Hence He could have created from all eternity, or at some definite time. All we can know about the time of creation, then, must come from some revelation, by which God makes known to us when He actually did create.

Fortunately, we do have such a revelation, and therefore can settle the question. This is one instance when the superiority of

3. Farrell, *Companion to the Summa*, I, p. 181.

theological knowledge over philosophical knowledge is evident. In the first line of Genesis we read: "In the beginning God created heaven and earth." Christ Himself speaks of a time "before the world was." He also mentions in the same context that the Father loved Him "before the creation of the world" (John 17:5, 24). These texts have been supplemented by the definition of the Church in the Fourth Lateran and Vatican Councils. We have seen already how these Councils refer to the creation of all things "in the beginning of time," and not from all eternity. Beyond this fact, the Church had defined nothing about the actual age of the world. That question will have to be determined scientifically if at all.

Some theologians prefer to say that the world was created in time and with time, since time is the measure of created things. In any case, this much is certain: there was a point at which God created, before which there was nothing but God and eternity.

D. Continued Creation

One last corollary is in order. We can deduce it from all we have learned thus far regarding the nature of creation. If all created things depend totally upon their creation, we cannot picture creation as an action that takes place and is finished. In a very real sense, there is a continued creation going on in the universe, insofar as God must continue to sustain in being, everything that he puts in being.

We can make something of wood or steel and leave it. Our product continues to be as it is because we have only rearranged the materials we worked with. But when God creates something, as we have seen, the totality of the product depends upon Him. We might compare this total dependence to our electric lights. We switch them on, and they continue to glow as long as they are connected with the central dynamo in a city. But once that connection is broken, the lights go out. Now God is the Central Dynamo of all being, and His universal causality as Creator is the all-important factor upon which all beings depend.

St. Augustine has described the total dependence of men upon God for their ultimate happiness: "Thou hast made us for Thyself, O God, and the heart of man cannot rest until it rests in Thee." But even more fundamental than this, is the utter dependence of all things on God for their very being. This one fact alone highlights the importance of theology for an ordered view of the world. Considering the world without God is like studying a shadow without the substance that casts it, or like looking at a reflection and ignoring that which it reflects. The Deists may like to think that God made the world and forgot about it, left it to its own devices, but metaphysically speaking, if God forgot about the world, there simply would no longer be a world.

Again, F. Sheed expresses this truth very clearly:

> This fact that God made us and all things of nothing by a sheer act of His will, is not simply a fact of history, something that happened an immeasurably long time ago. We may very well think of it as something that happened, because it did happen. But it implies as its corollary something that is happening here and now, happening from instant to instant, and of the most vital importance to us. Because we are made by God of nothing, then we cannot continue in existence unless God continuously holds us in existence. There is an emptiness at the very center of the being of all created things, which only God can fill; not an emptiness merely in the sense that it cannot be happy without God; but in the sense that it cannot *be* at all without Him. God does not simply make us and leave us . . .
> If I stand in front of a mirror, my image is in the mirror, but only while I stand there. If I go, it goes. Only my continuing presence keeps the image in being. The reason is that the image is not made *of* the mirror, but only *in* the mirror. The mirror contributes nothing but receptiveness; it is purely receptive, purely passive. So of the nothingness in which God mirrors himself: we may figure it as receptive or passive—carrying receptivity, passivity to the ultimate power. Thus the image is sustained by God's continuing presence. Take me away and the image (in the mirror) ceases. Take God away, and the universe ceases.[4]

E. Providence of God

The Vatican Council speaks of this dependence of creatures upon God in terms of Providence. "God by His Providence sustains and governs all the things that He has made, 'reaching from end to end mightily and ordering all things smoothly' " (Wisdom 8:1) (Denz. 1784).

This is perhaps the best note on which to end this consideration of the nature of creation. Certainly the whole matter, viewed in

---

4. Sheed, *Ibid.*, pp. 103–104.

any aspect, breathes of God. He alone can and did create. He alone is the divine Model upon which all the beauties of creation are patterned. He alone is the beginning, the continuation, and the end of the whole process, since all beings come from Him, are sustained by Him, and are destined to glorify Him.

But especially in the case of rational creatures, who are made to His image and likeness, who are destined to share His Life and His eternal Happiness, there must be a conscious recognition of the overwhelming importance of His place in life. Too often, all the emphasis is placed on the externals of the pattern to the detriment of its inner meaning. It is more than helpful, it is essential to realize that "in Him we live and move and are" (Acts 17:28).

It was with deep consciousness of the Providence that has planned creation and oversees the ultimate accomplishment of its ends that Christ Our Lord says: "Therefore do not be anxious, saying: 'What shall we eat?' or 'What shall we drink?' or 'What shall we put on?' for your Father knows that you need all these things. But seek first the Kingdom of God and His justice, and all these things shall be given you besides" (Matt. 6:31–34).

III. How God Created

Two problems are raised in the minds of contemporary thinkers by the account of creation given in Genesis: how to take the similarity of the Biblical account to the ancient mythological accounts and how to take the dissimilarity of the Biblical account to modern scientific accounts of the origin of things. We shall therefore discuss first mythological cosmogony and then scientific cosmogony.

A. Mythological Cosmogony

The position of the Catholic Church on the question of the relationship between the Biblical and the mythical accounts of creation was formulated in the letter of the Pontifical Biblical Commission to Cardinal Suhard in 1948. "This letter," Pope Pius XII said in his encyclical *Humani Generis* (§§ 68–69),[5] "clearly points out that the first eleven chapters of Genesis, although properly speaking not conforming to the historical method used by

---

5. The paragraph numbering is that of the Paulist Press edition.

the best Greek and Latin writers or by competent authors of our time, do nevertheless pertain to history in a true sense which, however, must be further studied and determined by exegetes; the same chapters, the letter points out, in simple and metaphorical language adapted to the mentality of a people but little cultured both state the principal truths which are fundamental for our salvation and also give a popular description of the origin of the human race and the chosen people.

"If, however, the ancient sacred writers have taken anything from popular narrations, and this may be conceded, it must never be forgotten that they did so with the help of divine inspiration through which they were rendered immune from any error in selecting and evaluating those events. Therefore, whatever of the popular narrations have been inserted into the Sacred Scriptures must in no way be considered on a par with myths or other such things, which are more the product of an extravagant imagination than of that striving for truth and simplicity which in the Sacred Books, even of the Old Testament, is so apparent that our ancient sacred writers must be admitted to be clearly superior to the ancient profane writers."

At one time it was fashionable to postulate the existence of documentary sources from which the Pentateuch as a whole and Genesis in particular was supposed to be constructed. This way of thinking has been superseded in recent years, however, by a tendency to think in terms of oral traditions. In Genesis one can discern the traces of three such traditions: the Elohistic characterized by the use of the name *Elohim* for God, the Yahwistic characterized by the use of the name *Yahweh* for God, and the Sacerdotal which presupposes the other two and adds dates, lists, genealogies, and the like. We have two of these traditions represented in the actual account of creation: the Sacerdotal tradition provides the narrative of the six days (Genesis 1:1–2:4a) and the Yahwistic tradition provides the story of Adam and Eve (Genesis 2:4b ff.). What we have here is a double account of the creation of man, one in the context of the creation of the world and the other in the context of the earthly paradise. In the Sacerdotal tradition God is called *Elohim,* and in the Yahwistic account of creation he is called *Yahweh Elohim* instead of the usual *Yahweh,* probably in order to make the narrative dovetail with the preceding. It is the Sacerdotal narrative of creation, the story of the six days, that exhibits the most noticeable similarity to the mythical accounts of creation, particularly to the Babylonian myth of creation, the *Enuma Elish,* which for this reason has been called by modern critics "the Babylonian Genesis."

The *Enuma Elish,* named for its opening words "When Above," is a cosmogonic epic of the first half of the second millennium before Christ. The hero of the epic is Marduk, the supreme god of Babylon, who establishes the present world order. In its original form, however, the epic must have been a much earlier Sumerian composition since Marduk's features in the story belong to the god Enlil of Nippur. There is, moreover, a later version, from the Assyrian period, in which Marduk has been replaced by Ashur. The epic thus serves successively as the Sumerian, the Babylonian, and the Assyrian Genesis. A quick reading of the poem, however, will not give one the impression of similarity to the Hebrew Genesis but rather of something like the battle of the Olympian gods against the Titans in the mythology of the Greeks. I would suggest that the student verify this for himself by reading one of the English translations of the *Enuma Elish* [6] and then reading immediately afterward the first chapter of Genesis. A closer examination, however, will reveal some striking points of resemblance.

When we read the epic as a story of the gods there seems to be no similarity at all to the first chapter of the Bible. The whole poem consists of seven tablets: the first relates the genealogy of the gods and the first victory of the younger gods over the older gods; the second relates how none of the younger gods is found but Marduk who will go against Tiamat, the Great Mother, who is seeking to reverse the previous victory; the third relates the gladness of the other gods at learning of Marduk's resolution; the fourth relates the victory of Marduk over Tiamat; the fifth relates the distribution of the spoils of the universe among the younger gods; the sixth relates the story of man's creation out of the blood of one of the defeated gods for the purpose of relieving the gods of work

6. The translation of the selections used in the text is based on a comparison of that of Heidel in his book *The Babylonian Genesis* (Chicago, 1951–2nd ed.) with that of Speiser in Pritchard's *Ancient Near Eastern Texts* (Princeton, 1950), pp. 60–72. A précis of the epic is available in Colum's *Myths of the World* (Universal paperbacks), pp. 17–19.

and how the gods in their gratitude build Babylon as a sanctuary for Marduk, and the seventh completes the listing of Marduk's fifty names which was begun in the sixth. If, however, we substitute for the proper names of the gods the common names of the various parts of the universe which they personify, the theogony turns into a cosmogony that does indeed resemble the Bible story.

The First Day

The Babylonian Genesis opens with the statement that when neither heaven nor earth had yet been named there existed only Apsu, the primeval fresh-water ocean, and Tiamat, the primeval salt-water ocean, and their son Mummu, the mist rising from the mingling of the two bodies of water:

> When heaven above had not been named,
> And earth below had not been named,
> Apsu primeval their begetter,
> Mummu, Tiamat, she who bore them all,
> Mingled their waters together. (I:1–5).

These waters would correspond to the waters mentioned in the second line of the Hebrew Genesis, the waters which were stirred by the breath of God. There is no mention in the Babylonian Genesis, however, of the creation of light, the work of the first day in the Biblical story, unless it be the birth of the gods from the primeval waters, and this because later on in the account these gods are allotted their stations in the universe which turn out to be the sun, moon, and stars. There is a struggle between these gods and those of the primeval waters leading to the emergence and victory of Marduk. This seems to represent a struggle between order and chaos ending in the victory of order. Marduk, who wins by using the four winds, is the Babylonian equivalent of the earlier Sumerian god of the storm, Enlil, corresponding, perhaps, to the breath of God that stirs the waters in the Hebrew account.

The Second Day

After the victory of wind (Marduk) over water (Tiamat), the wind divides the body of water in two and from one of the halves makes the sky raising it without let so that the waters will not escape:

He split her open like a mussel into two;
Half of her he set in place and formed the sky as roof;
He fixed the crossbar, posted guards,
And bade them let her waters not escape. (IV:137–140).

The fundamental image here seems to be the same as that of the Sumerian god of the storm, Enlil, who by his blowing holds heaven and earth apart. The separation of the waters corresponds to the work of the second day in the Bible story when God orders that a solid vault arise amid the waters to keep these waters apart from those, a vault which will separate the waters which are beneath it from the waters above it, a vault which God names the Sky.

The Third Day

What follows is the creation of the earth, i.e., the land, but the imagery in the myth is not as simple as it is in the Bible where the work of the third day is done by God having the waters below the vault collect in one place to make dry land appear. In the Babylonian story after the sky has been created Marduk measures the dimensions of the Apsu, the subterranean sea of fresh water, and then hangs the land over it like a canopy:

The lord measured the dimensions of the Apsu,
The Great Abode, its counterpart, he laid, Esharra,
The Great Abode Esharra which he made a canopy. (IV:143–145).

The Bible goes on to describe how God commanded the earth to yield grasses that grow and seed, and fruit trees each giving fruit of its own kind, propagating itself on the earth, but the *Enuma Elish* makes no explicit mention of this though it may be implied since it is said that when the primeval waters of Apsu and Tiamat still mingled, "no pasture land had been formed and not a reed marsh was to be seen" (I:6). With the separation of the waters, thus, the pasture land and the reed marshes are understood to have appeared.

The Fourth Day

On the fourth day in the Biblical account God created the luminaries in the vault of the sky to divide the spheres of day and night, to give portents and be the measures of time, to mark out the day and the year, to shine in the sky's vault and shed light upon

the earth. The next step in the mythical account is similar and has
similar purposes:

> He created stations for the great gods;
> He fixed stars, their images, the constellations.
> He determined the year, defined the divisions:
> Three constellations for each of the months.
>
> . . . .
>
> In the middle of it he put the zenith.
> He made the moon to shine, entrusted to her the night.
> He made her, thing of night, marker of the days. (V:1–13).

In the myth the luminaries are created in the order of increasing
(apparent) magnitude: the first of stars, then the moon, and finally
the sun, but in the Bible they are created in the order of decreasing magnitude: first the sun, then the moon, and last the stars.

The Fifth Day

There is nothing in the Babylonian epic to correspond to the
work of the fifth day in the Bible, the creation of fish and fowl. It
is true, however, that a considerable portion of the epic in this
section has been lost. Tablet V of the version which was found in
the library of King Assurbanipal contains only the first 22 lines
of a part which probably consisted of some 140 lines. In the portion which has been preserved there is described the creation of
the stars and the moon. There was undoubtedly more astronomical
lore and then perhaps an account of the creation of fish and fowl
corresponding to the fifth day in the Bible story. In any case, the
next tablet goes on to describe the creation of man, the sixth day's
work in the Bible.

The Sixth Day

In the Bible God creates man to His own image, giving him
authority over fish and fowl and all animal life on the earth and
over the earth itself; He blesses man by telling him to increase and
multiply and take command of the whole creation. In the myth,
on the contrary, man is not created to command but to serve, to
relieve the gods of the burden of labor. Marduk says:

> Blood I will mass and bone I will make.
> I will make a savage, "man" shall be his name.

> Yes, savage-man I will create.
> On him the service of the gods shall be imposed,
> That they may be at ease. (VI:5–8).

The image of God which man bears according to the Biblical story seems to be the authority over the creation which God confers upon him, an authority similar to that of God. In the myth the nearest thing we have to the idea of the image of God is the idea that mankind is made out of the blood of one of the gods who had been defeated by Marduk:

> They punished him and shed his blood,
> And from his blood they fashioned man.
> He (Ea) imposed the service of the gods
> And let the gods themselves go free. (VI:32–34).

In some of the parallel mythical accounts, in fact, man is made of clay mixed with the blood of the god.

The Seventh Day

It is interesting to see how the mythical account of man's creation leads directly into the divine rest which is the affair of the seventh day in the Biblical account. In the Bible story God had finished His work by the seventh day and so He rested and blessed and hallowed the seventh day as a day of rest to commemorate the day on which His divine activity of creation was finished. In the myth, on the contrary, the final work of creation, the making of man, enables the gods to rest and celebrate because now they can have man do all the work. The whole purpose of creating man, in other words, was to make possible the repose of the gods. This is undoubtedly a reflection of the social fact that in the early cities of Mesopotamia people were organized into temple communities and they supported themselves by working on the temple property.[7] Their whole life thus consisted of work in the service of the gods. The Bible story of the seven days with the seventh day of rest, in like manner, reflects the Jewish week with its six days of work and the Sabbath day of rest.

---

7. Cf. Frankfort, *The Birth of Civilization in the Near East* (London 1951), chap. 3, "The Cities of Mesopotamia."

Contrasting Ideas of God

One of the most striking differences between the story of creation as told in the Bible and as told in mythology is to be found in the conception of God. The gods in mythology do not create the world. They are the various parts of the world: Tiamat is the salt-water ocean, Apsu the fresh-water ocean, Mummu the mist and the cloud banks, Lahmu and Lahamu are the silt deposited at the borders of the fresh water and the salt water, Anshar and Kishar are the horizons of heaven and earth, Anu and Ea are heaven and earth themselves, Marduk is the wind, and other gods are the stars, the moon, and the sun.

The birth of the world is the birth of the gods themselves. There is no God in mythology who is no part of the world, who stands above the world, and creates the world out of nothing by a simple command. This absence of any idea of a transcendent God, this undifferentiated mentality which is unable to disengage the notion of divinity from that of the world is what creates the chasm between mythology and the Bible. Genesis is so far from conceiving the parts of the world as divine that it does not even call the sun and moon by their names (which were inevitably the names of Gentile divinities) but describes them by circumlocution as the "two great luminaries, the greater of them to command the day, and the lesser to command the night" (Genesis 1:16).

Contrasting Ideas of the World

From this it follows that the idea of the world in Genesis is not the same as it is in the myths where the world is "full of gods" as Thales said. The origin of the world in the myths is not a creation from nothingness but an emergence of order from chaos. It is true that even in the Bible story we have three phrases which suggest an original chaos: the void and empty earth, the darkness on the face of the deep, and the waters that are stirred by the breath of God (Genesis 1:2). In fact, the imagery of the primeval waters is the one which we found employed to describe the original chaos in the *Enuma Elish*. The difference, though, lies precisely in this— that the imagery of the waters is merely imagery in the Bible. Indeed the void and empty earth, the darkness on the face of the deep, and the waters that are stirred by the breath of God are probably three successive images of the nothingness from which all things were created. There was apparently no word for nothingness in a language so concrete as Hebrew, and we can infer with some probability that it is nothingness and not chaos that is meant because here and everywhere else in the Bible everything without exception is ascribed whole and entire to God the maker.

Contrasting Ideas of Man

These differences between the Bible and mythology in the conception of God and of the world result in a difference in the conception of man. In the Babylonian myth, since the gods are the various parts of the world, man is not the master of the world but its servant. He is created to serve the gods and this means subordination to the elements of the cosmos since these are the gods. In the Bible, on the contrary, man is created last of all because he is to be the crown and head of the whole creation. He is made to God's image in the sense that he, like God, is to have authority over all things. "Let us make man to our image and likeness," God says, "and let him have dominion over the fishes of the sea, and the fowls of the air, and the beasts, and the whole earth, and every creeping creature that moveth upon the earth" (Genesis 1:26). The conception of man as master of the world rather than servant of the world implies and reflects a different way of life. It is this conception that underlies the Ten Commandments, for which there is no parallel in the legal codes of the Gentiles, where the first table forbids the worship of the elements of this world and commands the worship of the transcendent God, and the second table enjoins the respect for the dignity of man that is consequent on his position as lord of the whole creation.

B. Scientific Cosmogony

The scientific account of the origin of things, whether we speak of the natural sciences or of the social sciences, is dominated today by the concept of evolution. Comparing the religious with the scientific version of the origins, in fact, almost boils down to comparing the idea of creation with the idea of evolution. The late Father Pierre Teilhard de Chardin, an eminent anthropologist, built up an entire Christian world view around the scientific notion of evolution. In his book *The Phenomenon of Man* (New York, 1959) he describes in detail his view that the world is in a state of evolution, matter evolving towards life, life evolving towards intelligence, and intelligence evolving towards God. Such a viewpoint, while undoubtedly understood in an orthodox sense by its author, lends itself easily to misunderstanding. One might conclude that intelligence or even God Himself is nothing but a product of evolution. In the encyclical *Humani Generis,* therefore, Pope Pius XII reprimanded those who "imprudently and indiscreetly hold that evolution which has not been fully proved even in the domain of natural sciences, explains the origin of all things, and audaciously supports the monistic and pantheistic opinion that the world is in continual evolution" (§ 5). Father Teilhard de Chardin himself, though, did not conceive God to be the final product of evolution but rather its transcendent goal, nor did he conceive human intelligence to be merely a product of evolution but rather an effect of the special intervention of God in the evolutionary process. Provided one makes distinctions such as these and provided one does not adhere to it in a dogmatic and uncritical fashion, one is free, as a Catholic, to accept the hypothesis of evolution.

1. The Evolution of Matter

The idea of creation and the idea of evolution are complementary, not contradictory, the one referring to the production of things and the other to the differentiation of things. There is no difficulty in supposing that matter was created from nothing and that once it was created it proceeded to evolve step by step into the variety of states and forms in which we now find it existing in the universe. The Bible itself is careful not to confuse the production of things from nothing with the differentiation of things from one another. The production of things from nothing, according to the creation story, is accomplished in the beginning whereas the differentiation of things from one another is accomplished in the six days. The story as it stands would seem to imply that matter came into existence in a somewhat undifferentiated form and that only afterwards and in successive stages was it differentiated until it attained its present state. In fact, unless we resort to some special

device of interpretation, the story as it stands would seem to positively exclude the idea that in the beginning of time the world
possessed the same shape and form which it possesses now.

I do not mean to suggest that the six days correspond to the actual
stages in the evolution of the world but only to exclude the assumption that a literal interpretation of the creation story would lead
to the belief that the universe came ready-made in its present form
from the hand of God in the beginning of time. There have been
attempts, it is true, to harmonize the details of the creation story
with those of modern scientific theories of the origin of the world.
Such attempts, though, seem to be based on the mistaken assumption that the purpose of the creation story is to provide us with
scientific information. We can say the same of the attempts that
have been made to calculate the age of the universe from the Bible.
The purpose of Genesis is not to tell us when the production of
things occurred nor how the differentiation of things was accomplished but to affirm that the one and the other were the work of
God. The intention of the sacred writer, in other words, was religious, not scientific.

The figures that have been obtained from the Bible for the beginning of time such as the year 3761 B.C., the one which is given
in the Jewish Calendar, correspond more to the beginning of history (history being defined as the recorded past of mankind) than
to the beginning of time. The idea that there was a beginning of
time, whether it was only some millennia ago or whether it was billions of years ago, seems to be part of the doctrinal content of
Genesis and of the dogma of creation defined by the Church in the
Fourth Council of the Lateran. There are two opposing standpoints
on the question of the beginning in contemporary science. According to the "evolutionary" theory of the universe championed by
such men as Lemaître and Gamow the whole world began several
billion years ago, but according to the "steady-state" theory of the
universe maintained by such men as Hoyle, Bondi, and Gold there
was no single beginning but matter is being continually created.
"Every cluster of galaxies, every star, every atom had a beginning,"
says Hoyle, "but not the Universe itself." [8] The question arises,
therefore, whether the steady-state theory is compatible with the
Christian doctrine of the beginning of time, whether the beginning

8. Hoyle, *Frontiers of Astronomy* (Mentor paperbacks), p. 134.

spoken of in Genesis is the beginning simply of our world or the beginning of the entire physical universe.

Everyone agrees that our own world had a beginning some billions of years ago. This can hardly be denied in the face of the evidence for the beginning which has been accumulated by the various natural sciences. If the atoms of radioactive elements, for example, had been formed too far back in time, they would by now have decayed completely and disappeared. Their age can be calculated by comparing the abundance of unstable isotopes of a given radioactive element like uranium with the more stable isotopes of the same element. The age of the rocks on the earth can be calculated from the proportion of radiogenic isotopes of lead to lead-producing radioactive substances locked together in the rocks. The age of the oceans can be determined by comparing the total amount of salt in the oceans with the amount of salt brought in yearly by rivers. The age of the moon or at least the duration of its separate existence from the earth can be measured by its distance from the earth together with its rate of recession from the earth. The life span of the sun and of other stars can be calculated from the ratio of the amount of hydrogen in the star to the rate at which the star consumes hydrogen since hydrogen is the fuel which a star burns. The age of clusters of stars within a galaxy can be estimated from their mechanical behavior since it is not mechanically possible for such a cluster to hold together indefinitely. The age of the whole Milky Way can be judged from the distribution of energy among the stars which according to the laws of statistical mechanics must reach an equipartition in which the velocity of each star is inversely proportional to the square root of its mass, the stars of the Milky Way being about two per cent away from this goal. In every one of these cases we get the same approximate result, namely that our world began a few billion years ago.

Everyone, therefore, admits that our own local world, our earth, the solar system, even the Milky Way, had a beginning. The question is whether the entire physical universe had a beginning. If it did have a beginning the way it would be determined or the way the age of the universe would be measured would be from the rate at which the universe is expanding. It is now well known that the universe is expanding since the spectrum of the distant galaxies exhibits the shift towards the red that is characteristic of a receding source of light (the Doppler shift). The rate at which the galaxies, other systems of stars like our Milky Way, are receding from one another is given by the formula

recession velocity = distance × Hubble's constant.

The meaning of the formula is that the more distant two galaxies are the faster they are flying apart from one another. Supposing that the universe had a beginning and that the beginning was the beginning of the expansion, the age of the universe would be given by the formula

age of the universe = 1/Hubble's constant.

For some time it was thought that this figure was of the order of 1.8 billion years, a figure that is obviously too small when we compare it with the figures obtained for the age of the oldest rocks on the earth's surface. Baade, however, has since shown that there was a mistake in the calculation of Hubble's constant due to a faulty method of measuring the distances between the galaxies so that the actual age of the universe would be five billion years or more.

Both of the current theories of the universe start from the generally accepted fact that the universe is expanding, but only the evolutionary theory concludes from this that the universe had a beginning. Using the definition of the density of the universe as the ratio of its mass to its volume, we can represent the differences between the two theories as follows:

$$\text{Evolutionary Universe: density (decreasing)} = \frac{\text{mass (constant)}}{\text{volume (increasing)}}$$

$$\text{Steady-State Universe: density (constant)} = \frac{\text{mass (increasing)}}{\text{volume (increasing)}}$$

In the evolutionary theory the fact of the expansion of the universe and the law of the conservation of mass lead to the conclusion that the density is decreasing and therefore to the conclusion that there was a maximum density in the past, that is, a beginning of the world. In the steady-state theory, on the contrary, the postulate that the universe is in a steady state, in other words, that the density of the universe is constant, excludes the possibility of a maximum density in the past constituting the beginning of the world. But the postulate of the steady state together with the fact of expansion also negates the law of the conservation of mass for the universe as a whole and leads to the conclusion that more matter is being continually created to maintain the constant density.

Is this state of maximum density in the past implied in the evolutionary theory of the universe an absolute beginning before which there was nothing or is it simply the beginning of the present era of the history of the universe? Gamow thinks that it is only the beginning of the present era of expansion and the end of a previous era of contraction. This previous era he calls facetiously "St. Augustine's Era" since St. Augustine, he thinks, was the first to ask the question what God was doing before he created the world. Seriously, however, he admits that this era is "metaphysical" and by that he means that it is impossible by definition to obtain any empirical evidence of such an era since all its features would have been obliterated in the contraction to the state of maximum density.[9] One may ask, therefore, whether it is scientific to speak of such an era and whether statements about it are statements of science, for a scientific statement or hypothesis is one that can be verified by empirical evidence. Hypotheses which cannot be tested are commonly eliminated from science as being unscientific.

Is the continual creation of matter postulated in the steady-state theory of the universe a creation of matter from nothing, creation in the theological sense, or simply the formation of matter from something else such as radiation? In contemporary microphysics one speaks of the creation and annihilation of particles, meaning by that simply the conversion of one particle into another or into radiation or vice versa. The term "creation" in the steady-state theory, however, does not mean the production of matter from radiation or from other matter but from nothing. "It should be clearly understood," says Bondi, "that the creation here discussed is the formation of matter not out of radiation but out of nothing."[10] The difference is apparent from the fact that the creation and annihilation of particles discussed in microphysics does not violate the law of the conservation of mass while the creation discussed in the steady-state theory admittedly does violate that law. The proponents of the steady-state universe maintain that the

9. Gamow. *The Creation of the Universe* (Mentor paperbacks), p. 134.
10. Bondi, *Cosmology* (Cambridge, 1952), p. 144.

conservation law is valid only on a small scale where the creation rate is not enough to make any significant difference. So the continual creation demanded by the steady-state theory is creation in the theological sense.

Now if the beginning of the world in the evolutionary theory is a beginning in the theological sense, a beginning before which there was nothing, and the continual creation of matter in the steady-state theory is creation in the theological sense, creation from nothing, does it follow that the two theories are not scientific hypotheses but simply excursions of scientists into the realm of theology? The answer, it would seem, is no. The theories are scientific and the proof of this is the fact that it is or will be possible to decide between them by the scientific method. When we look at the stars through a telescope we are looking into the past because all of the stars are light years away and the other galaxies are millions of light years away. If the evolutionary theory of the universe is correct the galaxies should have been closer together in the past than they are at present. If the steady-state theory of the universe is correct, on the other hand, the galaxies should be about the same average distance apart in the past as they are at present, for though they are always flying apart from one another new ones are always being created in the gaps. It should be possible, therefore, through observation of the parts of the universe that are distant from us in space and time to decide between the two theories. Since an empirical decision is possible it follows that the two theories are genuine scientific hypotheses.

It should not be thought that the evolution of matter is denied in the steady-state theory and admitted only in the evolutionary theory. The evolution of matter is required in both theories but in different ways. We might say, to borrow the terminology used to describe the evolution of life, that the evolutionary theory of the universe is a monogenistic account of the evolution of matter whereas the steady-state theory is a polygenistic account. In the one there is a single evolution of the whole universe but in the other each galaxy has its own evolution. No theological questions are raised by the detailed accounts of the stages of evolution in either theory unless one wants to interpret the six days of the Genesis story as the actual stages in the evolution of the universe. Such an interpretation, we have seen, is unwarranted since the purpose of

RESPONSIBLE ⟶

the story is religious, not scientific. Nor is any theological question raised by the evolution of organic from inorganic matter. There is nothing in the doctrine of the Church, for that matter, against the idea that man may be able to make living organisms from inanimate material in the laboratory.

2. The Evolution of Life

Theological questions are raised, though, by the idea of the evolution of the human body from organic matter. From the standpoint of biology man is a genus of the order Primates. The evolutionary progress of the Primates, according to G. G. Simpson, has been in the direction of greater adaptability rather than of greater adaptation. This is in sharp contrast to the tendency towards specialized adaptations which characterize other groups. Thus the order of Primates can be defined only in terms of the prevailing evolutionary trends which have set it apart from the other groups such as the development of large and complicated brains, the elaboration of the visual apparatus and a corresponding reduction of the olfactory apparatus, the abbreviation of the facial skeleton, the tendency towards the elimination of the third incisor tooth and of one or two premolars, the preservation of a relatively simple pattern of the molar teeth, the replacement of sharp claws by flattened nails, the retention of pentadactyl limbs with an accentuation of the mobility of the digits, and so forth.[11]

The theory of human evolution is the hypothesis not that man descended from ape but that man and ape descended from a common ancestral stock in the order of the Primates. The branch from this stock which terminates in the modern apes is called the pongids and the branch which terminates in man is called the hominids. From the fossil evidence which has been collected to date it has been inferred that the first step in the evolution of the hominids was the development of erect posture and gait and the second step was the development of the large brain. Both of these developments, it should be noted, were in the direction of greater adaptability rather than of greater adaptation. Le Gros Clark suggests that the evolution of ground-living forms in the ancestry of man was the

11. Cf. Le Gros Clark, *The Fossil Evidence for Human Evolution* (Chicago, 1955), pp. 12f., note. This is the principal source of the scientific data on biological evolution presented in this and the following section.

result of adaptations primarily concerned not with the abandon-
ment of life in the trees but with an attempt to retain it. In regions
undergoing gradual deforestation such adaptations would make it
possible to cross intervening grasslands in order to pass from one
restricted and shrinking wooded area to another.[12] This is analogous to the idea that water-living vertebrates first acquired terres-
trial and air-breathing adaptations in order to preserve their
aquatic mode of life; for in times of drought these adaptations
would make it possible to escape from dried-up rivers or pools and
go overland in search of water elsewhere.

It is not easy to determine whether a given hominid fossil is to
be classified as human or as subhuman. It is hard to decide this
simply on the basis of brain capacity since there is a good deal of
variation on this score even in the single species *Homo sapiens*
and it would seem to be somewhat gratuitous to deny intelligence
to a being merely on the grounds that its brain capacity falls short
of the range of present-day man. The most practical criterion that
has been proposed so far is that of tool-making. If a given specimen
was a tool-maker, it will be classified as human; if not, then as subhuman. Such a criterion is practical because man's tools, at least
those of stone, tend to be preserved as well as or even better than
his bones. The difficulty of deciding the borderline cases between
the human and the subhuman level is analogous to the difficulty of
drawing the line between life and non-life in such cases as that of
the virus. The difficulty, however, does not prove that there is no
borderline between very high animal skill and very low human
intelligence nor that there is no leap in passing from the one to
the other in the process of evolution.

It is at this point that theological questions arise. In the encyclical *Humani Generis* (§ 64) Pope Pius XII affirmed that "the
teaching authority of the Church does not forbid that in conform-
ity with the present state of human sciences and sacred theology
research and discussions on the part of men experienced in both
fields take place with regard to the doctrine of evolution in as far as
it inquires into the origin of the human body as coming from pre-
existent and living matter—for Catholic faith obliges us to hold
that souls are immediately created by God." The Catholic, in other
words, is free to accept the hypothesis of evolution provided he also

---

12. *Op. cit.,* p. 170.

maintains the necessity of divine intervention in the evolutionary process to bring about the emergence of human intelligence. This does not mean, however, that the Catholic must introduce the idea of divine intervention into the theory of evolution itself any more than he must introduce it into the biological account of ordinary human generation—though here too divine intervention is required for the creation and infusion of the immortal soul. The Church claims that there is divine intervention in the procreation of every human being but does not claim that such intervention is observable and therefore does not claim that it is a matter to be treated by natural science.

The Pope adds, however, that "some rashly transgress this liberty of discussion when they act as if the origin of the human body from pre-existing and living matter were already completely certain and proved by the facts which have been discovered up to now and by reasoning on those facts as if there were nothing in the sources of divine revelation which demands the greatest moderation and caution in this question." (§ 65) When it was first proposed, the theory of human evolution was almost a pure hypothesis, an inference from the similarity of ape and man to the existence of a common ancestral stock, with almost no fossil evidence to substantiate it. Since that time, though, a number of fossil remains of earlier types of hominids such as the *Pithecanthropus* and the *Australopithecus* have been discovered. At the present time, therefore, human evolution is no longer a pure hypothesis but a verified hypothesis. Contemporary logicians point out, however, that even a verified hypothesis is never more than probable unless one can prove that there is no other possible hypothesis which can account for the known facts. Moreover, as Le Gros Clark has pointed out, "fossil remains of hominids and anthropoid apes are still very scanty; indeed, to those paleontologists who deal with vertebrate groups richly represented in the fossil record they must appear almost ridiculously so." [13]

Pope Pius XII, however, did not leave Catholics the same freedom of discussion with regard to the question of monogenism and polygenism. "When," he says, "there is a question of another conjectural opinion, namely polygenism, the children of the Church by no means enjoy such liberty. For the faithful cannot embrace

13. *Op. cit.,* p. vii.

that opinion which maintains either that after Adam there existed on this earth true men who did not take their origin through natural generation from him as from the first parent of all or that Adam represents a certain number of first parents. For it is in no way apparent how such an opinion can be reconciled with that which the sources of revealed truth and the documents of the teaching authority of the Church propose with regard to original sin, which proceeds from sin actually committed by an individual Adam and which through generation is passed on to all and is in everyone as his own" (§ 66). Catholics must maintain, in other words, that Adam was an individual and was the father of the present human race on earth.

It should be noted, first of all, that this condemnation of polygenism does not exclude the existence of other human races elsewhere in the universe which do not take their origin from Adam. It is explicitly limited to men "on this earth." Certainly the existence of human beings or intelligent beings of some sort elsewhere in the universe would raise a number of interesting theological questions. These questions would not be difficulties with existing doctrines but simple questions as to whether such beings belong to the same economy of salvation as we do, whether Christ's command to preach His doctrine to the whole world would imply communicating it to such beings or whether it is strictly a message of redemption to the fallen race of Adam, whether the race of Adam is to be regarded as a chosen race destined to carry revelation to the whole universe or whether each human race in the universe is possessed of its own revelation, and the like. Such questions cannot be answered in anticipation of the facts, it would seem, but should be set aside until such time as the existence or non-existence of other human races in the universe has been established.

Secondly, it should be noted that the Pope took care not to exclude the possibility of pre-Adamites, human beings existing on this earth before Adam, but intended to exclude only the possibility "that after Adam there existed on this earth true men who did not take their origin through natural generation from him." One would be free, therefore, to propose the hypothesis that Adam was a *Homo sapiens* called by God like Abraham to be the father of a chosen race, a race which was to be given the supernatural gifts of holiness, integrity and immortality, and that the *Pithecanthropus* and the *Australopithecus* were pre-Adamites, races which became extinct, as indeed they did, leaving no posterity on the earth. It is truly difficult to imagine the decision which has so profoundly affected the lot of the human race being left to a *Pithecanthropus*. The same hypothesis, namely that Adam was a *Homo sapiens*, is suggested from a different point of view by the term "true men" in the papal decree. The word "Adam" in Hebrew means "man," and it is certainly unlikely that the author of Genesis had anything other than a *Homo sapiens* in mind when he spoke of Adam as the first man.

Thirdly, it should be noted that this decree while affirming the unity of the present human race on earth does not affirm the origin of the first woman from the first man. It is true that there is a decree of the Biblical Commission dating from 1909 which among other things forbids departure from the literal interpretation of the item in Genesis about the formation of the first woman from the first man, but that decree was disciplinary in nature, not doctrinal, and it is now generally conceded that the disciplinary norms therein imposed are no longer in force. As a result we find Catholic scholars today taking Genesis 2:21f. on Adam's rib in a metaphorical sense. Father DeVaux, for example, says that the words of the Bible about God making the first woman out of a rib of the first man were a way of describing in the language of imagery the intimate relationship which unites man and woman and commands their mutual attraction.[14] The purpose of the story of Adam's rib, perhaps, was to teach the ancients that woman was of the same nature as man and not to be regarded simply as chattel.

From a scientific point of view the hypothesis of monogenism is more probable and consequently more widely held than that of polygenism. To the scientist, however, the term "monogenism" does not mean the doctrine that all present-day human races have descended from a single pair but the theory that they have all descended from a common stock. The term "polygenism," in like manner, signifies for a scientist the theory that the present human races have descended from different ancestral stocks. The theoretical argument in favor of monogenism is that the whole idea of evolution is the reduction of present-day multiplicity to common ancestral stocks. Polygenists, on the contrary, have to appeal to the

14. DeVaux, La Genèse (Paris, 1953), p. 45 note *b*.

idea of parallel origin to explain the similarity of the present human races. "Parallelism," says Colbert, "should not be invoked to explain resemblances among related animals unless it can be proved, for to do this is to make the whole concept of evolution largely meaningless." [15] The empirical argument in favor of monogenism is the interbreeding capacity of the present-day human races, a very strong argument from the biological point of view, and one which renders the hypothesis of polygenism rather improbable. Monogenism in the sense of a common stock is of course compatible with monogenism in the stronger sense of a single pair of first parents while polygenism is not. So we can regard the scientific arguments in favor of monogenism as lending some support to or providing some framework for the Biblical doctrine of the unity of the human race.

3. The Evolution of Intelligence

There are three recognized genera of hominids: *Australopithecus, Pithecanthropus,* and *Homo.* Another and more primitive type which has been named the *Oreopithecus* was discovered in the summer of 1958 but its time and its nature have not yet been satisfactorily established. The genus *Homo* includes the two species *Homo sapiens* and *Homo neanderthalensis.* All of these types with the possible exception of the *Australopithecus* (and of course the *Oreopithecus*) seem to have been toolmakers and therefore human. If it could be established that the two more primitive genera were ancestral to the genus *Homo,* then it could also be established that evolution did not cease with the emergence of human beings but has continued at its customarily slow pace until the present. The three genera can be distinguished among other things by the progressive increase in brain capacity. The brain capacity of the *Australopithecus* ranged from about 450 to about 700 cc., that of the *Pithecanthropus* all the way from 775 to 1300 cc., that of *Homo sapiens* from 1200 to 1500 cc. and that of *Homo neanderthalensis* from 1300 to 1600 cc. This last example, however, indicates that the sheer size of the brain is not a direct index of intelligence, for Neanderthal Man in spite of his large brain seems to .have been mentally or at least culturally inferior to *Homo sapiens.*

There have been attempts to prove that the *Australopithecus* was

15. As quoted by Le Gros Clark, *op. cit.,* p. 18.

able to make fire, witness the title *Australopithecus prometheus,* but it is now agreed that this conclusion was based on mistaken evidence. It has not been proven, nevertheless, that this type of hominid was incapable of making tools, for the fact that no tools were found in association with its remains up until recently must be set beside the circumstance that the remains have been derived from fissures and caves, and tools are not generally to be found in such places in the region (South Africa) but rather in river beds of the main valleys. Moreover, another skull probably of an *Australopithecus* was found in Africa in the summer of 1959, this time in association with some crude pebble tools, though this specimen is not as yet completely analyzed. The large number of baboon skulls that have been found associated with the remains of the *Australopithecus* indicate that it may have used weapons of some kind, for most of these skulls show fractures which are rather consistent in size and position and which must have been the result of well-aimed blows with a weapon. The likelihood is, therefore, that the *Australopithecus* was endowed with skill superior to that of modern anthropoid apes. Whether this skill would amount to intelligence in the strict sense and therefore whether this hominid was endowed with an immortal soul would be a question.

Remains of the *Pithecanthropus* have been found both in Java and in China. No tools have been found associated with the remains in Java although chopping tools, hand axes, and primitive flake tools have been found in deposits of a slightly later age in the same region, and it is not improbable that they were made and used by hominids of this type. In China, on the other hand, the same deposits which contained the remains of the *Pithecanthropus* also contained the evidence of a crude stone and bone industry. There were crude cores and trimmed flakes of quartz and silicified rocks; there were animal bones, broken and chipped, apparently by design for use as tools; and above all there were the remains of hearths as well as charred animal bones. The *Pithecanthropus,* therefore, was able to make fire and use it for cooking. The nature of his diet is indicated by collections of deer bones and hackberry seeds which were found in the same places. What is also apparent in these deposits is the fact that these early hominids had already developed a communal life of a very active kind. The ability of the *Pithecanthropus* to make not only tools but even fire would seem to imply more than animal skill. It would seem probable from what we now know about him that he was endowed with true intelligence and thus, theologically speaking, with an immortal soul.

Neanderthal Man is generally regarded as a distinct species of the genus *Homo* (all the present races are considered to belong to the single species (*Homo sapiens*) which occupied the continent of Europe and possibly adjacent regions during the last glaciation of the Ice Age. What I refer to is sometimes called the "classic" or "extreme Neanderthal type" to distinguish it from the earlier "generalized Neanderthal type" which is morphologically indistinguishable from *Homo sapiens*. The type of man that exists today, in other words, seems to have existed before the Neanderthal Man appeared on the scene. So the Neanderthal would represent an aberrant and now extinct line of evolution which branched off from the precursors of modern man. The differentiation of the species, it may well be, was brought about by the isolation caused by the rigorous climatic conditions of the beginning of the last glaciation of the Ice Age. Neanderthal Man certainly made fire and used tools but no evidence has been found so far of anything like the splendid paintings discovered in the caves inhabited by early *Homo sapiens* in southern France and northern Spain. Neanderthal Man was definitely human but apparently inferior in intelligence or at least in culture to *Homo sapiens*.

The species *Homo sapiens* dates back at least to the Aurignacian phase of Paleolithic culture, and this, at a conservative estimate, means an antiquity of some 20,000 years. Probably, though, the species is much older than that. From time to time claims for a remote antiquity have been made for skulls and skeletons of modern human type. One of these, the so-called Kanjera Man, seems worthy of special consideration, though its geological dating still needs confirmation. In any case the species progressed through two distinct stages of culture before the dawn of history, that is, before the rise of civilization. The first stage, the Paleolithic or Old Stone Age, is characterized by rough or chipped stone implements. The second stage, the Neolithic or New Stone Age, is characterized by the use of polished stone implements and by many cultural advances such as pottery making, domestication of animals, the cultivation of grain and fruit trees, linen weaving, and so forth. The next great advance came with the rise of civilization in the Near

East in the third millennium B.C. Some, though, regard the whole history of man up to the present as essentially an extension of the Neolithic Era.

The hypothesis of the evolution of man from subman has suggested to many the further hypothesis of the evolution of superman from man. If man has evolved from subman, they argue, should we not expect some kind of superman to evolve eventually from man? One might well inquire whether this superman is conceived to have some power superior to intelligence, whatever such a power could be, or simply to have an intelligence superior to that of *Homo sapiens*. The latter version of the hypothesis is indeed suggested by the hypothetical sequence which we have been considering, the sequence that begins with *Australopithecus,* proceeds to *Pithecanthropus,* and ends with *Homo*. It is a sequence of increasing intelligence, and it inevitably raises the question why the evolution should cease with *Homo sapiens*. The answer depends on the answer to the question why evolution occurs in the first place.

Lamarck's theory was that changes in environment cause changes in the structure of animals and plants, and that characteristics acquired in this manner are transmitted to offspring. Darwin's theory was that evolution occurs through natural selection, the natural process tending to cause the survival of the fittest and the extinction of poorly adapted forms. The advance of technology, however, tends to bring the environment more and more under control and to make it easier and easier for the unfit or poorly adapted to survive. It is true that contemporary biologists, Neo-Darwinians and Neo-Lamarckians, have modified the old theories of evolution by the introduction of the findings of genetics. It has also been discovered that radiation can cause genetic changes and that nuclear energy can be dangerous not only to individuals but to the race as well (for who knows whether the genetic changes that might be brought about in this manner would be for better or for worse?). So in sum we might say that the advance of science and technology gives man power over his own evolution: he has the power to prevent natural selection, power to introduce artificial selection, and even power to bring about genetic changes.

What this really seems to add up to is the fact that evolution has passed from the biological level to the intellectual level. To be sure, man's bodily evolution did not cease with the emergence of intelligence if we concede that the *Pithecanthropus* (and perhaps even the *Australopithecus*) was endowed with intelligence. The growth of his intelligence too, if we make this concession, was not completely dissociated from the development of the physical brain. Yet the development of his intelligence eventually outstripped the development of his body. There is little bodily difference between *Homo sapiens* of Paleolithic times and *Homo sapiens* of Neolithic times, but there is an intellectual chasm. There is practically no difference at all, biologically, between prehistoric man of the Neolithic Era and historic man, but there is the intellectual difference that exists between a primitive man and a civilized man. On a time scale the intellectual development of man would appear as a burst of movement that is ever increasing in rapidity whereas the bodily development of man would appear as a growth which was so slow as to be almost indiscernible. Man would be missing the point of his own evolution, therefore, if he were to use the powers he has gained through the development of his intelligence in the fields of science and technology to produce genetic changes and bring about artificial selection in the human race with the idea that his progress is on a bodily level.

What is more, there is divine intervention in the evolution of intelligence just as there is divine intervention in the evolution of life and in the evolution of matter. The divine intervention in the evolution of matter takes the form of the creative activity by which God draws the evolving matter from nothingness. His intervention in the evolution of life takes the form of the creation and infusion of the immortal soul into the human body. God's intervention in the evolution of intelligence, finally, takes the form of revelation. Although it is not generally conceded by cultural anthropologists as yet, the evidence is accumulating that there was a primitive revelation, a prehistoric manifestation of the transcendent God to man. For primitive peoples that still exist today show the traces of a tradition of belief in a transcendent God, leading one to infer that monotheism did not evolve from polytheism and other "primitive" forms of religion but that "primitive religion" is the corruption of an original monotheism.[16] This divine intervention in the form of revelation continued down the ages until it culminated in the

16. This is the theme of Father Wilhelm Schmidt's great ten-volume work, *Der Ursprung der Gottesidee* (Munster, 1926–1952).

incarnation of the Word when the invisible God made himself visible by becoming man.

The evolution of man's intelligence, however, did not cease with the completion of revelation in the Word incarnate. On the contrary, the content of the revelation now became the subject matter of intellectual evolution. The Vatican Council declared that revealed doctrine itself has developed over the ages since the time of Christ, not that its content was increased or diminished or changed in any way but that man's understanding of it has grown and matured. The Council cites here the famous words of St. Vincent of Lerins on the development of doctrine: "Let the understanding, the knowledge, the wisdom of each and every one and of the whole Church increase and progress extensively and intensively but always in its own right, in the same doctrine, the same sense, and the same position" (Denz. 1800). Thus the ultimate goal of the whole evolutionary process becomes more and more apparent as one ascends from matter to life to intelligence. God is not only the Alpha but also the Omega, the beginning of all things and their end (Apocalypse 1:8). In this life, however, the goal is never attained but only approached more and more closely.

Note on the Unity of the Human Race

In conclusion, it must be noted here that the Christian truth of the unity of mankind in its first parents is most necessary in this day of racial snobbery, exaggerated nationalism, and class wars. Indeed, it was this basic truth, fortified by additional Christian reasons for mankind's natural unity in Adam, and supernatural unity in Christ, that Pius XII first recalled to the whole disunited world when he was elected to the Chair of Peter on the eve of World War II. We might well ponder a few of his words here in an attempt to relish the totality of Catholic Dogma on this point: 'that there is neither Gentile nor Jew, circumcised nor uncircumcised, barbarian nor Scythian, bond nor free. But Christ is all and in all' (Colossians 3:10–11).

Pius XII mentions an error which "renders impossible or at least precarious and uncertain, the peaceful intercourse of peoples. This widespread error is the forgetfulness of that law of *human solidarity* and charity which is dictated and imposed by our common origin and by the equality of rational nature in all men, to whatever people they belong, and by the redeeming Sacrifice offered by Jesus Christ on the Altar of the Cross to His Heavenly Father on behalf of sinful mankind.

"In fact, the first page of the Scripture, with magnificent simplicity, tells us how God, as a culmination to His creative work, made man to His Own image and likeness, and the same Scripture tells us that He enriched man with supernatural gifts and privileges, and destined him to an eternal and ineffable happiness. It shows us besides how other men took their origin from the first couple, and then goes on, in unsurpassed vividness of language, to recount their division into different groups and their dispersion to various parts of the world. Even when they abandoned their Creator, God did not cease to regard them as His children, who, according to His merciful plan, should one day be reunited once more in His friendship.

"The Apostle of the Gentiles later on makes himself the herald of this truth which associates men as brothers in one great family, when he proclaims to the Greek world that God 'hath made of one (man), all mankind, to dwell upon the whole face of the earth, determining appointed times and the limits of their habitation, that they should seek God" (Acts 17:26–27).

"A marvelous vision, which makes us see the human race *in the unity of one common origin in God,* 'one God and Father of all, who is above all, and through all, and in us all' (Ephesians 4:6); *in the unity of nature* which in every man is equally composed of material body and spiritual, immortal soul; in the unity of the immediate end and mission in the world; in the unity of dwelling place, the earth, of whose resources all men can by natural right avail themselves, to sustain and develop life; *in the unity of the supernatural end,* God Himself, to Whom all should tend; *in the unity of means* to secure that end.

"It is the same Apostle who portrays for us mankind in the unity of its relations with the Son of God, image of the invisible God, in Whom all things have been created; 'In Him were all things created (Colossians 1:16); *in the unity of its ransom,* effected for all by Christ, Who, through His Holy and most bitter Passion, restored the original friendship with God which had been broken, making Himself the Mediator between God and men: 'For there is one God, and one Mediator of God and men, the man Christ Jesus' (I Timothy 2:5).

"And to render such friendship between God and mankind more intimate, this same Divine and universal Mediator of salvation and of peace, in the sacred silence of the Supper Room, before He consummated the Supreme Sacrifice, let fall from His Divine Lips the words which reverberate mightily down the centuries, inspiring heroic charity in a world devoid of love and torn by hate: 'This is My commandment that you love one another, as I have loved you' (John 15:12).

"These are supernatural truths which form a solid basis and the strongest possible bond of union, that is reinforced by the love of God and of our Divine Redeemer, from Whom all receive salvation 'for the building up of the Body of Christ: until we all meet in the unity of faith, and of the knowledge of the Son of God, unto a perfect man, unto the measure of the age of the fullness of Christ' (Ephesians 4:12–13).

"In the light of this unity of all mankind, which exists in law and in fact, individuals do not feel themselves isolated units, like grains of sand, but united by the very force of their nature and by their eternal destiny, into an organic harmonious mutual relationship which varies with the changing of times. And the nations, despite a difference of development due to diverse conditions of life and of culture, are not destined to break the unity of the human race, but rather to enrich and embellish it by the sharing of their own peculiar gifts and by that reciprocal interchange of goods which can be possible and efficacious only when a mutual love and a lively sense of charity unite all the sons of the same Father and all those redeemed by the same Divine Blood."

Pius XII concluded this magnificent expression of the divine foundation and practical significance of the unity of the human race with a statement that is both a prelude and an explanation of World War II: "Forgetfulness of the law of universal charity—of that charity that alone can consolidate peace by extinguishing hatred and softening envies and dissensions—is the source of the very grave evils for peaceful relations between nations." [17]

In the face of this marvelous statement of the basic religious truth: the unity of all men in Adam and in Christ, how narrow are

17. Pius XII, *Summi Pontificatus*, Nos. 29–46, the Paulist Press, New York.

those petty unchristian attitudes of racial hatred or national exclusivistic pride. The man sitting next to you in America may be white or colored, he may be Irish or Chinese—but if you stop with this surface characterization of him, if you are prejudiced against him, if you are unlikely to offer him human kindness, equal opportunity, or even more, civil respect because of the color of his skin or the nationality of his forebears—then you are being more than slightly inhuman and unchristian. *Inhuman,* because if you go back far enough you are his blood brother, and it is inhuman to spurn your own flesh and blood. *Unchristian,* too, because whatever his color or nationality, Christ died for him and Christ will gladly dwell in his soul.

If every human being, just by being human, is potentially good enough to share the life of God by grace, and to be welcome in the eternal kingdom of God, then he should be good enough for our respect and human kindness. While Pius XII, in the above passage, specifically cited this forgetting of universal charity as the cause of international strife and world wars, the same forgetfulness of the unity of human kind breeds these petty, mean sins of racial prejudice, class hatred, and minority intolerance which are no less dangerous, since they cause no end of internal dissension, ill will and unhealthy tensions in this land of the free and home of the brave. Once more we can see how important are these basic Christian dogmas, for basic Christian living.

CHAPTER VI

The Elevation and the Fall of Man

THE STORY OF CREATION presents the logical setting for this present chapter. Now that we have considered the origin of our First Parents, Adam and Eve, the next step is to take a glance at what actually happened to them at the dawn of human history. Certainly, this first page of history is among the most significant of all human happenings of all time. Much of what is happening today is fully intelligible only in the light of what happened then.

To view the content of Theology constructively and positively, the acts of Redemption which parallel those of the Fall of mankind are of greater and more hopeful significance to us today. However, the full meaning and purpose of Redemption is only understood when seen against the backdrop of that Original Sin and Fall of mankind. It is this theological setting, so pregnant with implications for the whole course of human destiny on this earth, that we must now approach.

This present chapter in early human history might well be epitomized in two words: Elevation and Fall. The whole of man's earliest experience can be summarized in this fashion: Man was originally elevated to a share in God's life, and directed towards a share in God's own eternal happiness. Man then lost his original endowment of God's life, together with the special gifts that accompanied it in the beginning. Adam not only lost his heritage for

himself, but for us, his physical progeny, as well. Although mankind retained the original supernatural destiny to share God's happiness, man no longer came into being with the supernatural equipment which was necessary for the attainment of Heaven's glory.
The deprivation of these supernatural endowments constitutes
Original Sin for us. It also spells the obvious need of Redemption
for a fallen world destined to a glory beyond its reach. But that is
another chapter. For the present, then, our theological history of
man unfolds in this order:

    1. The Original Endowments of Man: His Elevation to the
Supernatural Order.

    2. The Fall of Man and Consequent Loss of His Supernatural
Endowments.

    3. The Theological Nature of Original Sin.

    4. Original Sin in the World Today: The Modern Reaction.

    5. The Immaculate Conception of Mary the Mother of God.

    The first step involves a treatment of what Adam originally had
from God in the line of spiritual gifts. Without an understanding
of these, it would be impossible to know exactly what he lost
through Original Sin. An actual and precise assessment of what
Adam did lose for himself is the matter of the second point. But
since Adam's loss was not merely personal to him, but a loss of our
nature as well, in the third place we will see just precisely how
Adam's sin affected all of us—indeed, the whole human race. We
shall then bring the whole question of original sin into the world
of our times, to see how men have reacted and are reacting to the
drama just outlined. The whole Chapter is ultimately summarized
in the doctrine of the Immaculate Conception.

I. THE ORIGINAL ENDOWMENT OF MAN

    It is no small feat to understand man as he is today. It is even
more difficult to imagine how he was in the beginning of his life
on earth. There are certain elements pertaining to the nature of
man, which both Adam and we have in common. Otherwise we
could not all be called men. Due to the Redemption of Christ, Our
Lord, we too have a supernatural life like Adam's but there still
remain other qualities of a preternatural kind, that distinguish
him from us. The simplest method of procedure, therefore, seems

to be this: to reconstruct theologically a picture of what Adam was before the Fall, in contrast to what we are now after the Redemption.

Theologians generally classify the original endowments of Adam (and Eve) into three categories: Natural, Preternatural, and Supernatural. While the preternatural gifts of Adam are most useful in distinguishing what Adam was from what we are, the most important terms for the whole study of Theology that follows are the correlatives: natural and supernatural. Here we must tread carefully, for heresies lie underfoot at every step. Here is the battleground where some of the fiercest theological struggles have taken place, such as those between St. Augustine and Pelagius in the fifth century, between the so-called reformers Luther, Calvin & Company and the Fathers of the Council of Trent in the sixteenth century. Here at the beginning of the twentieth century the Modernists were brought to bay. Here today we find great confusion and a renewal of ancient errors in the minds of many, even Catholic people. And here also, in the field of the natural and the supernatural, the speculations of one of the most brilliant theologians of our times, Père H. DeLubac, are being questioned by other top theologians in Europe and America.

Obviously, we are not looking for controversy, but rather, a firm footing and a clarity of ideas in a difficult theological matter. Let us first look to that of which we are most certain: the triple endowment with which Adam was constituted by God in His creation.

A. The Natural Endowment of Adam

Natural is one of those words we hear and use continually, and yet find most difficult to define. We say it is natural for a dog to bark, a fish to swim, natural for a lion to eat meat. Why? Well, because it is the nature of the beast. This, of course, is simplifying the matter by equivocation; defining natural by nature. As we have already seen in our discussion of the nature of God, we define nature philosophically in the dynamic sense as "that by which something acts, the principle of operation." This is useful to the philosopher, because by studying the specifically different actions of beings, he can reason to different natures, or different principles of operation.

Thus, specifically animal actions point to animal nature, human actions designate human nature, divine actions lead us to divine nature.

In our present discussion, we view nature in a more static sense, as the philosophical notion of *essence*. Here nature is viewed as that which is required to constitute the essence of a being, as for example, man could not be man if he did not have a body and a soul. More broadly, we also include these faculties which are necessary to the proper functioning of a nature so constituted. Thus, the intellect, will and sense faculties are natural to man. The concept 'natural' could be further amplified to include the intrinsic requirement of divine concurrence without which no creature could live or act, and the extrinsic natural requirements of air, food, etc., but in discussing the natural endowments of the first man, it seems sufficient to define natural as *that which fulfills the notion or essence of man,* those things without which he would not truly be called man.

Fortunately, we have already discussed at some length the creation of Adam's body and soul, and have seen some indications of his mind and will. You may wonder why we speak of this natural equipment of Adam as endowments or gifts. Of course, once God determined to make a man, He had to give him those things which constitute human nature. But they are gifts in this sense, that no creature has a right to be. God did make man the highest creature of the material universe, but He did not need to make *us*. He could have made millions of others instead, who would have served Him better. Therefore, even our individual existence and natures are pure gifts of God just as Adam's was.

Had He wanted to, God could have stopped right here in His creation of man, since with these natural endowments of body and soul, with his soul possessing the powers of mind and will, Adam would have had all he needed essentially to be a man. Michael du Bay (Baius) of Louvain contended that God could not have left man in a state of pure nature, without any preternatural or supernatural endowments, but his opinion was condemned by Pope Pius V, in 1567 (Denz. 1079). As a matter of interest, this concept of man with only natural endowments, is all that the philosophers can speak of, for this is all that can be known of man by human reason. Ethics, for example, in the strictest philosophical sense, considers man only as tending towards an end of natural human happiness. We shall now see from Theology that man, from Adam to us, has never existed in a purely natural order, has never had a solely natural end. From the beginning, he was constituted in a higher supernatural order, and was destined to a higher end than purely human happiness. But first, we must discuss some very special endowments of Adam which are neither strictly natural nor strictly supernatural; *preternatural* endowments that put him in a class all by himself.

B. The Preternatural Endowments of Adam

Preternatural is a word which we very rarely see. Etymologically, it explains itself quite well. The prefix 'preter' is derived from a Latin preposition meaning *beyond*. Preternatural then would mean 'that which is beyond nature'—not contrary to nature, not completely out of the line of nature, but just beyond what nature normally includes. Moreover, this word is theologically used in a *relative* sense, that is, in relation to the one particular nature under consideration. By way of illustration, if you came into the living room Sunday morning and found your dog Fido reading the comics and guffawing at the antics of the Dripples, that would be something preternatural for Fido, beyond the nature of a dog, while it is perfectly natural for you to read, and understand, and laugh.

In our present discussion, we use preternatural in relation to man's nature, although what is preternatural for Adam, is perfectly natural for an angel's nature. For example, it would be preternatural for a man to be completely free from death which goes with his mortal body, whereas it is perfectly natural for an angel to be immortal since it has no body. Preternatural in the present context, then, means simply this: *that which is beyond this particular nature under consideration, namely, man's.*

Now what were the preternatural endowments of Adam? Since they actually enriched the natural endowments he possessed as man they are best seen in connection with these natural elements which we considered in the last section. In outline form, we can view these special gifts as freedoms from certain natural consequences or infirmities that follow from man's complex nature. They are easily enough understood, as all of us today labor under these infirmities, deprived as we are of the preternatural gifts that Adam had.

Natural Endowments		*Preternatural Gifts*
	Soul {	Will —Freedom from concupiscence
		Mind—Freedom from ignorance
Human Nature {		
	Body	—Freedom from death, suffering and unrequited labor

Viewed in this fashion, we get a rather negative view of the gifts. To see all that they imply positively, we must view each of them singly. This is also necessary, because not all of them are equally contained in the teaching of the Church. Freedom from concupiscence and immortality are formally defined in the Council of Trent. Freedom from ignorance and freedom from pain and hard work are indicated in the scriptural story, and commonly held by theologians. We shall therefore discuss them in this order of importance.

1. Freedom From Concupiscence

Theologians in their technical discussions call this particular preternatural endowment the *gift of integrity*. Occasionally they also imply all the preternatural gifts by the term integrity, but we can easily see how it fits the reality of Adam's freedom from concupiscence. Integrity implies a complete, upright, and undivided man. St. Paul describes very well the revolution that goes on within us today, without this gift of integrity: "For I do not do the good that I wish, but the evil that I do not wish, that I perform . . . For I am delighted with the law of God according to the inner man, but I see another law in my members, warring against the law of my mind, and making me prisoner of the law of sin that is in my members. Unhappy man that I am, who will deliver me from the body of this death?" (Romans 7:19–24).

Adam could not have uttered such a plea before his fall. Due to his gift of integrity, in Adam there was a perfect harmony between the desires of his soul and the appetites of his body. Just as all of nature, the whole physical world, was subject to the first man as the masterpiece of God's visible creation, so too, his whole physical nature was completely and peacefully subject to his spiritual nature. Note that this was not *natural* to man, but *preternatural*, beyond the ordinary demands of human nature. Since man is a composite creature, he naturally has two sets of appetites. The appetites of the body clamor loudly for attention, since they are directed at visible, pleasurable and obviously attractive things that appeal to the senses and can be attained at once. On the other hand, the appetites of the soul are directed at less obvious, but more important, long-range objectives like happiness, honor, virtue and salvation.

Because of his two-sided nature, it is *natural* that the two sets of appetites in man will often be in conflict. This is the beginning of disorder in man's life: the temptation to live merely as an animal, to seek pleasure for pleasure's sake, and not in the line of reasonable endeavor. St. Paul again has epitomized the struggle: "For the flesh lusts against the spirit, and the spirit against the flesh; for these are opposed to each other, so that you do not do what you would. . . . Now the works of the flesh are manifest, which are immorality, uncleanness, licentiousness, idolatry, witchcrafts, enmities, contentions, jealousies, anger, quarrels, factions, parties, envies, murders, drunkenness, carousings and suchlike. And concerning these I warn you, as I have warned you, that they who do such things will not attain the Kingdom of God. But the fruit of the Spirit is: charity, joy, peace, patience, kindness, goodness, faith, modesty, continency. Against such things there is no law. And they who belong to Christ have crucified their flesh with its passions and desires. If we live by the Spirit, by the Spirit let us also walk" (Galatians 6:17–26).

This is the situation that Adam was spared in the beginning. In him, there was no lusting of the flesh against the spirit or of the spirit against the flesh. In Adam, all was unity, with the lower appetites of the body under the perfect and orderly control of the higher appetites of the soul. There was no danger of Adam becoming a drunkard, a sluggard, a glutton, or a pervert. Whereas for us, character development involves a courageous, hard-fought domination of the flesh by the spirit, a continual struggle to fit the clamoring appetites of the body within the orderly framework of the soul's higher appetites, in Adam all was in order and at peace. Our integrity is the fruit of a lifelong battle, in which the spirit is willing but the flesh is weak. Adam's integrity was God-given, ready made.

Even though God intended this condition as a gift to all mankind, we cannot stress too often the truth that our present condition

of life as a warfare is natural, while Adam's situation was preternatural. The fact that Adam had this special gift explains, as we
shall presently see, why he could only be tempted by the devil to a
spiritual defect such as pride, and not to sensuality, as we are.

Another question of attitude should be indicated here. Since the
conflict between the different kinds of appetites in man is natural,
we should avoid the puritanical attitude of condemning the so-
called lower appetites as bad in themselves, always and everywhere.
These appetites are an essential part of man's nature as God made
him. Bodily appetites are only called *lower* in comparison to the
higher spiritual appetites. While they are technically called passions, these passions of the body are never bad when directed at the
purposes for which God intended them. Take two obvious passions
like anger or venereal pleasure. Christ, for example, did not sin
when he became angry and drove the money changers out of the
Temple with a whip. Similarly, husbands and wives are not sinful
in deriving pleasure from marriage. Rather, their lives are sacra-
mentally consecrated to God.

Saying that Adam was free from concupiscence, simply means
that his passions were always used reasonably, and did not conflict
with the higher purpose of his life. Concupiscence indicates *inordi-
nate* drives of passion, inclinations of man's lower nature that are
directed against the higher good of his soul. We understand concupiscence best by seeing its results in the world today. Very often,
men so allow themselves to be dominated by their sensual passions
that they lose all chance of attaining any true *human* perfection.
Since it is the rational part of man's nature that differentiates him
from an animal, to be truly a man, one must rule the appetites of
the body by reason. Otherwise, the tail wags the dog, as the saying
goes, and man becomes more of an animal than a man.

All of you have seen the tragedy of homes ruined by infidelity,
of a business career doomed by laziness, of a professional life jeop-
ardized by drunkenness. In a word, "What a man sows, that he will
also reap. For he who sows in the flesh, from the flesh also will he
reap corruption. But he who sows in the spirit, from the spirit he
will reap life everlasting" (Galatians 6:8–9). Even the pagan Aristotle remarked that a man who is dominated by his passions is worse
than an animal. For an animal is ruled by instinct, a man by reason.
If a man is merely passionate and therefore unreasonable, not hav-

ing instinct, he has no rule whatever in his life. He is like a ship without a rudder. This is the ever-present danger of concupiscence from which Adam was freed.

It was certainly a singular blessing of God that man enjoyed this angelic property in the beginning of time, insofar as he was spared the disorderly influence of concupiscence which now makes difficult our achievement of integrity and character. The great German theologian, M. Scheeben, has a wonderful passage on this point in his classical work: *Die Mysterien des Christentums:*

> Therefore the integrity which the first man received from God, the integrity which consists in the complete and indissoluble unity and harmony between body and soul, and between the higher and lower faculties of man, was a great, supernatural marvel of God's power and love. It was a marvel of power, because by it God conferred on nature something that it could not in the slightest degree effect of itself. It was a marvel of love, because God did not owe this gift to nature, and granted it only through an extraordinary beneficence and grace.
>
> So great a marvel can in no way be regarded as a self-understood natural endowment. It is extraordinary, unexpected; it is sublime and inconceivable in a special sense; it is a mystery in the proper meaning of the word. Whoever takes such a privilege for granted has a wrong idea of man; and what is more, he fails entirely to understand the greatness and value of this remarkable blessing. He does not reflect that this kind of integrity involves an elevation of man above his own nature (preternatural) to that of the angels. This is a wonderful elevation in virtue of which man, in spite of his corporality and sensuality, remains untroubled in his spiritual life, and even perceives that this corporality and sensuality are, so to speak, spiritualized: the body shares in the impassibility and immortality of the soul (gift of immortality to be seen next), and the sensuality can stir only in accord with the regulations and commands of the spirit. He does not realize that this integrity, in St. Augustine's expression, was a marvelous state which was produced and conserved by a mysterious power; and that, according to the same holy doctor, a great grace of God had to be present where the earthly and sensual body was aware of no inordinate animal appetite.[1]

By now, you are wondering how we come to know of this preternatural gift of integrity. As in other theological proofs, we find definite indications in Holy Scripture and Tradition, corroborated by the authoritative teaching of the Church. The first text in point

---

1. Scheeben, *The Mysteries of Christianity*, p. 218, Herder, St. Louis, 1946.

we have already seen. After seeing Eve the first time, Adam declares his knowledge of God's plan for marriage, "two in one flesh." Then the condition of Adam and Eve is thus described: "And they were both naked; to wit, Adam and his wife: and were not ashamed" (Genesis 2:25).

Here the inspired writer is taking one of the most rebellious of body's appetites to exemplify the order that existed in man's life. Men are ashamed today because of their lack of control over their lower appetites. Adam had no reason to be thus ashamed before his fall, because all was in order, due to his gift of integrity. As St. Augustine says in commenting on this text: "Their (Adam and Eve's) condition was different before sin. For as it is written, 'They were naked and were not ashamed,'—not that their nakedness was not yet shameful, because not yet did lust move those members without the will's consent, not yet did the flesh by its disobedience testify against the disobedience of man." [2]

Even in St. Augustine's day, some said that this was due to the ignorance of our first parents, but he argues that it was due to a special gift of God which was held as long as they were free of sin.

> Their eyes therefore were open, but were not open to this, that is to say, they were not so observant as to recognize what was conferred upon them by the garment of grace, for they had no consciousness of their members warring against their will. But when they were stripped of this grace, then that their disobedience might be punished by fit retribution, there began in the movement of their bodily members a shameless novelty which made nakedness indecent: it at once made them observant and made them ashamed.
>
> And therefore, after they had violated God's command by open transgression, it is written: 'And the eyes of them both were opened, and they knew that they were naked; and they sewed fig leaves together, and made themselves garments' (Genesis 3:7). 'The eyes of them both were opened,' not to see, for already they saw, but to discern between the good they had lost and the evil into which they had fallen. And therefore, the tree itself of which they were forbidden to eat was called the tree of knowledge of good and evil, from the circumstance, that if they ate of it, it would impart to them this knowledge. For the discomfort of sickness reveals the pleasure of health.
>
> They knew, therefore, 'that they were naked,'—naked of that grace which prevented them from being ashamed of bodily naked-

2. St. Augustine, *De Civitate Dei* (The City of God), Book 14, Ch. 17.

ness while the law of sin offered no resistance to their mind. And thus they obtained a knowledge of which they would have lived in blissful ignorance, had they, in trustful obedience to God, declined to commit that offense which involved them in the hurtful effects of unfaithfulness and disobedience. And therefore, being ashamed of the disobedience of their own flesh, which witnessed to their disobedience while it punished it: 'They sewed together fig leaves and made themselves garments.' [3]

St. Paul furnishes us with another theological argument for this gift of integrity in his epistle to the Romans. He calls concupiscence 'sin,' not because it is formally deliberate sin, but because it inclines one to sin, and derives from the sin of Adam. Therefore there would have been no concupiscence before Adam's fall. Speaking to the Christians he says: "Let not sin reign in your mortal body, so as to obey the lusts thereof. Neither yield your members as instruments of iniquity unto sin; but present yourselves to God, as those that are alive from the dead, and your members as instruments of justice unto God" (Romans 6:12–14). Then he laments: "But sin taking occasion by the commandment wrought in me all manner of concupiscence . . . for I know that there dwelleth not in me, that is, in my flesh, that which is good. . . . For I am delighted with the law of God according to the inward man, but I see another law in my members, fighting against the law of my mind and captivating me in the law of sin, that is in my members. Unhappy man that I am, who shall deliver me from the body of this death? the grace of God by Jesus Christ, Our Lord" (Romans 7:8–25).

This doctrine of St. Paul has been officially promulgated by the solemn teaching of the Church in the Council of Trent which declared: "This Holy Synod realizes and admits that concupiscence remains in the baptized, which concupiscence, since it has been left for the struggle, cannot harm those who do not consent to it, or those who manfully resist it by the grace of Jesus Christ. . . . This concupiscence, which the Apostle Paul sometimes calls sin (Epistle to the Romans cited above), the Catholic Church has never understood it to be called sin in those reborn in Christ, but rather it is called sin because it originates in sin and inclines (man) to sin" (Council of Trent, Session V, Canon 5, Denz. 792).

---

3. St. Augustine, *De Civitate Dei*, Book 14, Ch. 17.

Some theologians add an argument of fittingness: since Adam's higher faculties were (by grace, which we shall see later) so perfectly subjected to God, it was only fitting that his lower faculties should have been perfectly subjected to his higher faculties.

This should suffice for the first, and perhaps most important, preternatural gift of integrity. We must now pass on to the other preternatural gifts. It might seem more logical to discuss the gift granted Adam's mind (freedom from ignorance) after that granted his will (freedom from concupiscence). However, we shall next speak of immortality, or the freedom from death granted his body. We do this because of the greater prominence given it in the documents of the Church. For example, the famous decrees of the Biblical Commission, cited above, mention: "The original happiness of our first parents in a state of justice, grace (or the supernatural gift), integrity and immortality" (Denz. 2123).

2. Freedom From Death

Here too is a special gift of God to man in the beginning, that we can readily understand. Someone has said that death is the most certain and most uncertain of realities for mankind. None of us knows when he is going to die, but nothing is more certain than the ever-present threat of death. It was part of man's original happiness that he did not have death to consider or expect, provided that he would obey God.

Even long after the Fall, the inspired writers of the Old Testament and the New linked death to Adam's fall. In the Book of Wisdom we read of God's original plan: "For God made not death, neither hath he pleasures in the destruction of the living. . . . For God created man incorruptible, and to the image of his own likeness he made him, but by the envy of the devil, death came into the world" (Wisdom 1:13 and 2:23–24). St. Paul gives us his own version of the same story: "Wherefore as by one man sin entered into this world, and by sin, death, and so death passed upon all men" (Romans 5:12). This is also the doctrine defined explicitly by the Council of Trent (Denz. 788).

The simplest way to express Adam's freedom from death is to say that he was immortal before the Fall. God expressed it quite clearly in putting man on trial: "Of the tree of knowledge of good and evil, thou shalt not eat. For in what day soever thou shalt eat of it, thou shalt die the death." Obviously God could not threaten man with death if he were not immortal to begin with (Genesis 2:17). The correlative words of God that impose this punishment of death on Adam after his fall are also quite clear: "Because thou hast harkened to the voice of thy wife and hast eaten of the tree whereof I commanded thee that thou shouldst not eat . . . in the sweat of thy brow shalt thou eat bread till thou return to the earth out of which thou was taken, for dust thou art, and into dust thou shalt return" (Genesis 3:17 and 19). These are familiar words that the priest quotes when he puts ashes on our foreheads at the beginning of Lent, reminding us of our present condition of frailty and mortality.

How can we understand the immortality of man before his sin? Certainly, like his freedom from concupiscence, it was preternatural, beyond the normal demands of his nature. Angels are immortal by nature because they are spiritual beings and spirit has no parts to disintegrate, as we saw above in speaking about the simplicity of God. Even the soul of man is naturally immortal. But man is by nature partly material, and it is natural for his body to wear out, for the various parts to become eventually incapable of sustaining the vivifying action of his immortal soul. Death then, the separation of soul and body, is the natural lot of man.

When we say that Adam was immortal, we do not mean to imply that he would have lived forever on earth, but rather, that his eventual passing from earth to heaven would not have involved a separation of soul and body such as we have to undergo. When his trial was over, man would have been translated, soul and body, into heaven. Just as God preternaturally disposed that there should be a wonderful harmony between the powers of Adam's soul and body which we call the gift of integrity, so too God originally planned that the union of body and soul would be permanent and indissoluble. Some theologians explain this by a special providence of God preserving Adam from external harm, and attribute his internal strengthening to the influence of the fruit of the tree of life spoken of in Genesis.

In any case, we do not know too much beyond the fact that in God's original plan man would not die. And we also know that part of the disrupting and disordering effect of sin was not only to disturb the unity of man's inner life (loss of integrity), but also the very physical unity of body and soul. From the very beginning the wages of sin were death.

It will not be until the final achievement of the kingdom of God on the last day that immortality of the body will reign again. The risen bodies of the just will not be able to die forever, for Christ has conquered death as well as sin in His Passion and Resurrection. St. Paul tells us, "Provided we suffer with Him (Christ), that Christ's final victory is ours, that we may also be glorified with Him" (Romans 8:17). St. Paul also beautifully connects Adam and Christ in this: "For since by a man came death, by a man also comes resurrection of the dead. For as in Adam all die, so in Christ all will be made to live. . . . For He must reign, until He has put all His enemies under His feet, and the last enemy to be destroyed will be death" (I Corinthians, 15:21 and 26–27).

There remain two other preternatural gifts that can be disposed of more briefly, since, as we mentioned above, they are not contained so explicitly in the sources of revelation and the teaching of the Church. One pertains to the prefection of his mind, the other to the inconveniences his body was spared. Together with the other two gifts discussed above, they complete the preternatural endowments of Adam's human nature.

3. Freedom From Ignorance

This gift is akin to Adam's gift of integrity, since it is a strictly intellectual endowment, perfecting his mind as integrity perfects the action of his will. Just how perfect was the knowledge and wisdom of the first man? The Scriptural story merely gives us two indications, from which the Scholastics, like St. Thomas, reasoned to further conclusions which seem in keeping with the general perfection of Adam as the Head of all humanity.

Genesis mentions that Adam viewed all the animals in Paradise and gave them a fitting name. This may seem like no argument at all if we consider names in the categories of pet names like Fido or Flicker. But in the scriptural sense, names indicate a knowledge of the essence or properties of beings. Remember that this was the dawn of human language, which is one of the best signs of man's superior intelligence. St. Augustine, in commenting on this passage of Scripture, quotes the ancient philosopher Pythagoras as saying that he was most wise who first made up the words for all things.

Any adult today might be hard pressed to classify correctly all the animals he would see for the first time in visiting a large zoo. At least, we can see in this first mention of Adam's knowledge, some broad acquaintance with the elements of nature that surrounded him on his advent into this world. Nor did he learn this in a science class.

The second indication of Adam's knowledge is shown in his immediate knowledge of the nature and purpose of woman, in his realization of the institution of marriage upon seeing Eve for the first time. He speaks of a man leaving father and mother and cleaving to his wife, and yet Adam did not have a father or mother. Nor had he ever before seen a woman, much less had a wife. Where did he get this knowledge? Since he came into the world as an adult, there seems only one possibility. He could not have attained it by experience or schooling, hence only by some special infusion of knowledge into his mind by God.

Beginning with these indications, theologians generally hold that Adam must have had a sufficient infused knowledge of natural and supernatural truths, to fulfill his function as father and teacher of the whole human race that was to follow. This would have been a strictly personal endowment. Of course, he could communicate the knowledge to his children. Moreover, we can suppose a supreme acuteness of mind in Adam since his mind was not clouded with passion or prejudice. One of the books of the Old Testament says of Adam and Eve: "He (God) filled them with knowledge and understanding; He created in them the science of the spirit; He filled their hearts with wisdom" (Ecclesiasticus 17:5–6). This facility to learn would have been translated to Adam's progeny as a result of their integrity.

St. Thomas gives three reasons for Adam's having a superior endowment of infused knowledge: 1) the Creator would not reasonably put an adult man on earth in ignorance of the fundamental elements of religion and morality; 2) Adam and Eve had no parents or teachers to give them the necessary instruction; and 3) Adam would have to instruct others as the first man, the head of the human race (*Summa Theologica*, I, q. 94, a. 3). This is a good example of theological reasoning. Going beyond this, we do not know just what was the extent of Adam's natural and supernatural knowledge. Certainly there is no necessity of supposing that he knew dif-

ferential equations or the quantum theory. However, we can suppose that in his pristine perfection, Adam had a magnificent grasp
of all those natural truths that would enable him and his descendants to live in accordance with the laws of reason. And of course, he
could progress in knowledge and truth as we do by experience. As
to supernatural truths, he would have to know those things necessary for salvation: the basic theological truths about God and man.

This freedom from ignorance in the first man was preternatural,
because man naturally comes into the world with a blank mind.
The whole process of education is concerned with filling the mind
with truth that a man might be truly wise. It is an understandable
gift of God that the first man was spared this schooling, this day-by-
day acquisition of the knowledge necessary for successful human
living. After all, Adam in one sense got a late start in life. He had
to begin to live as a mature adult immediately upon his arrival in
life. None the less, that his knowledge was infused directly by God,
and not acquired by human experience and schooling, was strictly
a preternatural gift.

4. Freedom From Suffering and Unrequited Labor

This last of the preternatural gifts can be considered in relation
to immortality, since this too is a perfection of the body. The technical theological word for this freedom from suffering is impassibility, derived from the negative form of the Latin word for suffering. Again, we do not have any more than a few indications of this
particular blessing in Scripture. For example, there is the description of Adam's original location on earth: "And the Lord God had
planted a paradise of pleasure from the beginning, wherein he
placed man whom he had formed. And the Lord God brought forth
of the ground all manner of trees, fair to behold and pleasant to eat
of: the tree of life also in the midst of paradise: and the tree of the
knowledge of good and evil. . . . And the Lord God took man,
and put him into the paradise of pleasure to dress it and keep it"
(Genesis 2:8–9 and 15).

Theologians also reason to Adam's original endowments from
the punishments that were inflicted upon him and Eve after the
fall. To Adam was said: "Cursed is the earth in thy work, with labor
and toil shalt thou eat thereof all the days of thy life, thorns and
thistles shall it bring forth to thee, and thou shalt eat the herbs of
the earth . . . in the sweat of thy brow shalt thou eat bread" (Gene-

sis, 3:17–19). And of Eve God said: "I will multiply thy sorrows and thy conceptions: in sorrow thou shalt bring forth children" (Genesis 3:16). Certainly we can sense the difference between their condition as indicated before and after the fall. Perhaps the culminating evidence is this: "And the Lord God sent him out of the paradise of pleasure to till the earth from which he was taken" (Genesis 3:23).

It is commonly held, then, that the immortality of Adam's body was enhanced by other preternatural gifts. While it is normal and natural for a body to suffer, to become seriously ill, to endure physical and mental hardships, to bear the yoke of hard work that often enough grants little yield, these things would be out of place in a paradise of pleasure. Even though children would have been conceived and born as they are today, here too the word of God indicates that the process of childbirth would not have been painful before the fall. We can see now how many of our trials and tribulations can be attributed to sin, how wonderful was the original plan of God for mankind, before Adam ruined it by his rebellion.

St. Augustine depicts a marvelous picture of the condition we might have known without sin:

> In paradise, then, man lived as he desired, so long as he desired what God had commanded. He lived in the enjoyment of God and was good by God's goodness. He lived without any want, and had it in his power so to live eternally. He had food that he might not hunger, drink that he might not thirst, the tree of life that old age might not waste him. There was in his body no corruption, nor seed of corruption, which could produce in him any unpleasant sensation. He feared no inward disease, no outward accident. As in paradise there was no excessive heat or cold, so its inhabitants were exempt from the vicissitudes of fear and desire. No sadness of any kind was there, nor any foolish joy. True gladness ceaselessly flowed from the presence of God who was loved 'out of a pure heart and a good conscience and faith unfeigned.' The honest love of husband and wife made a sure harmony between them. Body and spirit worked harmoniously together and the commandment was without labor. No languor made their leisure wearisome; no sleepiness interrupted their desire to labor.[4]

While St. Augustine is engaged here in theological speculation, we find an echo of his words in the folklore of many ancient peoples,

---

4. St. Augustine, *De Civitate Dei*, Book 14, Ch. 26.

who always seem to look back to a golden age of years gone by, with a deeply nostalgic sense of what has been and was lost in the obscurity of some primeval disaster. Perhaps it is the same sort of nostalgia that makes men press forward in hope of a future millennium when things will be different than they are in our troubled world of today. We know by Faith that Paradise Lost will be Paradise Regained, some day, but only fully in the world to come in the new Paradise of delights where "eye has not seen and ear has not heard nor has it entered into the heart of man (to imagine) what things God has prepared for those who love Him" (I Corinthians 2:9).

This completes our study of the preternatural gifts with which God endowed our first parents, that their human nature, wonderful in itself, might be blessed far beyond its natural requirements of body and soul, mind and will. While we today possess human nature deprived of these gifts, and wonder at the marvelous powers of Adam and Eve, we do have by the grace of God, something far more marvelous than these preternatural gifts. Christ has restored to us the essential power, the supernatural gift that Adam had and lost. It is this power to participate in the very nature and life of God that we now consider.

C. The Supernatural Endowments of Adam

Having defined *natural* as that which fulfills the notion or essence of a being, and *preternatural* as that which is beyond the requirements of any particular nature, we can now see that *supernatural* means that which is altogether above the rights, powers and needs of any created nature, even angelic. Supernatural denotes that which belongs strictly to God alone. In our present context, when we say that Adam was endowed originally with supernatural gifts, we mean that he was lifted completely beyond the scope of his created nature, to live and act on a plane proper to God, to partake in some ineffable way in the divine nature.

There is perhaps no aspect of theology so astounding to us as this elevation of man to the supernatural order. There are deeper mysteries in Christianity, like the Trinity, but here is a mystery wherein *we* are meant to come face to face with the Trinity. So great is this wonderful reality of grace, that, like the Trinity to which it is so closely related, it was not openly revealed in the Old Testament. Scheeben speaks thus of Genesis:

Concerning the mysterious benediction, the supernatural consecration spread over man, the sacred writer preserved a discreet silence, as the mystery was too vast to be understood by the people for whom he wrote. This folk was of too menial a frame of mind to have been capable of attaining a comprehension of the august dignity which is the portion of God's children. And in general, the men of the Old Testament, before the grace and the Spirit of God's sonship had reappeared in Christ, were treated by God not as sons, but as slaves, and as stiffnecked slaves at that. For this reason, the mystery of the Trinity, which is so closely interwoven with the present mystery, was not distinctly revealed in the Old Testament. What was revealed of it was but dimly apprehended.

Nevertheless, since the entire Old Testament was a figure of the New, natural things could be made to serve as types of supernatural things. So the spiritual sense of the words in which Moses relates the production of natural man suggests that the same words refer also to man's supernatural creation. As God makes man to His natural likeness by infusing a spiritual soul into the body as an image of His own spiritual nature, so He elevates man to His supernatural likeness by stamping upon his soul an image like to Himself, the image of His Son; and as God breathes a rational soul into man's body in order to give him natural life, so He breathes His own Spirit into the soul in order to impart to it His own divine life.

The words do not in themselves reveal this. . . . The types did not become manifest until the anti-types had appeared in the New Testament. Although in the present case, the typified supernatural object actually existed in Adam, it could not be discerned in the words of Moses until the idea of this object had again become vivid in the New Testament.[5]

It is to the New Testament, therefore, that we must go for an exact idea of the supernatural life that was restored by Christ Our Redeemer after it had been lost by Adam. One thing is very evident in the mission of Christ: He means to redeem or restore us by giving us a *new life:* "I am come that they may have life and have it more abundantly" (John 10:10). He insists that it is not merely more of the life we already have, but life of a different, higher, eternal order, so much so that we have to be *born again* to receive it: "Amen, Amen, I say to you, unless a man be born again of water and the Spirit, he cannot enter the Kingdom of God" (John 3:5). St. Paul insists on this new reality which is essential to our regaining what was lost in Adam: "Put on the new man who according to God is created in justice and holiness of truth" (Ephesians 4:24).

5. Scheeben, *op. cit.*, pp. 214–215.

St. John especially repeats himself continually to insist upon this truth which is at the center of Christianity: that Christ's whole redemptive mission was to give us life eternal, a participation in the very life of God, that we might live on a higher level of existence, God's level. Study the following texts to see how often the word 'life' occurs:

"These things are written (St. John's Gospel story of Christ) that you might believe that Jesus is the Christ, and that believing, you might have life in His name" (John 20:31).

"In this has the love of God been shown in our case, that God sent his only begotten Son into the world, that we may have life through Him" (I John 4:9).

"And this is the testimony, that God has given us eternal life; and this life is in His Son. He who has the Son has the life" (I John 5:11).

"And the life was made known and we have seen, and now testify and announce to you, the life eternal which was with the Father, and has appeared to us. What we have seen and have heard, we announce to you, in order that you also may have fellowship with us, and that our fellowship may be with the Father, and with His Son, Jesus Christ" (I John 1:2–4).

This last text gives us an indication of why the central theme in the revelation of the supernatural order is the insistence on the giving of new life, eternal life, a sharing of divine life by men. It is given for a purpose: that man from the very beginning might not just belong to the human family, but that God wished him to belong to His own family, so to speak, to be His children, to have fellowship with the Father, Son and Holy Spirit on earth as well as in Heaven. To belong so intimately to God, to share eventually the very happiness of God, man must be elevated beyond his stature as merely man. A man's actions may gain him human happiness, but God has destined him to share divine happiness in the Beatific Vision. To be able to do this, man must first begin to live with the life of God, that his actions might have a new value, that man himself might become "a new creature" (II Corinthians 5:17). As St. John puts it: "Behold what manner of love the Father has bestowed upon us, that we should be called the Children of God, *and such we are*" (I John 3:1). God does not merely give us His name, as human adopting parents do, but His very life. This is what

Adam had and lost. This is what Christ Our Lord came to restore: "In Him was life, and the life was the light of men . . . to as many as received Him, He gave the power of becoming sons of God. . . . The word was made Flesh and dwelt among us, and we saw His glory, glory as of the only-begotten of the Father, full of grace and truth . . . and of His fullness we have all received, grace for grace" (John 1:4, 12, 14, 16).

It is difficult for us to comprehend fully this tremendous reality, this new world proper to God alone, to which sanctifying grace elevates man. Theologians have vied with each other in attempting to state this truth in human language without lessening its amazing import, or slipping into pantheism. Two of the finest works in this matter are the French theologian, J. Bainvel's *Nature et Surnaturel* (Nature and Supernature); and the German, Scheeben's *Natur und Gnade* (Nature and Grace). Bainvel makes the point that the supernatural suppresses nothing that is reasonable or legitimate in nature. It does not lop off its powers and tendencies; it directs them to a higher end, to divine purposes, to a sharing of the life and happiness of God. The supernatural orders the workings of man's mind and will to the loftiest destiny possible: that of being a true son of God, and heir to His Kingdom of Heaven, a living Temple of the Holy Spirit. Bainvel insists that human nature is not destroyed by grace, but immeasurably perfected, for the most perfect specimens of humanity are those in which grace had the deepest influence: the Sacred Humanity of Christ, the Blessed Virgin and the Saints (cf. *Nature et Surnaturel*, pp. 156–161).

Scheeben has left us a summary of this theology on the supernatural elevation of man in these stirring words:

> It is an activity of a special, supernatural, and extraordinary beneficence and love, whereby God gives immeasurably more to His creature than the latter possesses in its nature or can claim for its perfection by virtue of its nature. It is an activity by which God builds upon the foundation laid in creation, and makes of it the substratum and basis of a higher creation, a higher order. It is, in a word, an activity by which God elevates the creature above its own nature and makes it participate in His nature.
>
> The mystery of God in the creature is a supernatural ocean of light that wells up from God's bosom and pours over the creature to make him a sharer in the divine nature and glory. Consequently it is as enigmatic and mysterious for us as is the nature of God. It

is a certain diffusion of the interior divine productions over the creature, and consists in the fact that God impresses the image of His Son on the creature in order to admit the creature to participation in His own nature, and thereby brings forth His own Son in the creature anew. It consists further in the fact that God once again breathes His own Spirit into the creature, thereby uniting the creature to Himself in closest supernatural fellowship of life and love. It is a rebirth and fellowship which, owing to their incalculable sublimity, are as mysterious and obscure for the creature as are the generation of the eternal Son and the spiration of the Holy Spirit.

The mystery of God in the creature is the outpouring upon the creature of the secrets hidden in the bosom and heart of God. It is raising up the creature from his lowliness and remoteness to the bosom and heart of God: to the bosom of God, that the creature may be reborn of Him, clarified by His light, and transformed into His image; to the heart of God, that the creature may be animated by His own Spirit, inflamed with His fire, and become fused with Him as of one Spirit.

This mystery is so sharply distinct from creation itself, and from everything belonging to creation that it is, so to speak, the opposite of creation. It extricates the creature in order to deify him, that is, to make him a sharer in the divine nature with all the majesty, sanctity, and beatitude of that nature.[6]

It may seem to unduly complicate our understanding of the supernatural to link it so intimately with the mystery of the Holy Trinity, the greatest of all Christian Mysteries. But we are left no alternative in this matter. E. Mersch, one of the greatest theologians of our time who was killed during World War II while going to the assistance of some wounded soldiers, makes this very connection in an unfinished book that was published after his death. He says that "the supernatural cannot be anything else but union with God, a relationship to God that perfects a finite being." Therefore, "to define it (the supernatural) in its internal structure, we must look to God." Making that more specific, since God *is* the Holy Trinity, "must we not say that the supernatural consists in a relationship to, a union with the Holy Trinity, precisely as the Holy Trinity." Finally, to show that how the life of the Holy Trinity really goes on in us by sanctifying grace (that is what Scheeben was striving to express above), Mersch concludes: "Just as Christ lives on in His members so the relationship that He has with the Holy Trinity is continued in His members (i.e. in *us*). The super-

6. Scheeben, *op. cit.,* pp. 205–206.

natural (life), such as it is realized in Him in its supreme and total expression, that is to say, such as it is realized by the union of the Word with the Holy Trinity, is prolonged in continuing the same union with the Holy Trinity in Christians." [7]

The above doctrine is difficult, but it is a theological effort to plumb the depths of words we have already seen: "The Life Eternal which was with the Father, has appeared to us. What we have seen and have heard we announce to you, in order that you also may have fellowship with us, and that our fellowship may be with the Father, and with His Son, Jesus Christ" (1 John 1:2-4). This is St. John's way of putting the reality of sanctifying grace as clearly as he could. He too must have realized how difficult it would be to comprehend for he had to promise the early Christians a much better view in the world to come: "Beloved, now we are the children of God, and it has not yet appeared what we shall be. We know that, when He appears, we shall be like to Him, *for we shall see Him just as He is.*" Heaven will not give us something we do not already possess, for heaven is merely the enjoyment of the possession of God, the Holy Trinity, who already dwells in us by Grace. Heaven will merely open our eyes to what we already have by Grace so that we can eternally enjoy our possession of God which we now know only by Faith. This is the word of St. Paul too, for he says that "we see now through a mirror in an obscure manner, but then face to face. Now I know in part, but then I shall know even as I have been known" (I Corinthians 13:12-13).

While we are faced with a deep mystery here, we cannot lose sight of the basic factors that we do know. Sanctifying grace did lift Adam to a plane that was out of the reach of any conceivable creature, to the divine level of the supernatural, God's life. It made his soul holy with the very holiness of God, and enabled him, because of his sharing of God's life, to merit a share of God's own eternal happiness of heaven by his deeds. It would be no fiction of the theological imagination to say that he became, by sanctifying grace, a very Temple of the Holy Spirit, and in fact, the adopted son of God. All this was certainly beyond the demands, almost we might say, beyond the wildest dreams of his human nature, therefore, a true supernatural gift to Adam. All this could only come from God, as only God can share His life with someone. Only God has a right

7. Mersch, *La Théologie du Corps Mystique*, Vol. I, pp. 168, 173, 174.

to divine life, and divine happiness. It is a tremendous thought that He originally planned to share His life with us in Adam, and has indeed restored this supernatural life to us in Christ, Our Redeemer. It is an equally tremendous thought that heaven, the sharing of divine happiness, is the only adequate reward for a life lived on this supernatural plane, in the state of grace. Such indeed was man's destiny as he came from the hands of God.

We attempted in the last paragraph to give a summary of supernatural order as seen from the vantage point we can best attain: what it does to man. A few illustrations may clarify the matter. What is the basic significance of a man elevated to the supernatural order?

1) He attains a new and completely higher value. He is no longer just another creature, but now, a creature on God's level. His worth touches the divine. He is like the drop of water that the priest puts into the chalice during the Offertory of the Mass. Four-fifths of the world is water, so its value is not tremendously great. But this drop is mingled with the wine, and at the consecration, all is changed into the Precious Blood of Christ. Who then can judge its value by human standards, economic worth, or chemical content? And who can value a human being by mere economic, social, biological or political standards after he has been elevated to the supernatural order? "He has granted us the very great and precious promises, so that through them you may become partakers of the divine nature" (II Peter 1:4). Who would rate paper as merely paper after it has been stamped as hundred dollar bills by the United States Treasury? Who would rate words as mere physical sound waves if they come from the mouth of Christ declaring our adoption as sons of God? Man is of the highest value in this world merely as a human person. Who can estimate his value as a partaker of God's divine life through grace?

2) Because life gives the power to act, this new supernatural power gives man an ability to do what was hitherto entirely impossible to him, to act on a completely higher level. He is enabled by beginning to live on God's level to attain the goal that is reached on that level, to share eventually in God's happiness.

3) Finally, the supernatural life makes of man a "new creature" in the eyes of God. This is because he receives, as we have seen, a "new life." It is difficult to imagine this heartland of the supernat-

ural order. Christ, Our Lord, has himself given us the best examples
to illustrate it. "I am the Vine, and you are the branches. . . . As
the branch cannot bear fruit unless it remain on the vine, so neither
can you unless you abide in Me. . . . He who abides in Me and I
in him, he bears much fruit, for without Me you can do nothing"
(John 15:4–6). St. Paul applies this illustration further. He says
that you take a wild olive branch that bears no edible food and
graft it on the domestic variety of olive tree, so that it becomes fruitful. So too, with our natural life alone, we cannot take one step
towards heaven, but after being incorporated into the Body of
Christ at Baptism, and after receiving Sanctifying Grace, the Life
of that Body, all our human actions can be so many steps towards
the Eternal Vision of God. Hence the folly of living in the state of
mortal sin, in spiritual death, cut off from the life of God and
wasting our human life and talents, for without God we can do
nothing of eternal value.

There are many more things that might be said about the supernatural order, but they are more fittingly treated in a later section
on the Redemptive grace of Christ. We can only indicate here, the
basic comparison between the natural and supernatural order,
stressing the fact that they are two completely different orders of
being.

In the natural order we have a principle of natural human life:
the soul; faculties for human activities: the mind and will; cooperation of the First Cause in their activity: the divine concurrence;
and finally a purely human goal: human happiness. Although man
is by nature a human being, we have already indicated that he has
never belonged to the purely natural order, as such, since from the
beginning he was constituted in the supernatural order. This supernatural order has a corresponding structure on a higher level of
being. The new principle of life is the soul elevated to a participation in divine life by sanctifying grace. The new principles of
activity are the human mind and will elevated by the infused theological and moral virtues, supernatural habits of action that you
have already learned about in Moral Theology. The Gifts of the
Holy Spirit also aid man to be receptive to the inspirations of God
in this new type of activity. What the divine concurrence does in
the order of nature, actual grace does in the supernatural order.
The power of the First Cause moves men to act through grace on a

divine level, not on a merely human level. And finally, there is a completely new goal, attaining a share in the happiness of God.

This is, in outline, the highest order to which Adam was elevated. We can now see how beautifully the preternatural gifts complemented the supernatural elevation of Adam, and how both of them gave an exquisite perfection to his human nature. Scheeben calls the preternatural gifts the "Spiritualization of sensual and corporal nature," and the supernatural gifts the "Sanctification and deification of the spirit." [8]

Sanctifying grace is certainly the essential element of Adam's original justice, since it is grace that elevates man and enables him to attain his supernatural destiny. While the preternatural gifts gave Adam a more complete harmony of body and soul, this is not essential to salvation. Indeed, we today must work out our salvation without these preternatural endowments. St. Thomas also teaches that in Adam, it was his grace that caused his additional preternatural perfections: "It is given to understand that if by the withdrawal of grace the obedience of the flesh to the spirit was broken, it was through grace existing in the soul, that the inferior part of nature was subject to the superior part."

In conclusion, we can summarize all the doctrine unfolded here on the original endowments of Adam. A good summary has been formulated for us by the Bishops and theologians who intended to present this statement for definition in the Council of the Vatican, which met in the middle of the last century. This Council was never completed, and many of the doctrines discussed never reached the stage of definition. However, this one was stated and restated four times. We can cite it as the result of much mature thinking on the part of eminent theologians.

"The Most High Creator and Lord of all things, whose power is not circumscribed by the laws and properties of created nature, wished of His boundless goodness to elevate the human race in our first parents to a state in which it would partake of the divine goodness in a measure above the condition of its own nature. And so, beyond the gifts with which it was perfected in its own nature (preternatural gifts), He endowed it with the admirable gift of sanctity and justice (supernatural gifts), so that man who is by nature a servant of God, by the divine command and the Gift of the

---

8. Scheeben, *op. cit.*, p. 219.

Holy Spirit now becomes a son of God, moreover, in virtue of works no longer performed by the power of nature alone, but following the infusion of grace from above, man may now merit an eternal heritage . . .

"This is that elevation of man which Catholic theologians, insisting on the tradition of the Holy Fathers of the Church, have rightly called supernatural, that they might indicate something which transcends both the powers and the demands of created nature, and so is due, neither to the natural condition or merits of man, but rather is a gratuitous benefit of divine generosity . . .

"If therefore, anyone should deny that there are divine gifts and endowments which exceed the demands and powers of created nature, and perfect it beyond its order, let him be anathema." [9]

This completes our first point regarding the original endowments of Adam. We have seen at some length, the three categories of gifts that were his from the beginning: natural, preternatural, and supernatural. We should now be in a position to study his fall, together with his consequent loss of the preternatural and supernatural gifts.

II. THE FALL OF MAN

There is something extremely familiar in the Biblical account of the first sin. The pattern of man's infidelity in the face of God's commands has not changed very much in the course of the centuries. Of course, it may appear that Adam, with all his marvelous endowments was incapable of sin. Indeed, he was preserved by his gift of integrity from temptations to what we call the grosser sins like gluttony, drunkenness and lust. But he was still a man, and he was free as all men are to glorify God or dishonor him in the inner reaches of his soul. There would have been no sense in God giving him a command if he were not free to obey or disobey it. After all, even the angels, who were of a higher nature than man, and like man constituted in the state of grace, they too had their trial. We know from revelation that with all their gifts of nature and of grace, even some of the angels succumbed to the fatal spiritual sin of pride. It is significant that the devil, a fallen angel, approached man and woman on this same ground of pride that had been his

---

9. Schema, *Constitutionis dogmaticae secundae de fide*, Chapter 3, Mansi, *Amplissima Collectio Conciliorum*, LIII, 288–289, 294.

downfall. Lest we get ahead of ourselves, let us first take a glance at the scriptural story of the first sin. Then we shall consider how the Church regards this story in her official teaching.

A. The Biblical Account of the Fall

As we have seen to some extent in the Biblical account of creation, there are two extremes of interpretation to be avoided here. This account of the revealed word of God cannot be dismissed as pure *allegory*. Some would cancel out any distinct command, and positive punishment or definite sin, saying that Adam merely sinned sometime or other during his life. The whole story is reasoned away as merely symbolic without any historical foundation in fact. The other extreme interpretation would be to accept the whole story in a strictly *literal* sense, with serpents walking and talking at first, and then committed to crawl as a penalty, with a definite kind of fruit involved, say an apple, as Milton supposed. Then finally, there is the middle position which we hold, seeing in the scriptural story a great deal of allegory, but with it, a basic account of some very definite facts. We shall consider three of these facts in order: the command given to Adam and Eve by God, the temptation by the devil and first sin, and thirdly, the immediate consequences of that sin.

1. The Command of God

"And the Lord God took man, and put him into the paradise of pleasure, to dress it, and to keep it. And he commanded him, saying: of every tree of paradise thou shalt eat; but of the tree of knowledge of good and evil, thou shalt not eat. For in what day soever thou shalt eat of it, thou shalt die the death" (Genesis 2:15–17). This command is given to Adam, not merely as an individual, but as the head of the human race, who has in trust for the rest of the race, all the marvelous blessings we have discussed. Death came not only to him, expulsion from the paradise of pleasure was not merely personal, but for all his descendants as well.

The command then is clear and definite. It confronts him with decisive alternatives: life or death, a life of pleasure or a life of trials and tribulations as we know it. Not much can be said of the knowledge of good and evil, except that Adam and Eve first knew evil upon breaking God's command and eating of the forbidden

fruit. A modern Anglican writer, C. S. Lewis, has written an interesting phantasy entitled *Perelandra,* about the mythical life of a first
man and woman on the planet Venus. He pictures them as having
the endowments of Adam and Eve before the fall, as they are undergoing a trial like that of our first parents. One of the things that
amazes the reader is their complete ignorance of evil or pain or
suffering. The trial of this mythical couple is this: they are forbidden to remain on a certain part of their planet after night has
fallen. This may seem like a trivial and inconsequential command,
but so have many people objected to the command of God to Adam
and Eve.

Such an objection misses the whole point of the narrative. It is
not the matter of the command that is important, but what is manifested by Adam's obedience to a command, no matter how simple
that command might be. We must remember that Adam was made
lord of the world. All creation on earth was subject to him and he
was to hold rule over it. But be a creature angel or man, he must
always remember that he is still a creature, still dependent on God
for whatever he has. Obedience is the test of his fidelity, of his
recognition that God is still above him and must be served. People
might also object that it is silly to hold Catholics to Sunday Mass or
Friday abstinence under pain of mortal sin. After all, it takes less
time to go to Mass than to a movie or a basketball game. But in
giving God that hour once a week, man shows God that he recognizes his duty to serve Him.

In a rather popular book, A. J. Cronin's *Keys of the Kingdom,* the
missionary priest-hero is made to say to his Protestant missionary
friend that he cannot picture God condemning a soul to hell for
eating a grilled pork chop on Friday. Here the author completely
misses the point. God isn't interested in the fish business, but he
does demand a conscious service and obedience from his creatures.
And God must punish infidelity, just as Adam and we are punished
for our infidelities. It is not the matter, eating meat or what not,
that is important, but what it signifies. Take a word. A word is not
important in itself, but if it is a word of treason, or love, or consecration, then it becomes tremendously important because of what
it signifies. Men have been hung for a word of treason, and men
have entered upon a lifelong marriage because of a word of love.
The eating of fruit may seem inconsequential, but if it is the only

thing God requires of a man as blessed as Adam was, and Adam refused to obey this one requirement of God, then surely God is
within His rights to punish Adam as he clearly threatened. If you
consider what God threatened, then surely you can gather that God
was serious about this command if he threatened death as a punishment for disobeying it.

2. The First Sin

"Now the serpent was more subtle than any of the beasts of the
earth which the Lord God had made. And he said to the woman:
Why hath God commanded you, that you should not eat of every
tree of paradise? And the woman answered him, saying, of the fruit
of the trees that are in paradise we do eat, but of the tree which is
in the midst of paradise, God hath commanded us that we should
not eat; and that we should not touch it, lest perhaps we die. And
the serpent said to the woman: no, you shall not die the death. For
God doth know that in what day soever you shall eat thereof, your
eyes shall be opened, and you shall be as God, knowing good and
evil. And the woman saw that the tree was good to eat, and fair to
the eyes, and delightful to behold. And she took of the fruit thereof,
and did eat, and gave to her husband who did eat" (Genesis 3:1–6).

Perhaps one of the first questions that comes into your mind is:
What was this serpent? Serpents could not talk even in the wonderful garden of paradise. Therefore, this serpent had to be the instrument of a spiritual intelligence. Certainly he was not being used
by God or by a good angel. The only alternative is a bad angel, or
the devil. It is interesting that even today, people instinctively shy
away from snakes as from something repulsive.

It is rather a surprising thing that in the centuries that have
passed since this first temptation, the devil has not changed his tac-
tics. Perhaps it is more surprising that people are still falling for
his line. Christ called him the 'Father of lies' and that is how he
began with Eve, telling her that she certainly had a bad situation
in paradise since she couldn't eat any of the fruit there. He tries to
get her to question the wisdom of God on a basis of this misrepre-
sentation: Why does He command you something like this? We
should certainly learn from Eve's experience that it is a waste of
time and a dangerous practice to argue with the devil. Better to tell
him to go where he belongs, namely to hell. But Eve told him that

they could eat of all the trees except one, and that they would die if they ate of it.

Backed out of one lie, the devil easily slips into another, and proceeds to ridicule God's truth, thus tempting her to pride. Why, they will not die. God is just afraid that they too will become gods. Here is the basis of every temptation, to put oneself in God's place, to make up one's own rules and disregard the law of God. We can see a repetition of this same routine in temptation today. People say that Christianity cramps their style. If you follow the moral law, life becomes unbearable. Why take God's word? You say mortal sin leads to hell. Why, who ever saw hell? Go on, try it and see for yourself that this is the new freedom, the easy way to happiness. Nothing will happen to *you*. All this talk about God's law and eternal punishment is mediaeval priestcraft. Be your own boss. Now look at what this fat juicy temptation has to offer.

Eve made that mistake right in the beginning. Instead of listening to her conscience, the voice of God, which told her to get away from this temptation, she looked at the forbidden fruit and found it good to eat, fair to the eyes and delightful to behold. You might say that there was something typically feminine in Eve's downfall: too much curiosity. The devil can always make temptation look attractive if you stay around and look at it long enough. When the story goes this far, when a person dawdles with temptation, the ending is always the same as in the story of Eve. "She took of the fruit thereof and did eat." And because we live so close to other people, as soon as the forbidden fruit turns to ashes in one's mouth, misery begins to look for company. Sin has a way of multiplying itself. That's why the devil is always on the job. Eve's sin did not stay with her alone. No sooner had she eaten of the forbidden fruit than she "gave to her husband who did eat." Adam's downfall was typically masculine too: a sympathetic siding with woman even though she was wrong, a common pride and open rebellion against the authority of God. That was the first tragedy in the earliest history of mankind. They reaped the effects of their sin immediately. We are still reaping its effects today.

3. Consequences of the First Sin

We have already discussed some of the results in speaking of the preternatural and supernatural gifts given to Adam and Eve on trial. When their wills rebelled against God's will, immediately there is rebellion of their lower appetites against their higher nature, a loss of integrity: "And the eyes of them both were opened, and when they perceived themselves to be naked, they sewed together fig leaves making themselves garments. And when they heard the voice of the Lord God walking in paradise at the afternoon air, Adam and his wife hid themselves from the face of the Lord God, amidst the trees of paradise, and the Lord God called Adam and said to him: where art thou? And he said: I heard thy voice in paradise, and I was afraid, because I was naked, and I hid myself. And He said to him (Adam): And who hath told thee that thou wast naked, but that thou hast eaten of the tree whereof I commanded thee that thou shouldst not eat?" (Genesis 3:11).

We might stop here for a moment and consider a practical conclusion. Here is the first indication of clothing, and we see it has a function of modesty, to hide the shame of fallen man. Today, however, clothing is designed, at least for women, not for a covering, but rather to make more seductive and alluring those parts that clothing was first used to cover modestly. This is so true, that one old character in Bruce Marshall's famous book, *The World, the Flesh, and Father Smith,* says that modern women would be much less tempting naked, than clothed in a modern bathing suit. The whole philosophy behind modern women's clothing is a denial that there was a Fall, or that modesty has any function in the Christian life. As Christian men it is good to have a firm conviction in these matters. If we can assume that women dress to please men, their dress might be more modest if their husbands, boy friends, brothers, or fathers were not afraid to evince displeasure at seeing them cater to the depraved minds of immoral fashion designers, or to the corrupt standards of a pagan and paganizing world. Right here at the beginning of history, we find that even such a common factor in human living as clothing has a meaning and purpose geared to the state of fallen nature. That meaning is quite generally disregarded today, and the lot of fallen mankind is not made any easier because of this pagan attitude which casts aside the natural gift of shame which God gave man and woman to replace their lost integrity.

To go on with the story, as soon as God accused Adam of eating the forbidden fruit, we find a rather human confession, with both

Adam and Eve shifting the blame. "And Adam said: the woman whom thou gavest me to be my companion gave me of the tree, and I did eat. And the Lord God said to the woman: Why hast thou done this? And she answered: The serpent deceived me, and I did eat" (Genesis 3:12–13).

Now comes the difficult part of the story, when God has to punish them in order: the serpent, then the woman, then Adam. We should try to get underneath the allegory that cloaks his words to Satan, "that old serpent," as St. John calls him in the Apocalypse (12:9). "And the Lord God said to the serpent: Because thou hast done this thing, thou art cursed among all cattle, and beasts of the earth. Upon thy breast shalt thou go, and earth shalt thou eat all the days of thy life" (Genesis 3:13). This seems to mean that the devil will have to crawl and grovel in the popular sense of these words. At the hands of Christ, Our Redeemer, he will be completely vanquished. Though he is of the highest order of creation, an angel, a much lower creature, man, whom he has tricked into sin, will also be able to despise and conquer him in the name of Jesus. He will bite the dust, or eat as a degraded creature. It is a common experience of Christians that the devil must obey them if they tell him to begone in the name of Jesus. While he was able to gain some domination in this world by inducing men to sin, Christ Our Lord said of his new kingdom that vanquishes Satan: "Now is the judgment of this world; now will the prince of the world be cast out. And I, if I be lifted up from the earth, will draw all things to myself. Now he said this, signifying by what death He was to die" (John 12:31–33).

God has yet one more word to say to Satan regarding his downfall. This verse is perhaps the most important in the Old Testament, since it is the promise of redemption that the rest of the Old Testament gradually unfolds. It is a verse of tremendous prophetic import. "I will put enmities between thee (the serpent) and the woman, and thy seed and her seed. She shall crush thy head, and thou shalt lie in wait for her heel" (Genesis 3:15). What a wealth of theology is hidden here. Here is the fall of man in reverse. Just as Eve was first tempted and induced Adam to fall, there will be a New Eve who will give birth to a New Adam to redeem mankind. The Church has always interpreted this verse in reference to Mary, the Mother of God. In her, Satan had no part. She was even conceived free from original sin as we shall see later on. She is the gateway to the new life from Christ, as Eve was the prelude of the spiritual death of sin. And as Satan conquered mankind from the tree, so Mary's seed, Christ the Redeemer, will conquer sin and death from the wood of the Cross. As we sing in the *Pange Lingua Gloriosi* on Good Friday:

> "Eating of the tree forbidden,
> Man had sunk in Satan's snare
> When his pitying Creator
> Did this second tree prepare
> Destined, many ages later,
> That first evil to repair."

We find this same thought in the Preface for Masses during Passion Time: "We give thanks unto Thee, O Holy Lord, Father Almighty, Everlasting God, Who didst set the salvation of mankind upon the tree of the Cross, so that whence came death, thence also life might rise again, and he that overcame by the tree, by the tree also might be overcome, through Christ Our Lord."

The whole story of the prophecy, so pregnant in meaning, is included in the statue you have so often seen depicting the Immaculate Conception, atop the Dome, or down at the Grotto: Mary stands upon the globe of the world. Across the world is coiled the fatal serpent, with an apple in his mouth. But her heel is upon his head, crushing him. Thus by reversing Eve's failure, and by completely dominating the influence of evil, Mary becomes the new Mother of all the living, for such is the meaning of the name Eve. And her divine Son, Christ, becomes the New Adam, the new head of redeemed mankind.

After this ray of prophetic hope in a final victory, God metes out His punishment to Eve: "I will multiply thy sorrows and thy conceptions: in sorrow thou shalt bring forth children, and thou shalt be under thy husband's power, and he shall have dominion over thee" (Genesis 3:16). Certainly women have had an ample share of the sorrows of the world. Modern psychologists have shown that women, by their lot in life, have demonstrated that they can bear much more suffering than men. In the enduring of pain, it is men, not women, who are the weaker sex. "The male is biologically weaker than the female. From the very beginning and throughout life the male is less resistant than the female, more often defective, and more likely to die under adverse conditions." [10]

---

10. A. Scheinfeld, *Women and Men*, p. 59.

Adam was the head of the human race, and consequently, his was the greatest responsibility. To him, then, went the lion's share of the punishment. God sounds somewhat gentle in his admonitions to Eve. His words to Adam have a tone of divine severity: "And to Adam he said: Because thou hast hearkened to the voice of thy wife, and hast eaten of the tree, whereof I commanded thee that thou shouldst not eat, cursed is the earth in thy work; with labor and toil shalt thou eat thereof all the days of thy life. Thorns and thistles shall it bring forth to thee, and thou shalt eat the herbs of the earth. In the sweat of thy brow shalt thou eat bread till thou return to the earth out of which thou wast taken: for dust thou art and into dust thou shalt return" (Genesis 3:17–19). This is the end of those wonderful gifts Adam had received. The alternative he had freely chosen became a reality. Witness the loss of his integrity, immortality, freedom from pain and hard work and above all, the loss of grace and friendship with God. The final words of the story are cruel in their finality: "And the Lord God sent him out of the paradise of pleasure, to till the earth from which he was taken. And he cast out Adam" (Genesis 3:23–24).

B. The Teaching of the Church on the Fall

There are two main sources here: the decrees of the Biblical Commission, and the Canons of the Council of Trent. We have already discussed the authority of the Biblical Commission above. It is helpful to mention here the remainder of the decrees which we began to discuss in the previous chapter. The following historical facts are said to be contained in the account of Genesis, and therefore, not to be called into doubt: "1) The original happiness of our first parents in a state of justice (supernatural gift), integrity and immortality (preternatural gifts). 2) The precept given to man by God to try his obedience. 3) The transgression of the divine command by the persuasion of the devil (in the form of a serpent?). 4) The casting out of our first parents from that primeval state of innocence, and 5) the promise of a redeemer to come" (Denz. 2123). Catholics are held to give both internal and external assent to these basic historical facts concerning the foundation of the Christian Religion. Obviously, other Catholic doctrines such as the Redemption, the Immaculate Conception, the necessity of baptism for infants, etc., would be meaningless without these primal facts.

The second source of the Church's teaching on the original justice and fall of Adam is of the highest order in the teaching authority of the Church. The following Canons have been solemnly
defined in the Council of Trent. We judge it best to give these decrees before going into a wider theological discussion on the nature of original sin for these outline the exact scope of the Church's
teaching against the Protestant heresies at the time of the Reformation. All of these points are given by the Council in negative
statements, following this traditional pattern, "If a man does not
admit this . . . let him be anathema." To simplify the presenta-
tion, we present the essential elements of what must be believed
by translating directly the positive points of doctrine.

1) It must be admitted that the first man, Adam, immediately
lost the sanctity and justice in which he had been constituted, when
he transgressed the command of God in Paradise. Moreover, by his
offense he incurred the wrath and indignation of God, and also
death with which God had already threatened him. By his fault,
the whole man Adam became worse in body and soul (Denz. 788).

This first point, as you can see, only has reference to the effects
of original sin on Adam who committed it. Specific mention is made
of the loss of his special gifts. The second point which follows has
reference to what we lost by original sin.

2) It must be admitted that the prevarication of Adam harmed
not merely him alone, but his progeny as well. He lost the sanctity
and justice, which he had received from God, not only for himself
alone, but for us too. He who had become guilty by the sin of disobedience, handed down upon the whole human race not only death
and the punishments of the body, but also sin, which is the death
of the soul. The opposite doctrine contradicts St. Paul who says:
"Wherefore as by one man sin entered into this world, and by sin
death; and so death passed upon all men in whom all have sinned"
(Romans 5:12, Denz. 789).

3) It must be believed that this sin of Adam which is one by origin and propagation, is not handed down by our imitation (of the
sin of Adam), but is in everyone and proper to each. This sin is not
taken away by the power of human nature or by any other remedy
except by the merits of our One Mediator, Our Lord Jesus Christ,
who has reconciled us to God in His Blood, "Who (Christ), of God,
is made unto us wisdom, and justice, and sanctification and re-

demption" (I Corinthians 1:30). These merits of Christ are applied to both adults and infants by the sacrament of baptism properly administered in the form of the Catholic Church. Because, "There is no other name under heaven given to men, whereby we must be saved" (Acts 4:12). Hence this saying: "Behold the Lamb of God, Behold Him who takes away the sins of the world" (John 1:29), and "As many of you as have been baptized in Christ, have put on Christ" (Galatians 3:27, Denz. 790).

This third point should remind you of the outline given at the beginning of this book. There we showed how God and man were united before the Fall; how sin separated them after the Fall; and finally, how the Christian Religion is centered in Christ, the God-Man who takes away sin, and becomes the one and perfect mediator between God and fallen mankind, now redeemed. You will note too in this last decree, that the baptism of infants was mentioned, since many of the new Protestant sects at the time of the Council of Trent refused to baptize infants. Many today still baptize only adults. All this has reference to the universal application of original sin, and is reiterated in the next decree.

4) It must be admitted that infants should be baptized soon after birth, even though they are born of parents who are baptized. Also they too are baptized for the remission of sins, for they contract original sin from Adam, which sin must be expiated in the baptism of regeneration that they may attain eternal life. Consequently, the form of baptism for the remission of sins is true and not false for them. The words of St. Paul (about sin entering the world by one man) are to be understood in the sense that the Catholic Church throughout the world has always understood them. Because of this rule of faith handed down by the Apostles, even infants, who could commit no actual sin by themselves, are truly baptized for the remission of sins, that they may be cleansed by baptism of what they have contracted in birth. For, "Unless a man be born again of water and the Holy Spirit, he cannot enter the Kingdom of God" (John 3:5, Denz. 791).

5) It must be admitted that the grace of Our Lord Jesus Christ, which is conferred in baptism, takes away all guilt of original sin. It completely takes away everything that has any true or proper notion of sin. It (sin) is not merely erased or no longer imputed. God hates nothing in the baptized, "who are buried together with

Christ by Baptism" (Romans 6:4), who, "no longer walk according to the flesh" (Romans 8:1), but who "put off the old man and
put on the new man who is created according to God in justice
and holiness of truth" (Ephesians 4:22), who are made innocent,
immaculate, pure, and beloved sons of God, "heirs indeed of God,
and joint heirs with Christ" (Romans 8:17), so that nothing at all
keeps them from entering heaven. This Holy Council realizes and
admits that concupiscence remains in the baptized, which concupiscence, since it has been left for the struggle, cannot harm
those who do not consent to it, or those who manfully resist it by
the grace of Jesus Christ. This concupiscence which the Apostle
Paul sometimes calls sin, the Catholic Church has never understood to be sin in the sense that it is really and truly (formal) sin
in those baptized in Christ, but it is called sin insofar as it originates in sin and inclines (man) to sin (Denz. 792).

This long decree is aimed specifically at the then new Protestant
errors which held that sin was merely covered over by baptism,
that man was internally sinful and corrupt even after baptism,
that the inclination to sin is itself a sin. Against these heresies,
the Council declares that a man is made internally holy by sanctifying grace, since he begins to live with the very life of God and
becomes truly a son of God. This is a point on which many Catholics today are hazy. They look on baptism as a negative thing,
merely taking away original sin. Rather, we must, as the Council
of Trent insists, see baptism as a rebirth, a new life in Christ. The
first effect of baptism is not a mere taking away of sin. Rather,
we are incorporated into Christ and the Church, we receive a new
life, and because of this new life, sin must go. Baptism is like the
dawn. At sunrise, the darkness is not taken away, and then comes
day. Rather, when the light strikes the earth, the darkness is dispelled. So with us, when the life of Christ comes into our souls at
baptism, or in confession, the darkness and death of sin is dispelled.
We become new creatures again.

6) This same Holy Council declares that it is not within its
intention to include the Blessed and Immaculate Virgin Mary,
the Mother of God, in this decree regarding original sin (Denz.
792).

This final decree is a marvelous example of the infallibility of

the Church Teaching. In the first five decrees, the universal application of original sin to all mankind is proposed. Then at the end,
while it does not specifically define that the Blessed Virgin Mary
was conceived immaculate, free from original sin, at least it declares that the Council does not wish to include her in the universal application of original sin. Thus, hundreds of years later,
in 1854, when the Church found it fitting to declare the dogma
of the Immaculate Conception to be of faith, it was not impeded
by these former decrees of the universal application of original sin,
since they had explicitly made exception of the Mother of God

We have given the above decrees from the Fifth Session of the
Council of Trent (July 17, 1546) at full length, since they are the
core of the Church's doctrine on original sin. Thousands of pages
have been written on original sin since then, but all must point
back to these decrees as to the best and most authoritative statement of the matter. Our next step is to view more deeply the exact
theological nature of original sin, in Adam and in ourselves. This
section has been the necessary springboard.

III. The Theological Nature of Original Sin

It is here that the story becomes difficult again. The facts of the
case are clear enough from revelation. We have seen from Holy
Scripture and the solemn teaching of the Church that the first man
rebelled against God, and that his sin caused a grave disorder not
only within his own life, but in the lives of all his descendants as
well. The mystery here, as in the other deep truths of theology,
lies not in the facts, but in the *how.* We know that this did happen, but how did it happen? How can all mankind suffer for the
sin of one man? We cannot completely explain the mystery, or it
would not be a mystery. But theology does try to see all that it
possibly can by reasoning about the facts that God has revealed,
and by comparing this mystery with other Christian Mysteries to
which it is closely related in the over-all pattern of theology.

There are two senses in which the sin of Adam may be called a
sin. First, it is his own personal and actual sin. Secondly, it gave
rise to a state of sin, or as some theologians term it, a sin of nature.
Since it is this state of sin, not the act of sin, that is transmitted to
all men, the mystery of original sin concerns the sin of Adam in

this second sense of the word. Before speaking of this sinful state, its transmission, its effects in the world today, we shall take a quick look at the sin of Adam, a personal sin.

A. Original Sin in Adam

From what we have seen in Holy Scripture, it is not too difficult to judge that Adam committed a grave sin. You recall the gravity of God's command. He was not trifling when he threatened death as a punishment for this sin. As to the formality of the sin, it contained the basic malice of every human sin since then: it was an act of disobedience motivated by pride. God has established His law for our conduct. It is not merely an arbitrary ruling, but one that declares the path we must follow if we are to be truly happy and at peace with God and ourselves. Pride enters in when a man cannot recognize his true position as a creature, subject to God in all things. Pride inspires a man to make himself God, to formulate his own rules for life instead of following the instructions of his Maker.

As we have already seen, the path of pride was the way that the devil approached our first parents. They succumbed to his suggestion that they should be gods themselves. It was an easy and logical step from pride to disobedience. Their fatal motto became that of the fallen angels: "We will not serve." All of us can recognize this trend, for what is the sin in any man's life that does not reflect a fatal pride, a turning of our wills against God's All-Holy Will, a disobedience of the law of God? And who has not felt the blasting of inward peace and order that results from this?

It is noteworthy that the Second Adam, who came to remake man to the divine image of God, gave us the very opposite example: humility and obedience as opposed to the pride and disobedience of the First Adam. "Have this mind in you which was also in Christ Jesus, who though he was by nature God, did not consider being equal to God a thing to be clung to, but emptied Himself, taking the nature of a slave and being made like unto man. And appearing in the form of man, He *humbled* himself, becoming *obedient* to death, even to death on a cross" (Philippians 2:5–9). And He made this our daily prayer for a better life: "Thy will be done on earth as it is in heaven." What better antidote to pride, which the Book of Ecclesiasticus tells us is "the beginning of all sin" (10:15).

We cannot say that Adam's sin was the worst sin in the book, as kinds of sin go. Blasphemy, for example, is certainly a worse kind of sin. But in viewing the results of sin historically, Adam's sinful deed was certainly the worst tragedy that has befallen human kind. Its gravity is also augmented by the special gifts which he had from God in the beginning. He was less prone to sin than we are.

We have already seen enough about the results of original sin in Adam himself. The real mystery is the result of his sin in us. Before leaving Adam and Eve to their misfortune, we might recall an ancient tradition in the Church that they repented of their sin and were ultimately saved. This is intimated in the Old Testament, speaking of Wisdom: "She preserved him that was first formed by God, the father of the world, when he was created alone. And she brought him out of his sin, and gave him power to govern all things" (Wisdom 10:1–2). In any case, because of this ancient belief, it is a touching point in a sad story, that we find the names of Adam and Eve listed in the Calendar of the Saints, for December 24, the day before the coming of the long-awaited Savior.

B. Original Sin in Us

Here is the real problem. We had best proceed once more from the known fact to its explanation, insofar as that is possible theologically.

1. The Fact of Original Sin in Us

There is no doubt here, as far as Catholic Doctrine goes. We have already seen the clearest and most definite statement of the Church's teaching in the Council of Trent. It may help, however, to elaborate upon the fundamental scriptural text in this matter. The Council itself judged it helpful to quote a section of this text twice during its statement. The famous passage is from St. Paul's epistle to the Romans. He is not primarily concerned with original sin here. Rather, he is teaching the Romans about the justification and sanctification of all men in Christ. But in doing so, he continually contrasts this supernatural oneness of all men with Christ in grace, with their like oneness with Adam in sin. This text is so important that we shall give the whole passage, and then explain it.

"Wherefore as by one man sin entered into this world, and by sin death; and so death passed upon all men, in whom (or, because) all have sinned. For until the law (of Moses) sin was in the world; but sin was not imputed, when the law was not. But death reigned from Adam unto Moses, even over them also (i.e., infants) who have not sinned after the similitude of the transgression of Adam, who is a figure of him who was to come (i.e., Christ).

"But not as the offence, so also the gift. For if by the offence of one, many died; much more the grace of God and the gift, by the grace of one man, Jesus Christ, has abounded unto many. And not as it was by one sin, so also is the gift. For judgment indeed was by one unto condemnation; but grace is of many offences, unto justification.

"For if by one man's offence, death reigned through one; much more they who receive abundance of grace, and of the gift, and of justice, shall reign in life through one, Jesus Christ. Therefore, as by the offence of one (Adam), unto all men to condemnation; so also by the justice of one (Christ), unto all men to justification of life. *For as by the disobedience of one man, many were made sinners: so also by the obedience of one, many shall be made just.*

"Now the law entered in that sin might abound. And where sin abounded, grace did more abound. That as sin hath reigned to death; so also grace might reign by justice unto life everlasting, through Jesus Christ our Lord" (Romans 5:12–21).

We have seen how God inflicted death as the punishment of Adam's sin. This death, St. Paul argues, passed on to all men, since all partake of Adam's sin. Even before the law of Moses, all those people who lived from Adam to Moses died. This universal punishment even affecting children who had not imitated Adam's sin, points to the universal transmission of Adam's sin to all his progeny. So that there might be no doubt about this belief, he specifically states that Adam's offense was unto all men to condemnation, that by his disobedience we are constituted sinners.

St. Paul has another passage in which he contrasts our oneness in sin (death of the soul) with Adam and our oneness in grace (life of the soul) with Christ. "For since by a man came death, by a man also comes resurrection of the dead. For as in Adam all die, so in Christ, all will be made to live" (I Corinthians 15:21–22). This sin we incur from Adam is not a personal sin in the sense that we commit it. Rather it comes with our nature, infected by the sin of Adam. Again as Paul puts it, we "were by nature children of wrath" (Ephesians 2:4). The opposite goal by our new union with Christ is, of course, to be children of God.

This belief in original sin runs through the whole Old Testament, although it is difficult to pin it down to this or that text. Certainly though, the constant, ever-growing desire for a savior to come, presupposes that there was something man had lost, something that must be restored to him. In the early Church, the belief in original sin is best shown by the practice of infant baptism. St. Cyprian explains it thus: "Since nobody is denied baptism and grace, how much more ought an infant not to be denied (these benefits), who being just born and done no sin, except that, by being descended from Adam in the flesh, he has contracted by birth the contagion of the ancient death" (*Epistola ad Fidum*, 64, 5). St. Augustine wrote so much about original sin against the Pelagians who denied it in his time, that they began to accuse him of concocting the doctrine. He was the wrong man to accuse falsely though. He simplified matters for us by citing many passages from the most famous Fathers of the Church supporting the Catholic belief in this matter. He then said specifically: "It was not I who devised the original sin, which the Catholic faith holds from ancient times; but you (he speaks to Julian the Pelagian) who deny it, are undoubtedly an innovating heretic" (*De Nuptiis et Concupiscentia*, II, 10, 33).

So much for the *fact* of original sin in us. The more difficult problem for theology is to explain the *nature* of original sin in us. The nature of original sin in Adam is a much more simple matter, for he personally and voluntarily committed the sinful deed. However, it is not the sinful deed, but the state of sin that is transmitted to us.

2. The Nature of Original Sin in Us

Apart from the teaching of the Church, there are reams of theological speculations in this difficult matter. For our purpose it seems best to summarize what is definite from the teaching of the Church, and to indicate the best results of theological speculation. First of all, we must admit that original sin is a real sin in us. That means, we bear its guilt, not merely its punishment. You remember how St. Paul distinguished between the penalty, death, and the sin which causes it, since we are constituted sinners in Adam.

This point has been reiterated in the Council of Trent which stated that original sin is in everyone and proper to each. How do we contract this sin? By being born of Adam's seed. He hands down to us the nature which he infected by his sin, not the originally endowed nature he received unsullied in the beginning. Lastly, we can be sure that everything that is sinful in original sin is taken away in baptism, when we are made new creatures. It might be well to reread the decrees of the Council of Trent as listed above, to see the precise statement of the Church on these points.

In their attempts to paint a positive picture of original sin, theologians have termed it a sin of nature. They do this to distinguish it from a personal sin which arises from a wilfully sinful act by this or that person. Obviously, we do not personally will original sin. Our will in the matter must be somehow connected with Adam's, since original sin is voluntary in the will of the first head of the human race. This is the core of the difficulty, the heart of the mystery.

Theologians generally teach that God, in His plan for the world, looked upon Adam as the *juridical head* of the human race, as well as its physical head, insofar as all men are descended from him. As juridical head, he had all the special gifts of grace and integrity in trust for all of us. In losing them, he lost them for us as well as for himself, just as a wealthy father, the juridical head of his family, can lose his wealth for his children, in losing it for himself. God created man for a supernatural end. He loved man so much, He wanted superhuman service from man, so that He might give man a superhuman reward. It is due to the result of Adam's sin that we are incapable of giving God what He demands. In receiving our nature from Adam, we receive it as he has left it, deprived of the grace we need to attain heaven, and also stripped of those special preternatural gifts he had. We are all spiritually stillborn, in a state of disorder and with a sin of nature. This sin of nature is essentially a privation of grace, death of the soul, and is voluntary by the will of Adam, our juridical head.

The key of this mystery, insofar as it can be clarified theologically, lies in a mysterious solidarity of all men with Adam. In itself, we know very little about this, except that such was God's plan. To understand it a little more clearly, we must somehow contrast it with our mysterious union with Christ. Here too is the way in which the revealed word of God manifests the mystery of original sin to us, not in itself, but contrasted to that correlative mystery of our union with Christ. Sin and Death come into the world by one man, Adam, just as grace and life come into the world by one man, Christ. We are made sinners by the disobedience of one man, Adam. We are made just again by the obedience of one man, Christ.

E. Mersch says of St. Thomas' treatment of original sin, which is very much like his explanation of Redemption: "Here are two unities, two solidarities that go together . . . here, the dogma of original sin appears in connection with the dogma of redemption, somehow fashioned on the same model. . . . To complete the doctrine of Saint Thomas, it would be necessary to search out this unity which is supernatural, mysterious, real, almost organic, vital in any case, a union that is had by all men in Adam, just as there is a like (union of all men) in Christ." [11]

We might well consider the doctrine of St. Thomas to which Mersch here refers. As Mersch remarks, we can profitably compare this wording of St. Thomas on original sin with his treatment of redemption, for the mysteries complement each other. We did not personally and voluntarily undergo Christ's passion and death, and yet we are saved personally because of His merits. But now let us see how St. Thomas summarized all the theological speculations up to his time on the problem of how we get original sin.

All men who are born of Adam can be considered as one man, insofar as they are one in the nature which they receive from their first parents . . . the many men derived from Adam are as many members of one body. The act of one member of the body, say the hand, is not voluntary by the will of the hand, but by the will of the soul which moves the member. Hence a murder which the hand commits is not imputed as sin to the hand, as if the hand were considered in itself as divided from the body, but it is imputed to it as something of the man which is moved by the first moving principle of the man. So too, the disorder which is in this man (by original sin) as derived from Adam, is not voluntary by the will of this man, but by the will of his first parents who move by the motion of generation all who are derived from him, just as the will of the soul moves all the members to act. Hence, the sin which is thus derived from the first parent in the offspring, is called original (sin), just as the sin which is derived from the soul in the member of the body is called actual (sin). And as actual sin which

11. Mersch, *La Théologie du Corps Mystique*, Vol. I, pp. 188–190.

is committed by some member is not the sin of that member, except insofar as that member belongs to the body of man and is therefore called human sin, so original sin is not the sin of this person except insofar as this person receives his nature from his first parent, and therefore it is called a sin of nature according to the word of God, "By nature we were sons of wrath." [12]

This, then, is the mystery of original sin: the mystery of our oneness in Adam, a oneness that in the original plan of God should have resulted in our sharing of his marvelous elevation to preternatural and supernatural gifts. Instead of being this, it has become a mystery of iniquity, a sharing of sin and the results of sin. It might be an almost unsupportable mystery of iniquity, were it not for God's redemptive plan, wherein we again share in the mystery of God's goodness. The mystery of our fall in Adam is now dwarfed by the mystery of our redemption in Christ.

> For He, as head, delivers us, His members, from our sins, just as a man by a meritorious work done by his hands, might redeem himself from a sin he had committed by his feet. For just as the natural body is one whole, composed of many members, so the whole Church, which is the Mystical Body of Christ, is *as one person* with its head who is Christ.[13]

Perhaps the world for a time became too individualistic to appreciate this doctrine, based as it is on the deep oneness of all men. But it is precisely this supernatural unity of all men that makes the historical fall and redemption of mankind more intelligible. Take away the universal influence of the First Adam bringing sin and death to mankind, remove the equally universal and more powerful influence of the Second Adam bringing grace and eternal life, then try, if you will, to view the supernatural history of mankind apart from this basic unity in Adam and Christ. It is like trying to get away from night and day, autumn and springtime. We can close our eyes to these supernatural realities, but we cannot destroy the basic fact: that we are all fallen together in Adam, and are meant to rise together in Christ. What was said previously about the unity of the human race in its common natural origin, is deepened immeasurably here, in the supernatural unity of our destiny in Adam and in Christ.

---

12. St. Thomas, *Summa Theologica*, I, II, Q. 81, art. 1, corp.
13. St. Thomas, *Summa Theologica*, III, Q. 49, art. 1, corp.

It is true that we individually contract original sin. As to the manner in which original sin is transmitted, all agree that it comes to us by generation—just as the divine life of grace would have come, had Adam not fallen. Who is immediately responsible for the infection of original sin? Luther and Calvin claimed that it could be attributed to the concupiscence of our parents in the act of generation. We certainly do not subscribe to such a doctrine. When we come into being, God creates our soul, our parents dispose the material for our body. Neither God nor our parents are responsible for original sin. God could not create a soul in sin. As St. Thomas puts it: "The infection of original sin is in no way caused by God, but by carnal generation it comes from the sin of our first parents alone" (*Summa Theologica*, I, II, Q. 83, art. 1, ad 4). This puts the full responsibility on Adam, where it belongs. He further explains the part of generation in the process: "Original sin is in the soul insofar as it (original sin) pertains to human nature. Human nature is passed on from the parents to the child by the giving of flesh into which the soul is then infused, and from this (joining of the soul to the body) the soul incurs the infection (of original sin which pertains to human nature as coming from Adam through the flesh) (St. Thomas, *De Potentia*, Q. 3, art. 9, and 6).

All of this is clarified by another statement of the well-known theologian, St. Robert Bellarmine: "The soul, as it is first understood to be created by God, has no connection with Adam, and so does not share his sin, but when it begins to dwell in a body generated from Adam, and to make one person with his body, then the soul contracts original sin" (Bellarmine, *De Amissione Gratiae*, 5:15). Therefore we get original sin when we get human nature, deprived of sanctifying grace. That is why it is called a sin of nature.

While we individually contract original sin, you will note that the whole spread of original sin is due to Adam, and to our union with him as human beings. The same parallel must be made in the case of redemption. We may think of ourselves as individually redeemed, but again, the whole efficacy of redemption goes back to the influence of Christ, and our individual redemption is first effected by our incorporation into His Mystical Body by baptism. We are saved because of our union with Christ as Christians, for

Christ is "the principle of all grace according to His humanity, just as God is the principle of all being" (St. Thomas, *De Veritate*, Q. 29, art. 5, corp.).

We have insisted on these aspects of our double unity in Adam and in Christ, because this is the heart of the theological history of man which we are now relating. There is much talk today of the United Nations and One World. Here beyond politics, in the world of theological reality, is a more basic unity and oneness. Man can refuse to be one in Christ, but there is no escaping our oneness in death and sin through Adam. It is this inevitable and primal oneness in defeat which makes so attractive and hopeful the possibility of our new oneness in victory through Christ. Perhaps the modern indifference to Christ is due to the fact that so many simply do not recognize what happened to us in Adam. We shall therefore terminate our discussion of original sin by a passing glance at the various reactions to this chapter in man's history, so dismal but yet so true.

IV. ORIGINAL SIN IN THE WORLD TODAY: MODERN REACTION

There are three possible reactions to the mystery of original sin. Many simply deny the reality of the mystery. Others distort the terms of the mystery and thereby distort man in whom the mystery is realized. Finally, there is the way of faith, accepting this truth as revealed by God to give us a clearer picture of what we are today in view of what has happened to us in the beginning. We shall discuss the three reactions in this order.

A. *Those Who Deny the Reality of the Mystery*

This is the familiar attitude of the rationalist or agnostic in the face of supernatural mysteries. He cannot see them. He cannot subject them to the microscope or the cyclotron. He cannot discover, or demonstrate, or understand the mystery by reason alone. Therefore he denies that there is any such thing as original sin. If he is paternalistic and indulgent to the simpler minded people who believe in revelation, he may benignly smile as he relegates Adam and Eve and their story to that pleasant realm of fairy tales where he places *Alice in Wonderland*. If he is vindictive and anti-God, he may inveigh against a religion that enslaves the minds of people with such poppycock as original sin, or any sin for that matter. Such doctrines are medieval. They impede the inevitable march of scientific progress in the modern world.

However widespread this attitude on original sin is in the world today, there are still many unanswered difficulties that arise to plague one who simply denies the mystery. "Without this mystery," writes Pascal, "the most incomprehensible of all, we are incomprehensible to ourselves. The node of our present condition has its entanglements and complications in this abyss, so that without this mystery, man is more inconceivable than the mystery is inconceivable to man" (Pascal, *Pensées*, Part II, a. 5, no. 4).

Cardinal Newman has expressed this same thought with an eloquence that has made this passage among the most famous of of his writings.

> To consider the world in its length and breadth, its various history, the many races of man; their starts, their fortunes, their mutual alienation, their conflicts; and then their ways, habits, governments, forms of worship; their enterprises, their aimless courses, their random achievements and acquirements, the impotent conclusion of long-standing facts, the tokens so faint and broken of a superintending design, the blind evolution of what turn out to be great powers or truths, the progress of things as if from unreasoning elements, not towards final causes, the greatness and littleness of man, his far-reaching aims, his short duration, the curtain hung over his futurity, the disappointments of mental anguish, the prevalence and intensity of sin, the pervading idolatries, the corruptions, the dreary hopeless irreligion, that condition of the whole race, so fearfully yet exactly described in the Apostle's words, 'having no hope and without God in the world'—all this is a vision to dizzy and appall, and inflicts upon the mind the sense of a profound mystery, which is absolutely beyond human solution.
>
> What shall we say to this heart-piercing, reason-bewildering fact? I can only answer, that either there is no Creator, or this living society of men is in a true sense discarded from his presence. Did I see a boy of good make and mind, with the tokens on him of a refined nature, cast upon the world without provision, unable to say whence he came, his birthplace or his family connections, I should conclude that there was some mystery connected with his history, and that he was one of whom, from one cause or another, his parents were ashamed. Thus only should I be able to account for the contrast between the promise and the condition of his being. And so I argue about the world: *if* there be a God, *since* there is a God, the human race is implicated in some terrible aboriginal calamity. It is out of joint with the purposes of its existence; and thus

the doctrine of what is theologically called original sin becomes to me almost as certain as that the world exists, and as the existence of God.[14]

One may, then, deny the reality of the mystery of original sin. But in doing so, many of the difficult facts of human existence today are left unexplained and largely unexplainable. As in many theological matters, the denial of mysteries creates even greater mysteries. It really is the truth that finally makes us free, free to understand things as they are.

B. *Those Who Distort the Terms of the Mystery*

Here we are not met with the blind incredulity of the first reaction. The mystery is accepted here, but it is so diluted or distorted that it becomes unrecognizable. Historically, there have been two classical ways of misunderstanding the terms of the mystery. Much can be gained by investigating these basic trends, for there is a pattern to error as well as to truth. The modern world is not so very original in the matter of error. Most of the prevalent heresies today are merely warmed-up versions of ancient heterodoxy. This is particularly true of our present mystery since our age abounds in erroneous ideas about the nature and destiny of man. Most of these stem from a distorted notion of the effects of original sin.

There are several ways of categorizing the two basic, erroneous trends regarding original sin. In reference to their consequent attitude on man, they may be called over-optimism or over-pessimism. In connection with their common inability to distinguish clearly between the natural and supernatural, they may be called naturalism and pseudosupernaturalism. Viewed in their historical origins as new philosophies of life, we must call them Pelagianism and Protestantism.

1. Pelagianism

This is by far the older of the two, and in its subtle way is still the more vigorous. It began with the writings of one Pelagius, a British monk, who lived in the first part of the fifth century. Like other monks living under the rigid monastic rulings of those days, Pelagius was deeply impressed with asceticism. Working hard by penance and mortification to conquer his vices and to increase in

---

14. Newman, *Apologia pro Vita Sua*, Ch V, pp. 241–243.

virtue, this monk lost sight of the inner workings of grace and began to view his purely natural efforts as the beginning and ending of the Christian life. Eventually, his emphasis on the natural abilities of man led him to an outright denial of the supernatural. We would be understanding the matter by saying that he was overly optimistic about man's natural power to attain virtue and heaven without God's help. For him, the supernatural grace of God was superfluous.

Getting back to Adam, Pelagius taught that there was nothing special in his endowments. While Pelagius would admit that Adam sinned, he openly denied that it had any effect on us beyond giving us a bad example. We only partake of this original sin if we imitate it in our own lives. His doctrine on redemption went in the same direction. The only help we have or need from God to avoid sin and acquire heaven is the teaching and good example of Christ, as opposed to the bad example of Adam. Our natural powers are, according to Pelagius, quite sufficient of themselves to get us to heaven without any help of any elevating or helping grace from God.

We call this system of thought naturalism because it begins and ends with nature, denying any and all trace of the supernatural in man's life and destiny. Catholic doctrine teaches that man's very destiny is supernatural, God's destiny, and that therefore man must be elevated to God's life—the supernatural order—to achieve this destiny. Besides this primary elevation of sanctifying grace, there is additional needed help in the way of actual graces, plus the means of grace: prayer and the sacraments, and the daily use of the infused virtues with the gifts of the Holy Spirit. For Pelagius, this whole supernatural order is superfluous and non-existent. Man gets along perfectly well enough without God's supernatural help. We may call the Pelagian view of man super-optimism and Pelagius, the Father of the Self-made Man. Heaven, salvation, perfection, perfect union with God—all these are within the reach of man's unaided natural powers. Here is the original idea of superman.

It is a long way back to the fifth century, but we are well acquainted with the echoes of this ancient error in the world today. Philosophically, it has reappeared most strongly in Jean-Jacques Rousseau's theory of the natural perfectibility of man. So deeply did this recrudescence of Pelagianism influence the eighteenth century that Rousseau has rightly been called the "Father of the Modern World." Note how closely his theory parallels that of the ancient heresy. We shall take Jacques Maritain, the foremost Catholic philosopher in the world today, as our guide in this analysis.

First of all, Rousseau not only denies the effects of original sin; for him, it is "a blasphemy" (Letter to M. de Beaumont, 3, 67, Edition Hachette). Moreover, according to Rousseau, the original state of man in paradise was purely natural. Since there was nothing preternatural or supernatural about Adam's endowments, since original sin, as a sin of nature, is considered a non-entity, man would be in exactly the same state today as Adam was in the beginning. This is the theory of natural goodness originally taught by Pelagius and reiterated by Rousseau:

> It means that man originally lived in a purely natural paradise of happiness and goodness, and that Nature herself will in the future perform the function which grace fulfilled in the Catholic conception. It also means that such a state of happiness and goodness, of exemption from servile work and suffering, is natural to man, that is to say, essentially required by our nature. Not only, then, is there no original sin of which we bear the guilt at our birth and still keep the wounds, not only is there in us no seat of concupiscence and unhealthy proclivities to incline us to evil, but further, the state of suffering and hardship is one essentially opposed to nature and started by civilization, and our nature demands that we should, at any cost, be freed from it. That is what the dogma of natural goodness amounts to.[15]

By removing the element of supernatural grace from Christianity, Rousseau left us a *naturalized Christianity* which was, in essence, a false Christianity trying to exist independently of Christ and God. Here is the birthplace of secularism. Maritain lists the signs of this new naturalized Christianity.

> To expect the resurrection of the dead and the universal judgment which will bring the kingdom of justice on earth as it is in heaven, to expect the revelation of the perfect Jerusalem where all is light, order and joy: but to expect all this in the very conditions of the present life and expect it from the strength of man, not the grace of Christ; to believe that we are called to lead a divine life, the very life of God—but to believe it of our natural life, not our life

15. J. Maritain, *Three Reformers*, p. 144. Charles Scribner's Sons, New York, 1929.

of grace; to proclaim the law of love of our neighbor, but in separation from the law of the love of God, and so to lower love, strong as death and stern as hell, to the level of what is most stupid and cowardly in the world, to the level of humanitarianism; to understand that there is in this world something awry, something horrible which ought not to be, but without seeing that the old Adam still falls, and the new Adam is still raised on the Cross and drawing souls to Him; and to want to have the world restored by man's power or the effort of nature and not helped and supported by the diligent humility of the virtues and by the divine medicines dispensed by the Bride of Christ, until the Bridegroom Himself shall come with fire and make all things new; in a word, to secularize the Gospel, to keep the human aspirations of Christianity but to do away with Christ! [16]

〜This is the full-blown flower of Pelagianism, in theory at least. We today have watched the fruition in fact. The development has been so variegated that it becomes difficult to trace. We can only give a few indications. Others will suggest themselves to you.

The natural-perfectibility dream of man which Rousseau introduced quite clearly was covered with blood during the French Revolution. In the following century, the same theory reappeared in Germany, glorified in the vigorously self-asserting 'Uber-Mensch' (Super-Man) of Friedrich Nietzsche. Many have indicated the connection between his theory of man and the vain boastings of the Nazis. Again the theory was drowned in blood, yet we still feed the children (and childish adults) on the antics of our own Super-man in the daily comics. Obviously, no one is going to take a comic strip too seriously, but an idea is not so easily dismissed.

Certainly, there is some justification for the oft-repeated opinion that Neo-pelagianism is the foremost heresy of our day. Think of the millions of people in our own country who have not had time for baptism, the gate to the supernatural order of living in Christ. Think of the millions who have no time whatever for prayer or sacrifice, whose total faith is in their own native abilities or natural talent. Think of the millions who may not express it, but actually live out this naturalistic philosophy of life: "I can get along. I don't need God. I've learned to have confidence in myself, to make friends and influence people. Here's the key to my success. I'm a self-made man. What I can't do for myself, I'll harness science to

---

16. Maritain, *Ibid.,* pp. 146–147.

do for me. Prayer is only for weaklings who don't have confidence in themselves or the progress of our age. We'll accomplish more by atomic fission than prayer will accomplish in a year of Sundays."

Thus is God unceremoniously ushered out of human living. The world becomes anthropocentric—centered on man, rather than theocentric—centered on God. Man discards the eternal laws of God and makes his own rules for dishonesty in business: "Everybody is doing it; business is business;" for successive polygamy: "If this marriage doesn't work out, we'll try it again with somebody else;" and for crass expediency in international policies: "Treaties are scraps of paper to be discarded when no longer useful. How many divisions does the Pope have?"

So it has come to pass that God, in fact, has gradually been exiled from His world, once man, in theory, has severed the connections between his nature and God. Man and the things of man are of primary value today. God and the things of God are out: out of politics, education, business, literature, recreation, family—even, to a great extent, God is out of religion and charity since these too have become man-centered and subservient to human desires, rather than to God's will. This is secularism, pure and simple.

It should be evident now that havoc is wrought when a theological error, even about so distant a fact as what happened in the Garden of Eden, is let loose in the world.

> One absolute essential of Christianity is the supernatural quality of grace. Remove that supernatural quality and Christianity goes bad. What do we find at the source of modern disorder? A naturalization of Christianity. It is clear that the Gospel rendered purely natural (and therefore, absolutely debased), becomes a revolutionary ferment of extraordinary virulence . . . you need only half-truths and maddened virtues, as Chesterton says, which once kissed but will now forever hate each other. That is why the modern world abounds in debased analogies of Christian mysticism and shreds of secularized Christianity.[17]

The best modern expression of the net results of Pelagianism and naturalism in our country today can be found in the Annual Statements of the American Hierarchy for the years 1947 and 1948.

"No man can disregard God—and play a man's part in God's

---

17. Maritain, *Ibid.*, pp. 142–143.

world. Unfortunately, however, there are many men—and their number is daily increasing—who in practice live their lives without recognizing that this is God's world. For the most part they do not deny God. On formal occasions they may even mention His name. Not all of them would subscribe to the statement that all moral values derive from merely human conventions. But they fail to bring an awareness of their responsibility to God into their thought and action as individuals and members of society. This, in essence, is what we mean by secularism. It is a view of life that limits itself not to the material in exclusion of the spiritual, but to the human here and now in exclusion of man's relation to God here and hereafter. Secularism, or the practical exclusion of God from human thinking and living, is at the root of the world's travail today" (*Bishops' Statement,* November 14, 1947).

The same train of thought was continued in the statement issued during the following year.

"Human life centers in God. The failure to center life in God is secularism—which, as we pointed out last year, is the most deadly menace to our Christian and American way of living. . . . To combat secularism, the individual Christian must get the full version of Christian truth. It is not divisible. One cannot pick and choose from it. Either it is accepted as a whole or it counts for little in real life. When the Christian does get this full vision, he becomes enthusiastic in trying to share it with the world about him. . . . The crisis is at hand. Today, every Christian must face the full Christian vision and with no thought of compromise must seek vigorously to live it. Every day he must ask himself: What am I doing to build a Christian world? No matter what his condition or state, there is much that he can do. The reconstruction must start with the individual. He must be vigorously Christian in thought and action—in the home, in the training of his children, in his office or workshop, and in his community" (*Bishops' Statement,* November 21, 1948).

This is the practical answer for the results of the first historical error about original sin. Enough of this first error for now. The second historical error starts off in a completely different direction, has had a difficult development, but in the end, it will coalesce with the first error in this, that it distorts the nature of man and the grace of God.

2. Conservative Protestantism

The so-called Reformation heralded an actual deformation of human nature, due to the basic theological error of Luther and Calvin regarding the early history of mankind. Unlike the Pelagians, the so-called Reformers admitted the original integrity and justice of Adam, but they viewed them as something natural, that is, due to the essential constitution of man as man. Man, therefore, not only becomes weakened by original sin and the loss of these original endowments, he becomes essentially corrupt. He can no longer do any good. Luther was the strongest on this point, but Calvin too claimed that fallen man could do no good in the moral order, and was therefore inevitably predestined to salvation or perdition, depending on the decree of God to save or damn him. Within the Church, and during the same sixteenth century, we find Michael du Bay (Baius) condemned for errors in this same tradition. Later on in the next century Cornelius Jansenius continued this pessimistic trend within the Church and was also condemned. We are still suffering from their malignant influence.

Perhaps the simplest way to approach this erroneous trend is to consider its origin in Luther. He was, as you know, a priest and a monk. He probably wanted to be a good one too, but found it increasingly difficult. Finally, convinced that moral victory was impossible for him, he gave up the fight. In his own mind, he rationalized it thus: Everything God gave Adam was necessary for his nature (even the preternatural and supernatural gifts). Adam lost this endowment for himself and us by original sin. That leaves us in a terrible situation. Even after baptism, the sin remains, for we still feel the movements of concupiscence. Thus (since he confused concupiscence with sin), we are still in sin, we are still totally corrupt and depraved, we can do no good, for we no longer possess even freedom. The deathlike burden of sin, i.e. concupiscence, vitiates every effort to be good. His final cry of defeat was this, "concupiscence (meaning for him, sin) cannot be conquered."

Luther then stated his famous dictum: *Pecca fortiter, sed fide fortius:* sin strongly, but believe even more strongly (Letter to Melanchton, August 1, 1521, cf. Enders, *Dr. Martin Luthers Briefwechsel,* III, 208). This was the logical conclusion of his pessimism. Believing us totally corrupt even after baptism, he could understand salvation only in this sense, that by having Faith in Christ, His merits would cover over our essential inward corruption. Thus good works avail us nothing; only faith can save us. And even while being saved, all we do is sinful.

This solved his personal problem. Unfortunately, he advised all others to go and do likewise: "Seek out the society of your boon companions, drink, play, talk bawdy, and amuse yourself. One must, sometimes, even commit a sin out of hate and contempt of the devil, so as not to give him the chance to make one scrupulous over mere nothings; if one is frightened of sinning, one is lost. If I could find some really good sin that would give the devil a toss" (Letter to Jerome Weber, Enders, *Dr. Martin Luthers Briefwechsel*, VIII, 160–161). Akin to this, but in a humorous vein, is a jingle written in jest by the late William Temple, Archbishop of Canterbury, after the foremost American Protestant Theologian, Reinhold Niebuhr, had spoken in England about his preoccupation with sin.

> At Swanwick, when Niebuhr had quit it
> Said a young man: "At last I have hit it.
>   Since I cannot do right
>   I must find out tonight
> The best sin to commit—and commit it."

We have seen how the Pelagian view of man, as unaffected by original sin, led to a false optimism, to a view of the self-sufficiency of man and of his innate goodness. Conversely, this Protestant view of man, as essentially corrupted by original sin, leads to a dreary pessimism. If Rousseau is the philosophical counterpart of Pelagius, we can see in Thomas Hobbes, the seventeenth-century Englishman, the philosophical counterpart of Luther. Rousseau taught that man was innately perfectible, only spoiled by society. Hobbes was in the opposite corner. For him, man is essentially a rapacious grasping individual, who must transfer his rights to society, the great Leviathan, if he is going to attain any peace or harmony. We can note here an overly pessimistic view of man, a dangerous forerunner of modern socialism and totalitarianism. Once more, you see the tremendous importance of thinking clearly about the nature of man. The great social upheavals we are witnessing began with bad ideas, as for example, Communism began with the bad ideas of Marx, Engels, Hegel and company.

As in the foregoing discussion of the Pelagian trend of thought on original sin, it is most difficult here to trace briefly, with any measure of historical accuracy, the classical Protestant trend of thinking about man as essentially corrupted by original sin. Christopher Dawson, an English Catholic author, has done much of this work in his outstanding books on the philosophy of history. A few recognizable indications must suffice here.

One obvious application is the influence of Protestant Puritanism on most Americans, even Catholics. If you follow the pessimistic view of man as essentially corrupt, then certainly pleasurable desires of the body become bad in themselves. Hence the evil nature of drinking, smoking, or dancing in the puritanical point of view. Note how religion has been so often identified with prohibitionism or blue laws in this country. Note also, how religion for many has been identified with an external respectability, such as being seen in Church on Sunday, but without any real concern with what goes on at home, in business or at the club. When all is corrupt interiorly, only external Christianity may be attained.

In a matter that strikes closer to us, actual surveys here at school reveal that only about one out of ten parents ever mention▮▮▮ to their children. They realize that some instructions are needed, they may admit that it is their duty to instruct their children for life, but somehow, they feel that sex is 'dirty' and that it is 'bad' to talk about it. This is hardly a Catholic idea. Rather, it goes back to the notion that man, and especially the body with all its appetites, has been totally depraved in the fall of Adam.

Perhaps the greatest modern indication of this pessimistic view of man's nature is the 'Frustrated Man' of our times, to borrow a term from Monsignor Sheen's recent volume on *The Philosophy of Religion* (1948). Many are the novelists, philosophers, and theologians outside the Church who are tremendously preoccupied with the obvious presence of evil in the world, and particularly, in man. We find a meeting with the beast, a classical name for evil, in the writings of Hemingway, Huxley and Dostoievski, in Berdyaev and Soloviev, in Kierkegaard, Barth, Brunner and especially here in America, in the theology of Reinhold Niebuhr. This is a varied company, and of course, the preoccupation with sin varies according to the man. Soren Kierkegaard, for example, is preoccupied with the evil in himself. He seeks the beast within, not in the social order. He is the father of the modern pessimistic philosophy—existentialism. Karl Barth reacts against modern humanistic optimism by reiterating the Lutheran doctrine about the intrinsic corruption of man. Barth inveighs against the modern do-goodism of the social Gospellers. He claims there is not much we can do except depend upon God for help in the mess we are in.

Reinhold Niebuhr has also rejected the false optimism of self-sufficient modern man by rediscovering original sin through its obvious effects in the world today. There is something hopeful in this new recognition of original sin, but yet something dangerous if it is to remain allied to the pessimistic over-statement of original sin that characterized the sixteenth century Reformers. As we have already mentioned many times, truth steers a middle course between the extremes of error. While we can approach those in error by recognizing the element of truth that lurks in every error, we can only save them by presenting the whole truth. This is the tremendous responsibility of Catholic Theology in our modern world which is torn between conflicting ideas of what man is, where he is going, and how he can ever arrive there.

C. The Catholic Position

Arriving at this point of our discussion is, as Newman says of his conversion, "like coming into port after a rough sea." While the greater part of our position has already been established in the foregoing parts of this chapter, we are now in a much better situation for summarizing the whole matter against the somber background of error. You may remember a famous passage in Chesterton's *Orthodoxy* where he compares the thrill of Catholic belief and life to a wild ride down a narrow mountain road. On either side lurks disaster. The coach may lurch to the right and to the left, but while death and disaster are imminent at every moment, the Church through the centuries has kept that dangerously thrilling but secure middle course of truth.

We have seen in the other doctrines already studied, how the truth of Catholic theology is always in between the opposing extremes of heresy. Here too, in a matter as close to us as ourselves, we can see again the calm serenity of truth in that middle path. On both sides of us here lurk false optimism and black pessimism about man. Pelagius and his followers tell us that man can do all good. Luther and the others tell us that man can do no good. The Church still combines the two half truths that each has taken from her, to give us the whole truth of the matter. Man can do the greatest evil in the world. As a matter of fact, he has done it in spurning God and losing His gifts in the beginning. All of us do it when we sin. But man can also do the greatest good in the world, by regaining his heritage in and through Christ. This is the whole matter in a nutshell.

You may have wondered why we spent so much time in differentiating the triple endowment of man in the beginning of this chapter. Our reason was this: failure to distinguish clearly between these three kinds of gifts has been the root of all the errors. Obviously, optimism or pessimism about man will depend upon how we assess his abilities and endowments. A Catholic view of the matter will show you clearly how we can steer the middle course between over-confidence and defeatism. We do have something to worry us, but something to give us confidence too.

First of all, we stated very definitely what man had coming to him as man. Essentially, he needs a body and soul, with the powers of mind and will to operate rationally. And, of course, the concurrence of God is needed to operate at all. With this basic equipment, man can live and operate as a man. The Church has vehemently defended the fact that man never lost this natural equipment, that he had it before the fall and after the fall. This fact takes the heart out of the main argument for pessimism, that man is essentially corrupt. How then, you may ask, is man worse in body and soul after the fall?

The key to the answer lies in those extra gifts that man had, over and above his natural gifts. Endow a man's body and soul, mind and will with the preternatural gifts and the supernatural gifts we have studied, and certainly he is better equipped than man with purely natural endowments. Strip him of those gifts and he is certainly worse off in body and soul, mind and will. Many theologians have compared man after the fall to a wealthy traveller who is set upon and stripped by robbers. As he stands naked by the wayside, he is certainly worse off than he was. However, he still has all that is essential to him as man.

There is one point that must be added to the comparison. Suppose that this man was going to a formal reception before he was robbed. He certainly cannot go now until he gets some suitable clothing. Adam was going some place too. Christ, Our Lord, has spoken of the wedding garment that is needed for the kingdom of heaven. While Adam retained all the natural endowments he needed, to live as man, he lost the supernatural endowment of grace which alone enabled him to enter the kingdom of heaven. He lost it for us too. Unless this gift of grace is regained, no man can go where God has destined all men to go—to a share of God's happiness in heaven. This aspect of the doctrine takes the polish off the main argument for false optimism. Man never was self-sufficient, and certainly is not now, after the fall.

Now we have all the theological groundwork that is necessary to establish the Catholic view of man in a fallen world. There is some ground for *pessimism* when we consider the high calling of man to share God's life and happiness, despite the fact that he comes into the world stripped of grace, the essential requirement of this high destiny, and without the original harmony of body and soul that God granted Adam in the beginning. There is some ground for *optimism* when we consider that God Himself has become man to remedy our situation, to take upon Himself the inconveniences of our natural state, to suffer the penalty of hunger and thirst, hard work and discouragement, yes, even to endure suffering and death that we might regain our lost riches as children of God and heirs to heaven.

As you see, the key to the mystery is our double oneness: a oneness of defeat and despair in Adam; a oneness of victory and new hope in Christ. If we have been wronged by Adam, we have been righted in Christ. If Adam's fall was a great disaster, a grievous fault, the Church can still see grounds for optimism when she sings in blessing the Pascal Candle on Holy Saturday: "O Happy Fault, that merited to have so great and so wonderful a Redeemer!" Insofar as it occasioned our new victory in Christ, the Second Adam, even this fault can be called happy, on the day before Easter.

Certainly, nature unaided has its difficulties. We can understand the feelings of St. Paul when he cries out: "Unhappy man that I am, who will deliver me from the body of this death" (Romans 7:24). But as Catholics, we know that we do not have to resign ourselves to the pessimism of nature unaided. For nature has been lifted up again, and we have the same answer to our difficulties that St. Paul had to his: "The grace of God through Our Lord, Jesus Christ" (Romans 7:25).

It is not difficult to endure inconveniences of our human nature, once we realize that Christ did not endow Himself with the preternatural gifts of Adam. Rather, He preferred to endure the natural hardships of human living that culminate in death. But he lifted these sufferings from a plane of animal endurance, and used them as a means of atoning for the sins that had brought them into the world. Sacrifice and suffering have an entirely different meaning since Christ endured them. The Christian sees them today, not as a cause for pessimism, but as a means of atoning for sin, and of co-redeeming the world with Christ: "I rejoice now in the suffering I bear for your sake," St. Paul writes to the early Christians at Colossae, "And what is lacking of the sufferings of Christ, I fill up in my flesh for His Body which is the Church" (Colossians 1:24).

Paul admits that he has suffered as much as anyone, in not having the preternatural gifts that Adam lost for us: "in many more labors, in prisons more frequently, in lashes above measure, often exposed to death. From the Jews five times I received forty lashes less one. Thrice I was scourged, once I was stoned, thrice I suffered shipwreck, a night and a day I was adrift on the sea; in journeyings often, in perils from floods, in perils from robbers, in perils from my own nation, in perils from the Gentiles, in perils in the city, in perils in the wilderness, in perils in the sea, in perils from false brethren; in labors and hardships, in many sleepless nights, in hunger and thirst, in fastings often, in cold and nakedness. Besides those other things, there is my daily pressing anxiety, the care of all the churches. Who is weak, and I am not weak!" (II Corinthians 11:23–29).

Do all these discouragements leave Paul in a mood of deep pessimism? When in addition to all these natural cares from outside and from within, he is given an additional temptation, the mysterious 'thorn in his flesh' to try him, he asks God three times that it might leave him. His answer from God and his reaction to that answer are the epitome of our Catholic attitude on life: of ourselves we can do nothing, and might well be pessimistic, but in Christ we can do all things, and this is true Christian optimism.

Here is Paul's solution: "And He has said to me: 'My grace is sufficient for thee, for strength is made perfect in weakness.' Gladly therefore, will I glory in my infirmities, that the strength of Christ may dwell in me. Wherefore, I am satisfied, for Christ's sake, with infirmities, with insults, with hardships, with persecutions, with distresses. For when I am weak, then I am strong" (II Corinthians 12:9–11).

This is the great victory of Christ and Christians, the great difference between cowardly surrender and saintly perseverance. The saint sees himself as clearly as the discouraged quitter. But he does not stop at self. His weakness drives the saint to His true strength in Christ. His humility is not a self-centered disappointment, but a God-centered lowliness which moves logically to confidence in God's mercy and Christ's help.

All in all, the story of our first parents has been inherently sad. We have certainly been profoundly influenced by what happened to them in the beginning. In a very true sense, we face the world today as they did after the fall. We enter the world as "abandoned children of Eve." But in another sense, while we must each regain the essence of what they lost—divine life—we need not look forward to a future Redeemer as they did. We now have our Redeemer, Christ Our Lord. In having Him reborn within us by the grace of Baptism, do we not have the heart of what Adam had before the Fall, and something more! Yes, the story has been sad in a sense, but in looking back upon what might have been, we can conjure up some slight picture of what will yet be, when all things will have been restored in Christ, when "we all attain to the unity of the faith and of the deep knowledge of the Son of God, to perfect manhood, to the mature measure of the fullness of Christ" (Ephesians 4:13–14).

V. The Immaculate Conception

The Tract of the Mass for Feasts of the Blessed Virgin Mary begins with these remarkable words: "Rejoice O Virgin Mary, thou alone hast destroyed all heresies." This statement may puzzle you at first. But not for long. During the first four centuries of the Church's existence, all of Christendom was torn by the myriad Christological heresies that in one way or another tried to distort the true divinity and true humanity of Christ, as well as the hypostatic union between the two natures of the Person of the Word. After centuries of strife, the Church triumphed when the truth of the Incarnation was summed up by the solemn definition of the Divine Maternity of Mary. In declaring that Mary was the true Mother of God, the Council of Ephesus (431 A.D.) epitomized the basic truths that Christ was true God and one person since Mary is His mother; also that Christ is true man since He is born of Mary. This orthodox belief about the glory of Mary sounded the death knell for the main heresies of those early centuries.

In much the same way, the solemn definition of the Immaculate Conception is the answer of the Church to the main modern heresies which have been propagated during the past four centuries, since the Reformation. These dealt mainly with original sin and the nature of man. We cannot believe that Mary alone, of all human beings, is exempt from original sin without declaring at the same time that we believe original sin to be the inheritance of all men. In declaring the exception, we declare our belief of the universal rule. Moreover, the popular modern confusion about the natural and the supernatural is clearly refuted by this dogma. Mary's exemption is portrayed as a singular privilege due only to the merits of Christ, the Redeemer of all men. Mary's possession of sanctifying grace is a gift of God, as is ours. Her singular freedom from concupiscence is an implicit statement that we do have concupiscence. Moreover, although it is beyond the strict scope of this dogma, in stating that she alone is free from even venial sin during life, the Church has given us to understand that man in a fallen world is not perfect. Thus has Mary destroyed all heresies. Neither Pelagianism, nor Protestantism, nor any of their present-day descendants can stand as true in the face of the infallibly defined truth of this dogma.

Here, as in our other doctrines, it is best to see, first of all, just exactly what the Church teaches in proposing for our belief the dogma of the Immaculate Conception. The following statement is a direct translation of the *ex cathedra* (i.e., an infallible declaration outside a General Council) declaration of Pius IX, entitled *Ineffabilis Deus:*

> Unto the honor and glory of the Holy and Undivided Trinity, unto the adorning and ennobling of the Virgin Mother of God, unto the exaltation of the Catholic Faith and the fostering of the Chris-

tian Religion, by the authority of Our Lord Jesus Christ and of the holy Apostles Peter and Paul, and by our own authority, we declare, we pronounce and we define that the doctrine which holds that the most Blessed Virgin Mary in the first instant of her conception was by the singular grace and privilege of Almighty God, in view of the merits of Jesus Christ, the Saviour of the human race, preserved free from all stain of original sin, is a doctrine revealed by God, and therefore to be firmly and constantly believed by all the faithful (Denz. 1641).

It is a remarkable tribute to the living and infallible teaching power of the Church that this marvelous truth of theology should have been finally defined after more than eighteen centuries of the Church's existence. We have already seen in our study of Genesis how the truth was indicated in the Old Testament promise of a Redeemer, the prediction of a final victory of the woman over the serpent whose head would be crushed. The early Church Fathers consistently interpreted this to mean that Mary is the New Eve, as Christ is the New Adam. As St. Ephrem wrote: "The one is the cause of our death, the other is the cause of our life" (*Sermo 4 In Divina Scriptura, Opera Syriaca*, II, 327).

The Fathers insisted that Mary was free from all stain of sin, more pure than the angels, the only one of our human kind who is completely holy and innocent. Thus they held that the prediction of her complete victory over Satan was realized. She would hardly have been fully victorious over him if she had been conceived under his domination, with the stain of original sin on her soul. Thus too have the Fathers interpreted the oft-repeated words of the angel Gabriel to Mary: "Hail, *full of grace*, the Lord is with thee. Blessed art thou among women" (Luke 1:29). This fullness of grace is a positive way of showing her unique freedom from sin.

Cardinal Newman summarizes this position by insisting on the comparison of Mary and Eve. Worlds of meaning are linked to their decision as an angel speaks to both of them. Both should have been equally prepared for their position in the scheme of history.

Have you any intention to deny that Mary was as fully endowed as Eve? Is it any violent inference, that she, who was to co-operate in the redemption of the world, at least was not less endowed with power from on high, than she who, given as a helpmate to her hus-

band, did in the event but co-operate with him for its ruin? If Eve
was raised above human nature by that indwelling moral gift which
we call grace, is it rash to say that Mary had even a greater grace?
And this consideration gives significance to the Angel's salutation
of her as 'full of grace'. . . . And if Eve had this supernatural inward gift given her from the first moment of her personal existence,
is it possible to deny that Mary too had this gift from the very
moment of her personal existence? I do not know how to resist this
inference:—well, this is simply and literally the doctrine of the Immaculate Conception. I say the doctrine of the Immaculate Conception is in its substance this, and nothing more or less than this (putting aside the question of degrees of grace); and it really does seem
to be bound up in the doctrine of the Fathers that Mary is the second
Eve.[18]

The feast of the Immaculate Conception was celebrated by the
Church as early as the seventh century in the East, and the ninth
century in the West. The real difficulty with the doctrine came
during the Middle Ages, when some of the greatest scholastic
theologians, including St. Thomas himself and his teacher St.
Albert the Great, faced this problem: Christ is the one Mediator
and Saviour of all men. If Mary is conceived without the stain of
original sin, then Christ would not seem to be her Redeemer,
and therefore, He would not be the universal Saviour of all mankind. It is to the eternal credit of a somewhat slighted theologian,
that Duns Scotus publicly proposed the answer to this problem at
the University of Paris in the year 1305.

The answer of Scotus proceeded thus: all human beings, including the Blessed Virgin, are due to contract original sin. We actually
do contract the stain of this sin, and our redemption is accomplished by repairing the damage done. But in the case of the Mother
of God, Mary was preserved from contracting the stain of original
sin which she normally would have contracted at her conception
in the womb of St. Anne, just as everyone else does. Mary's redemption then is by anticipation of Her Divine Son's merits. Her
redemption is preventive, rather than curative. All this is to pre-
pare her to be the Mother of God, the New Eve. We might better
understand it by a simple analogy. In the old days, people contracted diseases, then the doctor was called, and a cure applied.
Today, a child is given vitamins shortly after birth to prevent it

18. Newman, *Certain Difficulties Felt by Anglicans in Catholic Teaching*, Vol. II,
pp. 45-46, Longmans, Green & Co., New York, 1891.

from contracting the diseases to which all children are normally subject. Christ, Our Redeemer, *cured* us from the effects of original sin. He *prevented* His Mother from contracting the sin. Both of these actions are redemptive, so He is still the Universal Redeemer.

Once more, we can go to Cardinal Newman for a crystal-clear statement of our doctrine.

> We consider that in Adam she (Mary) died, as others; that she was included, together with the whole race, in Adam's sentence; that she incurred his debt, as we do; but that, for the sake of Him who was to redeem her and us upon the Cross, to her the debt was remitted by anticipation, on her sentence was not carried out, except indeed as regards her natural death, for she died when her time came, as others. All this we teach, but we deny that she had original sin; for by original sin we mean, as I have already said, something negative, viz., this only, the *deprivation* of that supernatural unmerited grace which Adam and Eve had on their first formation,—deprivation and the consequences of deprivation. Mary could not merit, any more than they, the restoration of that grace; but it was restored to her by God's free bounty, from the very first moment of her existence, and thereby, in fact, she never came under the original curse, which consisted in the loss of it and she had this special privilege, in order to fit her to become the Mother of her and our Redeemer, to fit her mentally, spiritually for it; so that, by the aid of the first grace, she might so grow in grace, that, when the Angel came and her Lord was at hand, she might be 'full of grace,' prepared as far as a creature could be prepared, to receive Him into her bosom.[19]

Perhaps we can better understand the difficulties that early theologians had with this doctrine, when we consider that today, almost a hundred years after its solemn definition, many Catholics still completely misunderstand it. Many confuse the Immaculate Conception with the virginal conception or birth of Jesus, whereas it has nothing to do with the birth of the Saviour, except as a remote preparation of Mary to be His Mother. The Immaculate Conception should not be confused with the sinlessness of Mary either, although it was the beginning of her positive sanctity and sinlessness. Neither does this doctrine mean that Mary was conceived in any other than the ordinary way by her parents, Saints Anne and Joachim.

To continue with the development of this doctrine, despite the

---

19. Newman, *Ibid.*, pp. 48–49.

difficulties that arose during the Middle Ages, devotion to Mary Immaculate spread far and wide throughout the Church. We can see the Holy Spirit guiding the development of this truth, for as we have already noted, when the Council of Trent proclaimed the universal application of original sin in its decrees of 1546, it made an explicit exception for the Mother of God, without defining, however, that she was conceived without original sin. It was not until December 8, 1854, that Pius IX solemnly defined this doctrine. And once more, we can see the Hand of God approving the teaching authority of the Church. Barely three years after the declaration of the dogma, the Blessed Virgin miraculously appeared to a peasant girl, Bernadette Soubirous, at a Grotto near the town of Lourdes in the department of Hautes Pyrenees in Southern France. Eighteen times she appeared between February 11 and July 16, 1858. When little Bernadette asked the Lady her name, the Lady answered in Bernadette's own southern French dialect, saying: "I am the Immaculate Conception." Millions of pilgrims have visited this holy spot since then, and thousands of cures have attested to the powerful intercession of Mary conceived without sin.

It would not be right to conclude this section without mentioning the intimate relationship between this doctrine and the Church in our own country. Over a hundred years ago, in the Sixth Provincial Council of Baltimore, the American Bishops requested that the Holy See would add the word "Immaculate" to the Mass and Office for the Conception of Mary on December 8. They also requested that this invocation be inserted: "Mary conceived without sin, pray for us." [20] During the next Provincial Council (May 13, 1849), Mary Immaculate was invoked as the Patroness of our country. It was also during this Council that the American hierarchy petitioned the Holy Father to make an infallible declaration of the doctrine of the Immaculate Conception.[21] It is an interesting fact of history that only five years later Pius IX did so.

These are only the highlights of a long history that began when Columbus arrived in the New World aboard a ship named after Our Lady—*The Santa Maria*. This history is beautifully portrayed

20. P. Guilday, *History of the Councils of Baltimore*, pp. 149–150, Macmillan, New York, 1932.
21. *Ibid.*, pp. 157–159.

in a book of Daniel Sargent's *Our Land and Our Lady*. We can take leave of the story in the present chapter, for here history is in the making. The depth of the influence of Mary Immaculate needs no explanation to those who have lived under her care. Certainly, at the University named after her where these lines are written, all realize that there is a serene peace and calm imparted to all parts of the campus from this Lady on her focal point atop the Golden Dome. One needs only to stand for a few minutes at the Grotto patterned after Lourdes, to realize that many troubled paths converge at Mary's feet, and take confidence from the sight of the serpent's head being crushed beneath her heel. But here or elsewhere, Mary Immaculate continues to lead the way to victory. We are reminded of the Epistle for the Mass of the Vigil of the Immaculate Conception: "I am Mother of the fair love, and of fear, and of knowledge, and of holy hope. In me is all grace of the way and of the truth, in me is all hope of life and of virtue. Come over to me, all you who desire me, and be filled with my fruits . . . he that hearkens to me shall not be confounded, and they that work by me shall not sin" (Ecclesiasticus 24:24–30). This promise is fulfilled in the Epistle for the Mass of the Immaculate Conception itself: "He that shall find me shall find life and shall have salvation from the Lord" (Proverbs 8:35). Despite all the effects of original sin, Christians can continue to have new confidence in her, who is in the words of Wordsworth, "Our tainted nature's solitary boast" (*Ecclesiastical Sonnets*). And for all of us who begin life under the baneful influence of original sin, what better prayer is there than that engraved on the miraculous medals that most of us wear: "O Mary, conceived without sin, pray for us who have recourse to Thee."

Conclusion and Summary

With Chapter VI we have taken a long step forward into the realm of theology as it affects man. You recall that at the beginning of this book, we remarked that all theology was a study of the Divine Life, in God, and as shared by men. This past chapter has given us a close-up view of man in the supernatural order. We approached the matter historically, considering the case of the first man, in whom all men were destined to share God's life on earth, and enjoy His happiness in eternity. We saw how God prepared

Adam and Eve for this magnificent destiny by endowing them with wonderful natural, preternatural and supernatural gifts.

Then came the drama of their lives, the mystery of iniquity when they abandoned the way of God for their own way of pride, and consequently lost their preternatural and supernatural gifts. Now they were in anything but an enviable state: destined to heaven and unable to get there of their own efforts. As we saw that is that state of affairs that we inherit at birth, born as we are in original sin without the endowment of divine life that alone enables man to attain eternal life in heaven. Besides we are bereft of the additional gifts of the preternatural order, left in a state of internal strife wherein the natural order of things makes life more difficult than God had originally planned it.

The next step was to check the various trends that stemmed from the two historical reactions to original sin. We followed the vagaries of Pelagianism and Protestantism from the time of their origin to the present day. We concluded that the true concept of man must take into account both the weaknesses of our Fall in Adam, and the additional strength that has accrued to us through our Redemption in Christ. This is the view of Christian optimism: "I can do all things *in Him* who strengthens me."

Lastly we turned to Her who is our life, our sweetness, and our hope. She, at least, has emerged victorious from this somber picture of what man might have been and what he is today. She is all that we might have been and more. Spiritually, and in every other way, she is perfection. Despite the many unhappy events of this chapter, we can glory in a happy ending when we conclude with the thought of Mary, the Immaculate Mother of God, and our Mother.

Having thus viewed man in his beginnings, our next step is to look to the end of this life, to view theologically what awaits him after that tremendous step we must all take: from time into eternity.

CHAPTER VII

The End of the World and of Man

THEOLOGY SPEAKS OF ULTIMATES. This present chapter should easily pass for theology, since its technical title is *De Novissimis:* Concerning the final things. Sometimes in English the subject matter of this chapter is called Eschatology, a term derived from the Greek word, Eschatos, meaning last. We first viewed the world and man in their beginnings. Now we look at the last things that each particular man faces: Death, Judgment, Heaven, Purgatory or Hell. Normally we speak of the four last things, since Purgatory is an intermediate stage, whereas the other four are definitive.

There will be an end to the world as well as to man. While the world antedates man as far as origins go, individual men leave the world before its ending. This is the reason why we consider the end of each particular man first. But since the world too will end, we finally consider the four last things of the world, and of mankind in general. These comprise the Last Day, the Resurrection of the Body, Final or General Judgment, and the End of the World.

The whole chapter naturally falls into two main divisions:

1. The End of Each Particular Man: Death, Judgment, Heaven, Purgatory, and Hell.

2. The End of the World and of Humanity on Earth: The Last Day, Resurrection of the Body, The General Judgment, The End of the World.

This is the briefest tract in Theology. One reason may be that Our Lord was very outspoken about theological realities that affect us now, and purposely vague about some of the details of the life to come. He did state the fundamental divine truths about the future life with no equivocation. However, we do not have too many details with which to fill in the picture. We know we shall die, that we shall be judged. We know that there is a horrible place prepared for the devil and his followers, another eternal kingdom of peace and joy for those who love God. But even this heavenly kingdom is presented as a pleasant surprise that awaits. Our Lord says in substance: "You can't imagine what it will be like, how wonderful it is."

We have the same assurance regarding the final end of the world and of mankind on earth. The last day will come, but its time is a mystery, and its suddenness like lightning flashing out of a dark summer sky. There will be a complete separation of the good and bad elements in all humanity, and ending of this world and a beginning of a new and wonderful kingdom in which God will be all in all. The best we can do for the present reign of faith is to trace out what we do know theologically about these basic final facts. For the fuller picture, we shall have to await eternity.

I. The End of Each Man

No one of us was intellectually conscious of his beginnings. Our conception, birth and early years are shrouded in the wispy months that were part of our lives and are yet unremembered. It will not be so with the end of our earthly existence. Many are the theories of the pagans who either deny the existence of a future life, or picture it as a world of darkness and oblivion, or imagine man as being continually reincarnated in the form of other men or of animals. Our doctrine, however, makes the end of man's earthly life a drama that each of us will witness and in which we shall all consciously take a part. For while the time of life's ending is not of our making, its destination certainly is. This is the matter of our present section: to see precisely how the end comes to be, and what the possible destinations are.

A. Death

Here is a word that chills even one who has learned to view it as a Christian. It disturbs us because even when death is peaceful and calm, it represents the disruption and breaking up of a unity of body and soul that is ourselves. The instinct of self preservation is basic to every living being. And we so closely associate the idea of life with this living together of body and soul, that for us, the separation of body and soul means the end of life. While actually it is only the body that dies, our whole concept of living is so related to life in the body, that the death of the body is actually the end of life as we know it.

Everyone instinctively shrinks from death, but there is some consolation in the thought that there are no exceptions in this matter. Rich or poor, man or woman, intelligent or stupid, all human beings must be born, and all must die. "It is appointed unto all men once to die" (Hebrews 9:27). Nothing is quite so personal as dying. Everyone must do it for himself. There is no escaping it. Some may delay it by medical care, some may hurry it along by suicide, but sooner or later, it awaits everyone.

Theology finds in death a meaning quite apart from its obvious natural meaning: the corruption of a body that is by nature corruptible. Theologians have always viewed death as a punishment for sin, the fulfillment of the threat that God made to Adam in the beginning, the return to dust that he foretold after the Fall. We have read in God's revealed word that "The wages of sin is death" (Romans 6:23). Moreover, we have seen at some length in the last chapter how "By one man sin entered into this world, and by sin death; and so death passed upon all men" (Romans 5:12).

It may at first seem difficult to understand how we consider death as both a natural thing and a punishment for sin. St. Thomas has put the answer in a nutshell. "Death is natural because of the condition of (our) nature, and a penalty because of our loss of that divine blessing that preserved from death" (St. Thomas, *Summa Theologica*, I, II, Q. 164, a. 1). To understand the full Christian concept, we must see the atoning power of death. It is the great means given to everyone to atone for the temporal punishment due to sin. In itself, it is merely a natural phenomenon, but related to the death of Christ, and accepted in the atoning spirit of His death it becomes a great means of grace and salvation.

The aspect of death that strikes us most deeply is its utter finality. When faced with difficulties in life, men will always say, "Well, things will be different some day. Times will change." All through life, men can change for the better or for the worse. This moment we are all for our self will against God's will, the next moment we may be on our knees, asking God to forgive us. Life is one continual series of ups and downs, bad endings and bright new beginnings. Yet, things never get so bad in life that we cannot hope for a better day. But with death, the curtains come down with a decisive thud. The strivings of life are over. The day of vice has passed, and so has the acquisition of virtue. There is no more sin, but also no more merit, and no more time for repentance. What is done, is done, and that forever. The alternatives at the end of this life are startling in their decisiveness. Christ Our Lord stated them in less than ten words: "He who is not with Me is against Me" (Luke 11:23).

We must see the providential nature of death over against its decisiveness. Since it is so definitive a moment, we can understand how God in His Providence wishes us to die at a time when we will be best prepared to attain heaven. This thought has softened the impact of many sudden and youthful deaths. God may well take a soul when it can best face Him in judgment.

Someone has well said that the best way to die well is to live well. This is the gist of Our Lord's own advice: "Watch therefore, for you do not know at what hour your Lord is to come." Work now, for "night is coming when no one can work" (John 9:4). Nothing so clearly emphasizes the true value of things in this life, as to see them outlined against the life to come. Money, position, clothes, influence . . . all these things pass with death. The same can be said of the normal worries of life. What may seem tremendously important now, may be really quite unimportant when viewed against the timelessness of eternity. St. Teresa of Avila composed a little verse that expresses the thought quite well:

> Let nothing disturb thee
> Let nothing affright thee
> All things are passing
> God alone is changeless.

All Catholics, realizing the utter certainty, and yet complete uncertainty of death have been accustomed to pray for a happy death. One of the most famous of these prayers is that composed by Cardinal Newman. We have often in these notes read his statement of basic theological truths. His prayers are no less eloquent.

"O My Lord and Saviour, support me in that hour in the strong arms of Thy Sacraments, and by the fresh fragrance of Thy consolations. Let the absolving words be said over me, and the holy oil sign and seal me, and Thy Body be my food and Thy Blood my sprinkling; and let my sweet Mother Mary breathe on me, and my Angel whisper peace to me, and my glorious Saints . . . smile upon me; that in them all, and through them all, I may receive the gift of perseverance, and die, as I desire to live, in Thy faith, in Thy Church, in Thy service, and in Thy love. Amen."

B. *The Particular Judgment*

"It is appointed upon men once to die, and after this the judgment" (Hebrews 9:27). It is probably the thought of this judgment immediately following death that makes death a somewhat unpleasant thought to us. There may be some small consolation in the thought that the whole world will be present at the general judgment. But in the particular judgment, the individual soul stands alone before God.

We are somewhat in the dark about many of the details of this particular judgment. Most of the testimony of Holy Scripture regarding the judgment has reference to the general judgment. We do have enough indications, however, both in Scripture and in the teachings of the Church, to show that there *is* a particular judgment. There are many indications that something happens to the soul after death. We make a special point of this, for many of these outside the Church have followed Calvin's belief that there is an interval of semi-consciousness between the time of death and the general judgment (cf. Calvin, *Institutiones*, III, 25). Others teach practically the same thing, referring to the soul after death as if existing in a kind of suspended animation.

We can take a better lead from the Old Testament: "Man shall go into the house of his eternity, and the mourners shall go round about in the street . . . and the dust return into its earth, from whence it was, and the spirit return to God, who gave it" (Ecclesiates 12:5–7). What happens when the soul returns to God? We have several indications of immediate reward and punishment. You recall Christ's words to the Good Thief: "This day thou shalt be with me in Paradise" (Luke 23:43). You also remember the famous parable of Lazarus and the rich man. Lazarus died and went to the bosom of Abraham, "and the rich man also died, and he was buried in hell" (Luke 16:22). What theologians conclude from this is that an immediate reward or punishment presupposes some immediate judgment consigning the individual soul to reward or punishment.

Just how does this judgment take place? The best opinion is that of St. Augustine (*De Civitate Dei*, 20:14) who speaks of a special illumination of soul whereby the individual sees clearly the divine judgment upon his life, and realizes that there is only one place to go in view of his status before God. We do not have to imagine a formal judgment scene, with the devil accusing and the guardian angel defending. Nor do we say that the soul sees Christ the Judge, either as God or as man. St. Thomas indicates that the soul, seeing itself with all the false values of earth stripped away, realizing clearly its standing in the eyes of God and eternal justice, simply moves of its own accord to the place it deserves.

> Just as a body is moved by its heaviness or lightness to its proper place, unless something retains it, so the soul, once it is freed from the chains of the flesh by which it is restrained during its earthly time of trial, immediately attains its reward or punishment, unless something impedes it . . . and because the place is already arranged for souls according to the fittingness of reward or punishment, as soon as the soul is freed from the body, it is either sunk into hell or rises to heaven, unless it is impeded by some fault by which its ascent to heaven must be held up that the soul might first be purified.[1]

On the further question of where the judgment takes place, again we simply do not know. The simplest opinion is that it takes place on the spot where real death occurs. The important element is that it takes place *soon* after apparent death. As we have already mentioned in another connection, no one knows exactly when real death occurs. It would be safe to say that it is within an hour or so of apparent death in the case of sudden deaths, and even sooner in the case of death following a long drawn-out weakening of the body. In any case, the Church allows the priest to administer the last sacraments after respiration has ceased, as long as the body is still warm. Real death is marked by the separation of the soul and body, a reality that cannot be seen.

1. St. Thomas, *Summa Theologica, Supplement,* Q. 69, a. 2.

It is the constant belief of the Church that reward and punishment, and consequently a previous judgment is the next reality for the individual soul upon death. We have the official statement of this belief by Pope Benedict XII in 1336. He defined that "the souls of those who depart this life in the state of mortal sin, descend into Hell directly after death and are there subject to infernal torments" (Denz. 531). We have an earlier statement regarding the souls of the just. The second Council of Lyons (1274) declared that "the souls of the just are received directly into Heaven" (Denz. 464). The Church has always believed that martyrs go directly to Heaven.

Despite the apparent vagueness of revelation on some of the details, it should be clear by now that there is no doubt about the fact of the particular judgment or of reward or punishment that immediately follows it. Sometimes we tend to think too often of judgment in terms of condemnation, whereas the justice of God will also assure that every good thing we have ever done in the state of grace will be rewarded. Our Lord says that not even a cup of cold water *given in His name* will go unrewarded. For those who spend their lives doing good, the judgment may well hold many pleasant surprises of good deeds long forgotten and now brought to light again.

This was the spirit in which St. Paul anticipated the judgment with hope: "For I know whom I have believed and I am certain that he is able to keep that which I have committed unto Him, against that day" (II Timothy 1:12). Despite his trials in life, he still looks to the judgment with hope in his heart: "I have fought the good fight; I have finished my course; I have kept the faith. As to the rest, there is laid up for me a crown of justice which the Lord, the just judge, will render to me in that day; and not only to me, but to them also that love his coming" (II Timothy 4:7–8).

The particular judgment then, is just the prelude to the state in which a person will spend his eternity. It will not merely inform a person of his salvation or reprobation, but will also include the degree of his happiness or misery. Obviously, the just judge will not pass the same exact judgment upon the Catholic who just barely makes heaven, and the saint; upon the lifelong sinner and him who only failed for a time. In the particular judgment each of us will see exactly where he stands. There will be no argument. We will simply see, and that will be that.

C. *Heaven*

Here is the only real ending to any human success story. The poor boy may become a millionaire, the page boy may become a senator, the altar boy may become a pope—but all of these successes are trivial and meaningless, unless a man also achieves the ultimate success of heaven. "For what does it profit a man, if he gain the whole world, but suffer the loss of his own soul? Or what will a man give in exchange for his soul?" (Mark 8:37). Heaven is the only substantial goal of all human endeavor. Heaven alone is success unending, security unthreatened, happiness and peace and joy beyond our dreams.

Heaven can only be all of these things because it goes to the very source of all happiness, peace and joy, because it consists in possessing this source which is God. While we know this for a fact, it is still a mysterious fact like the possession of God on earth through grace. That is why, even in this matter of the goal towards which we are heading, we must invoke faith again, and believe in our destination because God has told us about it, rather than see and understand it clearly by our own reasoning.

All this can be very disappointing. But here is the supreme test of faith: that we must have faith even in our destination, while we use the means known by faith to arrive there. Actually it must be so, for heaven is not a natural fact about natural happiness. Rather, like the state of grace, which is intimately bound up with the mystery of our sharing the very life of God, heaven is also intimately bound up with the mystery of our sharing the very happiness of God. Heaven is the state of grace come to fruition, the eternal enjoyment of what we already possess.

This fact has been greatly obscured by popular concepts of heaven. One would get the idea that entering heaven involves meeting St. Peter at a pearly gate, presenting the trivial passport of a few good deeds done with Boy Scout regularity and motivation, being issued a white nightgown, a more or less shiny halo and an instrument approximating a harp, and finally finding sitting space on a convenient cloud. In view of such a prospect, it is understandable that we can have popular titles like "Heaven Can

Wait" or mercenary types who say "I'll take my heaven now, you can have yours later!" If heaven held nothing more attractive than harps or halos as indicated above, we could not blame people for not being too interested in getting there, especially while tempted by Miami Beach, Lake Placid or Sun Valley.

The sober fact of faith is simply this: Heaven does not consist in being given a lot of insipid and inane things. Heaven means being happy unendingly and tremendously as God is happy. It means enjoying forever the God we already possess by grace. We are not given anything, except the power to see and enjoy the divine life that already exists in our souls, to the extent that it does exist there. If we could understand so mysterious a thing as our sharing of divine life, we could also understand how marvelous it will be to be happy as God is happy.

At least we can see where the mystery lies, and seeing the mystery clears up a good number of misconceptions. The mystery is the central fact of all theology: divine life in itself and as shared by men. We have already seen something of what is involved by our being in the supernatural order by sanctifying grace. Since this present sharing of divine life is so mysterious, obviously the result of this sharing, participation of God's happiness in the next world, will be even more mysterious. But this much is certain, there can be no happiness in heaven for those who do not possess God by grace at death. Those who die in the state of mortal sin already have the makings of hell—separation from God—in their souls, just as those who die in the state of grace have in their souls the essence of heaven—the possession of God. This explains the constant insistence of the Church on living in the state of grace. This explains too why all the works of the Church are aimed at this: to keep us from sin which is the death of the soul, and to help us grow in grace which is the life of the soul. The total mission of the Church adds up to one thing: helping us get to heaven.

Heaven, then, is essentially mysterious. There is nothing in the world that can faintly be compared to the beauty or the peace or the joy or the happiness that heaven holds. Christ enjoyed on earth the happiness of heaven by His Beatific Vision, but when it came to explaining what heaven is like, words failed. You can understand this difficulty, if you imagine how you would stammer in trying to explain the beauty of a sunset at sea to a blind man who has no idea of color, or sky or sea or sun. Or how could you explain the thrilling majesty of a perfectly executed symphony to a deaf man who has no idea of sound, or range or tone quality or harmony. We are in a very true sense blind and deaf when it comes to supernatural realities. That is why the best revelation we have of heaven is this: "Eye has not seen, nor ear heard, nor has it entered into the heart of man what things God has prepared for those who love him" (I Corinthians, 2:9).

While the inevitable mystery is rather disappointing when we speak of our true home, at least we have this security of knowing that we shall see God in the Beatific Vision. You have read many times the two basic texts from Scripture: "We see now through a glass in a dark manner: but then face to face. Now I know in part: but then I shall know even as I am known" (I Corinthians 13:9–12). "We are now sons of God; and it hath not yet appeared what we shall be. We know that when He shall appear, we shall be like to Him: because we shall see Him as He is" (I John 3:2).

The Church has defined this doctrine contained so clearly in revelation. There had been some controversy in the matter, so in 1336, Pope Benedict XII settled it by defining: "They (souls after death) see the divine Essence with intuitive vision and face to face, no creature acting as a medium by way of object of vision; but the divine Essence shows itself to them directly, nakedly, clearly and plainly, and thus seeing, they enjoy this very divine Essence, and through such vision and fruition the souls of the dead are truly blessed and have life and rest eternal" (Denz. 530).

Immediately following upon this perfect vision of God is a tremendous love, compared to which the loves we have known in human life are cold ashes. So great is this sight of God and the love that follows that the soul needs a special help of God, technically called the 'light of glory,' to buoy it up. You might get the idea of what would happen without it, if you would try to conduct the current from a giant cyclotron through an ordinary table lamp and wire connection. This comparison is nothing compared to the tremendous impact upon a creature who sees the Holy Trinity face-to-face and begins to love in proportion to the infinite beauty of what he sees.

All this is but a shadow of the reality of heaven, of that life everlasting which all but one of the twenty-seven books of the New

Testament explicitly mention. Remember that there is nothing dull, staid and static about heaven. It is life at its fullest, the highest activity of human life geared to a sharing of divine life, with mind and will attuned to the highest object of all knowledge and love. Again, we cannot imagine all that this implies. You can think of all the fleeting moments of your life when you were happy. Whatever made you happy then, was the slightest spark from God whom you will possess fully in heaven. You may remember moments when you were struck with created beauty and grandeur. He who created them, whose beauty and glory they only slightly reflect, is to be your possession in heaven. You may add up all the human happiness and joy that has existed since the beginning of the world, and all that will ever exist, and all together, it cannot begin to equal the happiness and joy of one soul in heaven, any more than the beauty or grandeur of all creatures can begin to compare with the beauty and grandeur of God from Whom they all come.

So you see, we are lost for comparisons. One drop of water cannot adequately explain the breadth of the oceans, nor can one star portray the glory of the sky at night. This is why the best definitions of heaven that we have from the best theologians and philosophers seem empty compared to the reality of what heaven is. For example, St. Thomas said that heaven is "the ultimate perfection of rational or intellectual life" (*Summa Theologica*, I, Q. 62, a. 1). And Boethius defines it as "a state made perfect by the accumulation of all good things" (*De Consolatione Philosophiae*, III, 2). We can perhaps appreciate heaven more by seeing it as the achievement of all we have ever hoped for, and more, the ultimate in peace and security and happiness. In a very homely way, the Gospels have portrayed it for us as a marriage feast, a banquet, a returning home.

There is no reason why the little earthly joys we now experience should be excluded by the celestial joys of Paradise. We learn that even in this life, grace perfects nature. Certainly then, there will be a perfect love of family and friends in heaven, with no threat of separation by death or misunderstandings. There will be the happy associations with Our Blessed Mother and the Saints. None of the boors that spoil social life on earth will be present in heaven to disrupt its harmony. They will have a place of their own. With the resurrection, will come the fullness of joy spreading from soul to body. And here too, there will be no more threat of sickness or pain or death. "Behold the dwelling of God with men, and He will dwell with them, and they will be His people, and God Himself will be with them as their God. And God will wipe away every tear from their eyes, and death shall be no more, neither shall there be mourning, nor crying, nor pain any more, for the former things have passed away. And He who was sitting on the throne said, "Behold, I make all things new" (Apocalypse 21:3–5).

This will be the final victory over death and sin. Some wonder why the blessed in heaven are unable to sin any more. This should be clear from the notion of what heaven is. On earth we possess God by faith and grace. When faith is weak, it is easy to be attracted by the false values of the world as Eve was, and to barter the Creator for the creature. But in heaven, we see God face to face and realize fully his glory. Nothing can begin to compare with Him. It would be as inconceivable for someone in heaven to prefer something to God, as for one of you to trade a new yellow Thunderbird for a worn-out jeep. On earth, we might be compared to some ignorant native on a Pacific island who has only seen a jeep. He has to take someone's word for the fact that there is something better. And so, only knowing something better by faith, the native might be willing to settle for a jeep, rather than wait for a Cadillac. And so often when faith is weak, people on earth barter their priceless possession of God for some cheap trinket. Such is the story of every mortal sin. In heaven, when faith gives way to sight, this will no longer be possible.

Another point of doctrine that many Catholics do not understand is that happiness in heaven differs with each individual. The reason for this is that our share in God's happiness for eternity depends upon our share in his life at the time of death. Now obviously, there is a difference between the sanctifying grace possessed by a great saint, and that possessed by a lukewarm Catholic, or a non-Catholic who did not have the help of the sacraments in building up his life in Christ. The Scriptures indicate this difference of merits very clearly: "In my Father's house there are many mansions" (John 14:2). St. Paul puts it three different ways: "Each shall receive his own reward according to his toil" (I Corinthians

3:8) and "He who sows sparingly shall also reap sparingly" (II Corinthians, 9:6). His clearest expression is this: "The glory of the heavenly is different from that of the earthly. There is the glory of the sun, and the glory of the moon, and the glory of the stars; for star differeth from star in glory. And so it is with the resurrection of the dead" (I Corinthians 15:41–42).

Some wonder how it is possible for the blessed in heaven to have unequal glory, and yet all be perfectly happy. St. Theresa had an apt way of explaining this. She said: "You can fill a thimble and fill a rainbarrel. Both are perfectly full, and yet one holds more than another. The same with the saints in heaven. Those who love God more on earth have a greater capacity for sharing his happiness in heaven. But all the blessed in heaven have all the happiness that they can hold. All are filled to capacity."

If we were press-agents for heaven, as we all should be, we would undoubtedly stress one aspect of its happiness that should impress all earthly dwellers. The happiness of heaven will be eternal and unending. It might help to go back and read the few paragraphs on the eternity of God in Chapter III. This eternity of God is the measure of heaven's eternity, for heaven is the possession of God and the enjoyments of His happiness. If anything mars the enjoyments of earth it is their short duration. You perhaps remember how eagerly you looked forward to Christmas as a child, only to have the day come and go. Before you knew it, you were looking at a very forlorn sight: stripped and faded Christmas trees cast aside in vacant lots. That dismal sight is typical of all earthly joys, which are often better by anticipation than in reality, so short-lived are they. The vacation is just beginning to get enjoyable when it is time to go back to work again. The house is finally paid for in full when the children have grown up and left, leaving it quite empty and barren. A man comes to full achievement of his art, or work, or profession and he dies before he can really sit back and enjoy the fruits of his labor.

The Word of God has summed up this truth in a sentence: "We have not here a lasting city, but we seek one that is to come" (Hebrews 13:14). The earth is truly, at best, "a vale of tears." If anything is disappointing about life here below, it is this transitory nature of even good things. Nothing good endures. It either wears out, or passes, or dies. This can certainly make us appreciate the eternity of heaven. For eternity, in the words of Boethius, "is the perfect and all-at-once possession of life without end" (*De Consolatione Philosophiae*, V, 6). In heaven, the life possessed is the very life of God, the happiness is the very happiness of God, and the duration of all this is forever, with no increase for it is perfect to begin with, and no letup for the God we possess is eternal.

Luther denied our doctrine about the degrees of happiness in heaven, for according to him, all were saved in the same measure and for the same reason—not because of any good works on their part but simply and solely by faith in the merits of Christ. The Church has defined our doctrine explicitly in the Council of Florence, where it declared that those who are received in heaven see the Holy Trinity clearly, "some however more perfectly than others depending upon the diversity of merits" (Denz. 693).

Certainly, here is success worth talking about, worth working for. This is the "pearl of great price" that Our Lord spoke about, this is the "everlasting kingdom" which is our true home. If we cannot say more about it, at least we can be sure of this much on God's own word: that of all the goals a man might strive to reach there is none more perfect, more satisfying, more enduring than heaven. Not only is no other goal comparable to heaven, no other goal is even worth considering, for after trying most of the other goals first, Saint Augustine came to this final conclusion: "Thou hast made us for Thyself, O Lord, and the heart of man cannot rest, until it rests in Thee." This is the reason that we put the R.I.P. after the names of our Christian dead—meaning "Requiescat in Pace"—"May he rest in peace." Such is also the meaning of heaven, the abiding peace of the Church Triumphant after the warfare of the Church Militant in this world.

D. Purgatory

This might be called the half-way house of eternity. It partakes of heaven insofar as the souls in purgatory are happy at the thought of being saved. It likewise resembles hell insofar as the souls in purgatory are suffering for their sins and deprived of the sight of God. But it is unlike both heaven and hell in one important aspect. Purgatory is strictly a temporary state. It will not exist after the general judgment at the end of the world.

What we know of purgatory from the revelation of God and the official teaching of the Church is extremely limited. There has never been any doubt, however, that purgatory does exist. Even before the coming of Christ and His revelation, we find this rather clear statement of the fact in the Old Testament: "It is therefore a holy and wholesome thought to pray for the dead, that they may be loosed from sins" (II Machabees 12:46). Obviously prayer cannot have any meaning in reference to the souls in heaven or the souls in hell. The only souls of the dead that can be helped by prayer are those who are in some intermediate state, not good enough for heaven, not bad enough for hell, still needing to be "loosed from their sins," that they might enter heaven.

Beyond these words of revelation, there has been a general line of reasoning for the existence of purgatory. St. Thomas has summarized it very well, so we shall reproduce his thought as found in one of his works very rarely quoted in these pages:

> There may be some impediment on the part of the good in the way of their souls receiving their final reward in the vision of God immediately upon their departure from the body. To that vision, transcending as it does all natural created capacity, the creature cannot be raised before it is entirely purified: hence it is said that nothing defiled can enter into it (Wisdom 7:25), and that the polluted shall not pass through it (Isaias 35:8). Now the defilement of the soul is by sin, which is an inordinate union with lower things; from which defilement it is purified in this life by penance and other sacraments. Now it sometimes happens that this process of purification is not entirely accomplished in this life and the offender remains still a debtor with a debt of punishment upon him, owing to some negligence or distraction, or to death overtaking him before his debt is paid. Not for this does he deserve to be entirely shut out from reward: because all this may happen without mortal sin, and it is only mortal sin that occasions the loss of charity, to which the reward of life everlasting is due. Such persons, then, must be cleansed in the next life, before entering upon their eternal reward. This cleansing is done by penal works of satisfaction: otherwise the negligent would be better off than the careful, if the penalty that men do not pay here for their sins is not to be undergone by them in the life to come. The souls of the good, then, who have upon them in this world something that needs cleansing, are kept back from their reward, while they endure purgatorial pains. And this is the reason why we posit a purgatory or place of cleansing.[2]

---

2. St. Thomas, *Summa Contra Gentiles*, 4, 91; trans. Rickaby, *Of God and His Creatures*, p. 415.

Our Lord has given us some slight indications that can be interpreted in reference to purgatory. He spoke of some sins that will not be forgiven in this world or in the next (Matthew 12:32), which would seem to indicate that some sins *will* be forgiven in the next world. He said that we would have to given an account of every idle word in the day of judgment (Matthew 12:36) which seems to indicate some place of accounting for venial sins before heaven begins. He says that some sins will be punished with many stripes (of the lash), and some with few (Luke 12:47), which can easily refer to a place of temporary punishment. Moreover, He tells us that this life is the time to work for heaven and to do penance for our sins: "Walk while you have the light" (John 12:35); for, "then night cometh in which no man can work" (John 9:4).

That there has always been in the church a deep realization of what Christ means, can be deduced from the ancient and constant tradition of praying for the dead. The only serious break in this tradition comes with the Protestants who say with Calvin that purgatory is "a pernicious invention of Satan which renders the cross of Christ useless" (*Institutiones* III, 5, No. 6). As far back as the catacombs of the early church, we find inscriptions of prayer for the dead, asking that they may be admitted to peace and refreshment (*pax et refrigerium*). It was in those early days that the custom of anniversary masses for the dead (Months Mind) began. As to the martyrs, no one prayed for them as they were believed to have gone straight to heaven because of the purification of their deaths. Their intercession was asked. This early custom of praying for the dead continues century after century with its obvious implication that the dead may be hastened by prayers through some purgatorial state to heaven. As St. Monica, the mother of the great St. Augustine, lay dying, this was her only wish: "Lay this body anywhere at all; the care of it must not trouble you. This only I ask of you, that you remember me at the altar of God wherever you are" (St. Augustine, *Confessions* 9:11). Obviously, a doctrine as old and venerable as this one which antedates the Christian Era and is even found in the Old Testament cannot truly be called "an invention of the Papists," in late Middle Ages.

This doctrine of the Church on purgatory has been defined by both the Council of Florence and the Council of Trent. We find this statement in the prior Council (1439): "The souls are cleansed by purgatorial pains after death, and in order that they may be rescued from these pains, they are benefited by the suffrages of the living faithful, namely by the sacrifice of the Mass, prayers, alms and other works of piety" (Denz. 693). About a hundred years later, the doctrine was reiterated by the Council of Trent: "The Catholic Church, instructed by the Holy Spirit, has, from the sacred writings and the ancient tradition of the Fathers, taught in sacred councils . . . that there is a purgatory and that the souls detained in it are helped by the suffrages of the faithful and especially by the sacrifice of the Mass" (Denz. 983). There is, therefore, no doubt about our belief in the existence of purgatory. In denying such a place, the Protestants have lost all reason for praying for the dead, and have thereby deprived their dead of this help which is at the same time such a consolation to the living. Moreover, the denial of purgatory leaves a rather serious gap in theology: where to put those souls who at death are not bad enough for hell or yet good enough for heaven?

Once the existence of purgatory is established, the real difficulty for theology is to discuss its nature, duration and location. We almost instinctively call it a place, although we might just as theologically refer to it as a state or situation. There have been innumerable speculations as to the nature and duration of the pains of purgatory, but here we are beyond the strict scope of the Church's teaching which merely says: "The souls are cleansed by purgatorial pains after death."

It is interesting to read the many private revelations and visions that have been granted the saints in this matter, more perhaps than in any other. While these private revelations do not pertain to the general deposit of faith to be believed by all Catholics, still they do give us some leads as to the nature of the pains of purgatory. St. Catherine of Genoa is the most famous name in this regard. She has written that "this sense of the grievousness of being kept from beholding the Divine Light, coupled with that instinctive longing which would wish to be without hindrance to follow the enticing look of God—these things, I say, make up the pains of the souls in purgatory." This description seems to parallel what we speak of as the 'sense of loss' in hell. There is some distinction to be made, however.

The pain of purgatory can best be described as a pain of love.

Love seeks union. It is those who love most deeply who suffer most when separated. Witness the grief that attends the separation of husbands and wives, parents and children, when separated by disaster, war or death. While they know that they will see each other again, and are consoled by the thought of reunion, the present separation causes them untold mental anguish and homesickness. It may be difficult to transfer this idea to purgatory, since our love of God is burdened by so many earthly distractions in this life. Yet the great saints tell us that only pure love of God will usher us into heaven. They insist that for those trying to be saints, and this is the calling of all Christians, even in this life our love of God should lead us along a purgative, illuminative and unitive way to God. This means that our love must be purged of the attachments that draw us away from God, enlightened by prayer and grace to know him better, and finally joined to Him above all else.

Now we know that love of God on earth hardly gets started along this path in many people's lives. And yet, without the love of God at least to the degree of dying in His friendship and grace we cannot even enter purgatory. Hence, either in this life or in the next, our love of God must be purified of the things that tarnish and disfigure it. We must completely break with all that is not of God either in this life or in purgatory.

Imagine that you have died, and all the distractions of this life have slipped away. There comes that tremendous realization that God is the answer to all your dreams of happiness. There comes the overpowering urge to possess Him fully, the heart-filling realization that you have been saved, that you do love God, however unworthily. All the earthly distractions that keep you from possessing God fully during life have now passed away. Now all that keeps you from Him is the unworthiness of your love, the horde of little sins that have betrayed it during life, the temporal punishment for serious sins yet unatoned for by penance and good works. What the fire of divine love burned out in the soul of the martyr, purgatory must purify in your soul. The more deeply divine love has been tarnished by attachments to things not of God, the more wide is the barrier between you and God, the more intensely must you suffer before heaven is yours.

So it is, the saints tell us, that the souls of the just willingly cast themselves into the pains of purgatory as the only means of attaining what they so vehemently desire. They are happy at the thought of being saved, and yet tortured by the separation from God which their own sins have occasioned.

It is a rather common belief that there exists in purgatory a material purgatorial fire, analogous to the fire of hell. While the Church has issued no definition of faith in this matter, many theologians argue from the famous passage of St. Paul: "Foundation can no man lay other than that which is (already) laid, which is Jesus Christ. But if a man build upon the foundation whether it be gold, silver, precious stones, wood, grass or straw—the work of each man shall become manifest. For the Day shall declare it, because that day is to be disclosed in fire, and the worth of each man's work shall that fire assay. If any man's work abide, which he hath built thereupon, he shall receive reward. If any man's work be burnt up, he shall lose his reward, but himself shall be saved, yet (as one who has passed) through fire" (I Corinthians 3, 12–15).

In any event, all are agreed that the time to progress in the love of God, the time to atone for sin, is during this life. Imperfections in our love and atonement are somehow obliterated in purgatory, but at the cost of great suffering in purgatory where St. Thomas believes that the slightest suffering is worse than all the sufferings of this life (St. Thomas, *Commentarium in Sententiis Petri Lombardi*, IV, D. 21, Q. 1, A. 1). You recall Our Lord's advice to work while it is still day because the night is coming in which no man can work (John 9:4).

We should not leave our considerations of purgatory without recalling the Catholic belief that the souls in purgatory can be helped effectively by us, whereas they can do nothing for themselves but suffer. The Church has defined that the souls in purgatory are especially helped by the Sacrifice of the Mass. When the Bishop ordains a priest he gives him the power to offer the Holy Sacrifice "for the living and the dead." The whole month of November is dedicated to prayer for the Poor Souls, and on All Souls Day the priests are authorized to offer three Masses, to highlight the needs of the suffering souls. Here is one of the practical conclusions of the Communion of Saints: that even after death we will be helped by the Masses, prayers and good works of the faithful on earth, and that we now can help those who have died. Catholics who are thoughtful and generous now in helping the souls in purgatory can

be sure of obtaining help themselves when they are in purgatory
for Our Lord has said: "Blessed are the merciful, for they shall obtain mercy" (Matthew 5:7).

E. Hell

This is undoubtedly the most unpleasant topic in all of theology.
We cannot avoid reality, however, even though it is unpleasant.
Many people who like to formulate their own dogma and morals
abhor the thought of hell, but we who profess Faith in Christ must
accept His word on all things. We may not pick and choose to fit
our likes. We must take both sides of the picture. There is a reality
called light, but also one called darkness. Virtue exists, but so also
does vice. We profess an eternal reward for those who choose to be
friends of God, and an eternal punishment for those who die reject-
ing God.

This is a hard saying, but it is Christ Himself who said it. "All
nations shall be gathered together before him, and he shall separate
them one from another. . . . Those on the right shall receive eternal bliss in the kingdom of the Father, those on the left shall hear:
Depart from me, you cursed, into everlasting fire, which was prepared for the devil and his angels. And these shall go into everlasting punishment, but the just into life everlasting" (Matthew 25:32,
33, 41, 46). There are even many Christian religions today which
have rejected this doctrine. How they can do this is hard to say, for
there is perhaps no other doctrine in the Christian religion more
explicitly and continuously reiterated in the New Testament.

Back in the earliest days of the Church, St. Ignatius of Antioch
wrote the following words to his Christians at Ephesus while he was
on his way to martyrdom under Trajan: "Do not err, my brethren;
. . . if any man by false teaching corrupt the faith of God, such a
one shall go in his foulness to the unquenchable fire, as also shall he
who listens to him" (*Epistola ad Epheseos*, 16:2). Perhaps the reason why people find it so hard to believe in hell is that they wish to
quiet their consciences by denying that there is any foundation to
the inner warning against evil ways. It is not the good people who
generally reject hell.

Perhaps too, some find it difficult to accept hell, because during
this life, we are accustomed to experience the never-ending mercy
of God. But then, God is perfect in all His ways, in His work of

heaven as well as in His work of hell. God is completely perfect, and that involves being perfectly just as well as perfectly merciful. It is good that He is predominantly merciful to us during this life, since this is the time of trial. But as we have seen, He has given us ample warning that there will be an end to the time of trial, a judgment upon our lives, a finality of reward or punishment on the last day. St. John Chrysostom summed up the matter for the world of his day: "All of us—Greeks and Jews, heretics and Christians—acknowledge that God is just. Now many who sinned have passed away without being punished, while many others, who led virtuous lives, did not die until they had suffered innumerable tribulations. If God is just, how will he reward the latter and punish the former, unless there be a hell and a resurrection" (*Homilia In Epistolam ad Philemonen,* 6:6).

Early in the Church's history, the doctrine on hell was stated briefly in the Athanasian Creed: "Those who do evil will go into eternal fire." About eight hundred years later we hear this echo of the doctrine in the Fourth Lateran Council: In the end "all will receive according to their works, whether they were good or bad, the evil will receive perpetual punishment with the devil, the good will receive eternal glory with Christ" (Denz. 429).

Once the existence of hell is established, the next step is to determine, as well as possible, just what hell is like. While the Church has made no solemn definitions on the nature of the punishments, there are sufficient indications in Holy Scripture and Tradition to establish a clear picture of the Catholic Faith which has always been held in this matter.

Hell is the bitter fruit of sin. There is a twofold pain in hell because of the twofold nature of sin. Every sin is primarily a turning away from God. Hell makes this action definitive, for the greatest punishment of hell is the pain of loss, the privation of the sight of God. Secondly, sin involves a turning to creatures instead of God, a preferral of some created good in the place of God, and in hell there is also a pain of sense, a torture inflicted by some created thing called fire. Our Lord's words in judgment, "Depart from me you cursed," will indicate the pain of loss, while the pain of sense will be shown in the words "into everlasting fire."

It is difficult for us to imagine the depth of pain that is involved in this eternal loss of God, just as it is hard for us to realize how the possession of God in heaven makes for unspeakable happiness. Once more, we are hindered by the many distractions of earth from realizing what it means to lose God forever. Two modern writers have captured a bit of the atmosphere that is the necessary setting for what we must consider here. It is the moment of leaving life.

> The agents of hell disappear, the human, they shrink and dissolve
> Into dust on the wind, forgotten, unmemorable; only is here
> The white flat face of Death, God's silent servant,
> And behind the face of Death the judgment
> And behind the Judgment the Void, more horrid than the active
>   shapes of hell;
> Emptiness, absence, separation from God;
> The horror of the effortless journey, to the empty land
> Which is no land, only emptiness, absence, the Void
> Where those who were men no longer turn the mind
> To distraction, delusion, escape into dream, pretense,
> Where the soul is no longer deceived, for there are no objects, no
>   tones,
> No colours, no forms to distract, to divert the soul
> From seeing itself, foully united forever, nothing with nothing
> Not what we call death, but what beyond death is not death
> We fear, we fear. Who shall then plead for me,
> Who intercede for me, in my most need? [3]

For the soul that has died in mortal sin, there is no more room for intercession, for mercy, for penance or pardon. The die has been cast, the fatal decision has been made, eternity will witness the horrible choice of self over God, only eternity is long enough to proclaim the horror of sin, the refusal to accept the saving grace of Calvary, the preference of inane, fleeting earthly goods to the all-wonderful timeless God. In hell, the emptiness of the choice, the necessity of living with it forever, the utter and complete failure in the one important matter of life will be the deepest torture. Our Lord spoke of it in this way upon referring to Judas: "It would have been better for him, if that man had never been born" (Matthew, 26:24).

George Macdonald has also caught a true picture of the misery involved in the pain of loss:

---

3. T. S. Eliot, *Murder in the Cathedral*, p. 69, Harcourt, Brace & Co., New York, 1935.

I think I have seen from afar something of the final prison of all, the innermost cell of the debtor of the universe. . . . It is the vast outside; the ghastly dark beyond the gates of the city of which God is the light—where the evil dogs go raging, silent as the dark, for there is no sound any more than sight. The time of signs is over. Every sense has had its signs, and they were all misused; there is no sense, no sign any more—nothing now by means of which to believe. The man wakes from the final struggle of death, in absolute loneliness—such a loneliness as in the most miserable moment of deserted childhood he never knew. Not a hint, not a shadow of anything outside his consciousness reaches him. . . . Soon misery will beget on imagination a thousand shapes of woe, which he will not be able to rule, direct, or even distinguish from real presences.[4]

If utter loneliness were all there were, it would be bad enough, but here being without God means being without the one eternal reality that can spell happiness, success, security, or fruition in life. One who dies in mortal sin dies of his own choice without God, and thus he must live, meaninglessly for all eternity, faced with a failure that can never be corrected or undone. You have seen how discouraging it can be to work on a job which seems to be getting you nowhere. Such is the horror of the pain of loss, spending an eternity getting nowhere, never a hope of a better day, never a dream of a homecoming.

A modern theologian, J. P. Arendzen, has compared this state to a man who is slowly dying of thirst at sea. What he craves with all the fervor of his being is water. It is all about him, miles deep under him, but he cannot drink any of it, and he will shrivel up and die without it. God is the driving need of every soul in hell, and while God is everywhere, each lost soul has wilfully put God out of his life and is in agony without Him.

Think of the agony of a man with his arm out of joint. In hell, the whole life and being of a man is out of joint. The lost soul is eternally on the outside of God's blessed Kingdom, looking in, realizing that he passed up hundreds and thousands of chances to enter, remembering how he hardened his soul against God who endured agonies Himself to entice him into the Kingdom. Is not this thought the "worm that dieth not" of which Our Lord spoke,

---

4. C. S. Lewis, *George Macdonald, an Anthology*, p. 59, New York, Macmillan, 1947.

the biting, tearing, soul-agonizing remorse that leads to hatred of God instead of repentance, for there is no more chance of possessing God, no slightest hope of even the few crumbs of pleasure that people substitute for God on earth, nothing now but the deepest pain at having lost God who is our all and losing all in losing Him.

Here is truly utter despair. Here is the only final failure, for failures on earth can always be rectified somehow. But this loss is really infinite and eternal, infinite because it is the loss of the Infinite Good who is God, eternal because as far ahead as the imagination can reach, it still spells nothing but a complete and irrevocable lack of all that is worth having, a sole possession of the nothingness of self which has chosen to be empty and stripped of God. And the empty self is a torture of itself, like a starving man who eternally is reaching for food that is real but cannot be grasped. And so the agony of the pain of loss goes on, and on, and on, forever.

But this is not all. It may seem that the pain of loss is sufficient suffering for sin, but sin means more than the rejection of God. Positively, sin involves the wilful choosing of some created good instead of God. And so in hell, beyond the negative pain of loss stemming from the absence of God within the soul, there is the positive pain of sense caused by some ever-present created force, existing outside the soul to torture it. The sinner has deliberately chosen some created thing instead of God. For all eternity, he will have a created thing called hell fire, not merely in his mind, or in his stomach or in his arms, but penetrating all the inner recesses of his being.

Again you may say, "this is too much." But again, we must say, this is no fabrication of the Church, nor of medieval theologians. The same merciful Christ who canonized the repentant thief on the cross, who thoughtfully forgave the adulterous woman and the profligate Magdalen, this same Christ spoke again and again of hell as the "unquenchable fire" (Mark 9:44), as the "furnace of fire" (Matthew 13:42 and 50), and as the place "where the worm dieth not and the fire is not extinguished" (Mark 9:43 and 45). The latter two expressions are both repeated twice for emphasis within the same chapter.

You cannot read the words of Christ in the New Testament and escape this insistence on hell as a place of torture by fire. Indeed it is mentioned no less than thirty times. It is no empty figure of speech. While we have to admit that fire in hell is not precisely the same as fire on earth, the pain suffered by burning on earth offered God the best description of what is suffered by the damned in hell. But fire in hell is worse, for it burns without destroying and it sears even the fallen spirits and the souls of the damned before the resurrection, and it is not limited to one place as the devils are in torture even while they tempt us on earth.

Just as all the created universe gives glory to God, and is used by Christ to be a means of grace in the sacraments, so for those who abuse the created good things of God during life, one of his creatures, the fire in hell, serves for their punishment in the next life. This horrifying creature is theirs forever, theirs in the very depths of their spirit. And it is a great grace of God that man who is drawn away from God by so many material temptations during life, should also have this thought of hell fire to win him by fear at least, if he will not respond to the love of God. Many have been drawn from attachments to sinful pleasures in this life by the thought of the torture that awaits body and soul in hell for those who misuse God's creatures in this life. Materialists may have difficulty in comprehending the pain of loss, but they do know what it means to suffer by burning. Knowing that this pain, however great, is only secondary to the pain of loss, may more effectively draw them from sin. Even the great St. Teresa of Avila was brought to her senses by a vision of the place in hell reserved for her if she did not mend her ways.

There are two final characteristics of the pains of hell that the Church insists upon in her definitions. The first is the eternal nature of the punishment. The Athanasian Creed, as we have seen, calls it *eternal* fire, and the Fourth Lateran Council, *perpetual* punishment. These are merely repeating the words of Christ's revelation, wherein He often contrasts the duration of hell to the duration of heaven, using the same adjective for both. This is a stumbling block for many today who indulge in wishful thinking that there will always be another chance even in hell. Many outside the Church who have rejected our doctrine on purgatory, make a kind of purgatory out of hell. Mohammedanism with its popular appeal says that heaven is eternal but hell only temporary (*Time*, 54:1, July 4, 1949, p. 19). This makes a mockery out of the words of Christ. The Catholic doctrine has been succinctly expressed by St.

Gregory the Great: Hell is "death without death, the end without an end, failure without fail, because death lives on, and the end is always beginning, and the failure knows no failing" (*Moralia,* 9:66).

The second characteristic is the fact that there are different degrees of suffering in hell, according to guilt. The Council of Florence (1439) states that those who die in mortal sin descend forthwith into hell where they are punished with unequal pains (Denz. 693). This doctrine parallels the degrees of happiness in heaven. Obviously, different men in life reject God to a different degree, and are attached to creatures in a greater or less degree. Our Lord said that it would go worse on the day of judgment for the inhabitants of Corozain and Bethsaida than for the people of Tyre and Sidon, for the former were obstinate in the evil and had the vision of Christ's miracles besides. We can see a germ of truth in the imaginary punishments meted out for different crimes in Dante's *Inferno.* Certainly, the more a man has rejected God and asserted himself against God, the greater will be his pain of loss. And the more he has abused creatures, the more deeply will he be penetrated by hell fire.

We began this subject by saying that it was unpleasant. Like all the other doctrines of Christ and His Church, it can be helpful in promoting our eternal salvation. Certainly God would not have revealed this horror, unless He wanted us to accept or reject Him and His salvation with our eyes wide open.

When speaking of preparations for the 1950 Holy Year, Pius XII made a special plea to Pastors to preach on hell fire. "It is sorrowful to see so many today—among them many Catholics—living as though their only aim is to form heaven on earth, without any thought of the beyond and of eternity. Propaganda for an earthly life without God is open, seductive and continuous. Often God is not denied. He is not cursed. He is as though absent. With reason it has been observed that even in films considered morally without reproach, men live and die as though there were no God, nor redemption, nor church. There is added deliberate ominous propaganda for the formation of a godless family, society and state.

"There is, therefore, no time to be lost in halting with all our forces the slipping of our ranks into irreligiousness and to awaken the spirit with prayer and penance. Preaching of the first truths of faith is more than ever urgent, and so is the preaching of hell. Without doubt such a subject must be handled with dignity and wisdom. It is true that desire for heaven is a motive in itself more perfect than fear. But from that it does not follow that it is for all men the most effective means of holding them far from sin and converting them to God" (Associated Press, Vatican City, March 23, 1949).

Let no one imagine that a man wakes up surprised at death to find himself in hell. No one is in hell but those who have deliberately asked for hell. And everyone in hell has passed up innumerable graces that would have kept him from going there. As we have already seen, this very thought of rejected graces is part of the horror of hell. Rather than say more about it, it is better to stop here with the salutary advice of St. John Chrysostom: "Do not inquire where hell is, but how to escape it" (*Homilia in Epistolam ad Romanos*, 31:5). That is the burden of the Catholic Religion: not to live in fear of hell, but in seeking heaven.

Thus ends our first section on the end of each particular man. Now that we have traced the steps through death, the particular judgment, heaven, purgatory and hell, we pass to the final section of this book, to consider the end of the world and of all humanity on earth.

II. The End of the World and of Humanity on Earth

In contrast to God's plan for the end of each particular man, there is a complementary plan for the end of the world and of humanity in general. This second plan highlights the social nature of man on earth, and the corporate being of Christ's Mystical Body, the Kingdom of God begun on earth and consummated in heaven. St. Thomas says that as God created all things and set the world in being, he too will consummate the final ending of the world and mankind as we know it (*Supplementum*, Q. 47, A 1).

A. The Last Day

There is no mystery about the fact that there will come a last day, called so often 'the day of the Lord,' but just precisely when it will occur is more of a mystery than the last day of each particular man, because of the larger time element involved. There is also much mystery about what will take place on the last day, although most theologians derive from divine revelation this order of events: the last day preceded by some signs, the resurrection of the bodies of all mankind, and the final or general judgment of all men. This will be the end of the world as we know it.

We should not conclude from the signs connected with the last day that anyone wil have certain knowledge of the event before it happens. As a matter of fact, men have been predicting the end of the world as far back as apostolic times. All such prognostications which have persisted even in our day must however be regarded with suspicion. Leo X in the Fifth Lateran Council (1512–1517) forbade anyone to pretend to certain knowledge regarding the end of the world. He condemns such conjecture as false. The signs which are contained in Holy Scripture are themselves shrouded in mystery since we are told nothing of their duration or the interval between them. There is further confusion from the fact that Our Lord gave at the same time with the revelation of the last day, certain signs referring to the imminent destruction of Jersusalem.

These are, in general, scriptural signs that are to precede the last day and the second coming of Christ. The first sign which is probably most certain indicates that the coming of the Lord will be sudden and unexpected: "As the lightning cometh out of the east, and appeareth even into the west, so shall also the coming of the Son of Man be" (Matthew 24:27). This sudden coming will be accompanied with great disturbance of nature: "But the day of the Lord shall come as a thief, in which the heavens shall pass away with great violence, and the elements shall be melted with heat, and the earth and works which are in it shall be burnt up" (II Peter 3:10). All these disturbances are to usher in the magnificent appearance of Christ in glory which He foretold to the High Priest when He was on trial.

The Church records a parallel passage in the Gospel for the last Sunday of the Liturgical Year: "And immediately after the tribulation of those days, the sun shall be darkened, and the moon shall not give her light, and the stars will fall from the heaven, and the powers of heaven shall be moved: and then shall appear the sign of the Son of man in heaven, and then shall all tribes of the earth mourn: and they shall see the Son of man coming in the clouds of heaven with much power and majesty" (Matthew 24:29). Perhaps this much should be most insisted upon: that Our Lord will come quickly, unexpectedly and with much majesty and glory, in contrast to his first humble coming amid angel song and a bright star at Bethlehem.

There are other signs that are more mysterious, or at least, harder to locate and place in sequence of time. Our Lord indicated that the Gospel would be preached to the whole world before the consummation (Matthew 24:14). Some find in the famous text of St. Paul to the Romans (11:25–31) a prediction that the Jews will be converted to Christ before the end, but this is not an article of faith. There seems to be indicated as well, a great apostasy of Christian nations, possibly led by the antichrist. There has been much speculation as to whether the antichrist designates a particular person or an anti-christian way of life (such as communism). The many scriptural indications in St. Paul and St. John seem more in favor of a person, the antithesis of the Saviour. If you care to, you can read more about this in the article entitled "Antichrist" in the Catholic Encyclopedia (Vol. 1, pp. 559–562).

The final word in this matter is to remember that Our Lord, as Man, refused to reveal the time of the last day: "But of that day and hour no one knoweth, no not the angels of heaven but the Father alone" (Matthew 24:36). And just as all men must be ready individually for the uncertain hour of death, so he wishes the Church to be always prepared and expectant for the triumphant day of the Lord. "Watch therefore, for you do not know at what hour your Lord is to come. . . . Therefore you must be ready, because at an hour that you do not expect, the Son of Man will come" (Matthew 24:42 and 44).

B. *The Resurrection of the Body*

These are words that you have said from your earliest years as you finished reciting the Apostles' Creed: "I believe . . . in the resurrection of the body and life everlasting." Most Catholics may be a little distracted when they get to the end of the creed, with the result that they affirm this doctrine many times over without realizing how great a part of it plays in God's plan for mankind. This is the doctrine that brings us back to Genesis and God's original plan for the glorification of His special creation on earth. The resurrection is the fulfillment of God's promise to restore mankind. Christ Our Saviour is victorious in the soul's Baptismal

birth to eternal life, but His victory only comes to its fullest fruition in the ultimate glorification of man's body in the resurrection. Here is where we fully partake in the Victory of our Risen
Saviour, when He finally makes all things new.

Like most other dogmas, it is easy to take the resurrection for
granted, even though many pagans and many non-Catholics have
not even heard of this future grandeur, and consequently do not
have this hope. If you look back in the history of Christianity, you
will find that it is especially those people who despise the body and
the things of the body who have explicitly denied this belief.
Some followed the Platonic view of the body as the prison house
of the soul, some like the ancient Manichaeans and the medieval
Albigensians looked upon the body as evil, a creation of the devil.
Of course, they would not profess the glorious resurrection of the
body on the last day. We, however, cannot despise anything that
God made. The body is an integral part of His plan, and He has
especially consecrated the human body by becoming man. His
body rose gloriously from the dead to partake in the bliss of eternal
life, and so will ours.

Unlike most Christian dogmas, the resurrection is quite clearly
indicated in the Old Testament. The most outstanding text is
from Job: "Who will grant me that my words may be written?
Who will grant me that they may be marked down in a book with
an iron pen and in a plate of lead, or else be graven with an instrument in flint stone? For I know my Redeemer liveth and in the last
day I shall rise out of the earth and I shall be clothed again with
my skin, and in my flesh shall see my God, whom I myself shall see,
see, and my eyes shall behold and not another: this my hope is laid
up in my heart" (Job 19:23–27). There are other indications which
you can read in Isaias (26:19–21), Daniel (12:2) and in the second
book of Machabees (7:9, 13, 23 and 46).

We can get an idea of the special importance that Christ Our
Lord placed on this doctrine if we view briefly four passages in
which He revealed it to us. One day the Sadducees who
denied the resurrection came to Our Lord with a problem that
was typical of their materialistic way of arguing with Him. They
spoke of a woman who had married seven men, each of whom
died successively. They wanted to know whose wife she would be
if there were a resurrection. The answer of Our Lord would fit

any objection to his revelation of the truth of the resurrection: "You err, not knowing the Scriptures nor the power of God. For in the resurrection they shall neither marry nor be married, but shall be as the angels of God in heaven" (Matthew 22:29–30).

At the death of Lazarus, his sister Martha remarked to Our Lord at the tomb, "I know that he shall rise again in the resurrection at the last day." And before Christ brought Lazarus back from the dead as a sign of what was to occur for all of us on the last day He said: "I am the resurrection and the life. He that believeth in me, although he be dead shall live. And everyone that liveth and believeth in me shall not die for ever" (John 11:24–26).

On another occasion, when the Jews at the pool of Bethsaida were in astonishment at Christ's healing the man who had been ill for thirty-eight years, Our Lord answered them: "Wonder not at this, for the hour cometh wherein all that are in the graves shall hear the voice of the Son of God. And they that have done good things shall come forth unto the resurrection of life; but they that have done evil, unto the resurrection of judgment" (John 5:28–29).

The last passage which has always been a subject of meditation for Catholics connects the resurrection of the Body with the reception of Holy Communion. The Body of Christ so sanctifies our bodies which have already been made Temples of the Holy Spirit at Baptism, that the resurrection is most fitting in God's plan for the final glorification of our bodies. The occasion for Our Lord's word on this subject is his famous discourse after the multiplication of the loaves. He promises a bread, even better than the manna from heaven. He himself is the bread of life coming down from heaven to give life to the world. "Because I came down from heaven, not to do my own will, but the will of Him that sent me. Now this is the will of the Father who sent me: that of all that he hath given me, I should lose nothing, but should raise it up again in the last day. And this is the will of my Father that sent me that everyone who seeth the Son, and believeth in Him, may have everlasting life, and I will raise him up in the last day. . . . I am the living bread which came down from heaven. If any man eat of this bread he shall live forever; and the bread that I will give is my flesh for the life of the world" (John 6:38–40; 51–52).

If you take these passages from Our Lord's teaching in their obvious sense, He means that all of us will be reconstituted in the union of body and soul that we now have, and added to this will be the glory of eternal life. He has of course made this even more obvious by His own resurrection, wherein His dead body was reunited to His living soul to share its glorified life. For St. Paul, the whole matter of our resurrection hinges upon Christ's resurrection. His teaching in this matter is so famous that we shall cite it at some length.

"Now if Christ is preached as risen from the dead, how do some among you say that there is no resurrection of the dead? But if there is no resurrection of the dead, neither has Christ risen; and if Christ has not risen, vain then is our preaching, vain too is your faith. Yes, and we are found false witnesses as to God, in that we have borne witness against God that He raised Christ—whom He did not raise, if the dead do not rise; and if Christ has not risen, vain is your faith, for you are still in your sins. Hence they also who have fallen asleep in Christ have perished. If with this life only in view we have had hope in Christ, we are of all men the most to be pitied. But as it is, Christ has risen from the dead, the first fruits of those who have fallen asleep. For since by a man came death, by a man also comes resurrection of the dead. For as in Adam all die, so in Christ all will be made to live" (I Corinthians 15:12–22).

St. Thomas draws together in a few summary words, the basic theological argument that underlies these words of St. Paul. "The gift of Christ is greater than the sin of Adam, as is clear from the fifth chapter of the Epistle to Romans (this is the basic text we used in the Chapter on Original Sin). But death was introduced by sin, for if there had been no sin, there would have been no death. Therefore, by the gift of Christ, man shall be restored again from death to life. Furthermore, the members of Christ's mystical body ought to be conformable to the Head. But our Head lives and shall forever live in body and soul, because 'Christ rising from the dead dieth now no more' (Romans 6:9). Therefore men also, who are His members, shall live in body and soul. And so there must be a resurrection of the flesh" (St. Thomas, *Supplementum*, Q. 75, c.).

St. Thomas does not infer from this argument and its conclusion a real necessity of the resurrection, since like all the other supernatural gifts given to man, the resurrection is freely given by the Goodness of God without any merit or demand on our part. But he does conclude that it would be very fitting that we who are likened to Christ as members of His Church during life, should also be likened to His glory after death.

Such has been the traditional teaching of the Church from the beginning. We have already noted that it was contained in the earliest Apostles' Creed. It is also found explicitly in the Nicene Creed, which we recite in the Mass: "And I await the resurrection of the dead" (Denz. 86). The Athanasian Creed of the fourth or fifth century adds: "At whose (Christ's) coming, all men are to rise again with their own bodies" (Denz. 40). It would take a book in itself to recount the many passages of the Fathers that explain the Catholic belief in the resurrection. So strong has been this belief from the earliest days of the Church, that there has been little development of the dogma, beyond some theological speculation as to how the body arises. The fact of the resurrection is incontestable as far as revelation goes.

The Church has always insisted on the *universality* of the resurrection. As is proclaimed in the Fourth Council of the Lateran: "*All* men shall rise again with their own bodies, which they now have, to receive according to their deeds" (Dez. 429). Our Lord made this very specific when He spoke of some coming forth unto a resurrection of life, and others unto a resurrection of judgment (John 5:29). Certainly if it is fitting that the bodies of the just, which have undergone so much to achieve salvation, share in the glory of the soul, it is also fitting that the bodies of the damned which have contributed to their damnation should also share the shame and punishment of the lost souls.

It is among the unique privileges of the Mother of God that her body has already been assumed into heaven to share in the glorious beauty and joy of her soul. Certainly, the body which nourished the Son of God should never go into earthly corruption. Pope Pius XII, on November 1, 1950, fulfilled the fond hope of all Christendom by solemnly defining this doctrine as a dogma of the Church.

We can derive yet one more point from the data of revelation on the resurrection. It is obvious that our own bodies will arise, for this is a resurrection, not the assumption of a new body. As the Fourth Lateran Council phrases it above, we will rise with the bodies which we now have on earth. Most of the difficulties that have been proposed against the resurrection are based on this matter of *identity*. But then, we must not take this matter of identity in so strict a sense that it becomes ridiculous. After all, we are not at all certain as to what establishes our total identity in this life. We do know from metabolism that the actual matter of our bodies changes every seven years or so. And yet we persist in being the same individuals we were decades ago. Certainly, no matter how the basic elements of our body change, we do recognize a substantial identity of bodily, emotional and spiritual life during these years. The Church indicates that this total vital identity will be renewed in the resurrection.

After all, if God originally made all the basic elements from nothing, He will in His omnipotence have no difficulty in resurrecting us in the future life with elements that establish our complete identity of these years on earth. We will be recognizable as what we were. Much more could be said about this. Theologians have speculated at great lengths on the subject in recent years. But when all is said and done, we can derive our maximum belief in the face of all objections from the words of Christ to the Sadducees, and to all others who reject this doctrine: "You err, not knowing the Scriptures nor the power of God" (Matthew 22:30).

Our final consideration has to do with the *nature* and *qualities* of the risen body. Here we depart from the teaching of faith and enter the realm of speculation. About all we can derive from revelation is contained in the words of St. Paul: "What is sown in corruption rises in incorruption; what is sown in dishonor rises in glory; what is sown in weakness rises in power; what is sown a natural body rises a spiritual body . . . the first man was of the earth, earthy; the second man is from heaven, heavenly" (I Corinthians 15:42–44 and 47). All of which means that we will have a true body in the resurrection, but it will in some sense be spiritualized.

We can find the basis for such theological speculation in these words of St. Paul. Perhaps we should begin with a distinction. Some qualities of the risen bodies are common both to the just and unjust, such as immortality and integrity. But in the case of the just *immortality* will be a cause of untold joy, with none of the sorrows that go with the body in this life, whereas in the case of the unjust, immortality will be a token of endless suffering. As to integrity, we mean that all will have a body of mature development, not a child's body or that of an old man or with crippled members. No one will be blind, or lame or tongue-tied in the next world.

We must also add that this integrity of body requires that there be a distinction of sexes in the next world, even though there will no longer be need for the propagation of the species. The same can be said of the nutritive faculties. They will be present but there will be no need of them: no hunger, no thirst, no drowsiness, but here too, the integrity of the body will be an increased cause of joy for the blessed and an occasion of greater pain for the damned. Certainly different things will strike the eyes and ears in heaven and in hell.

Then there are finally those qualities which pertain only to the glorified bodies of those in heaven, not to those of the damned in hell. In general theologians in their speculations mention four basic qualities of the glorified bodies: Impassibility, Clarity, Agility and Subtlety. These words may sound strange, since they are transliterations of technical theological terms. We are mainly interested in what they mean.

Impassibility is the fulfillment of one of the preternatural gifts given to Adam. In the resurrection, it means that the body is freed from the forces of corruption, waste, change and wear. What cannot hurt the soul can also no longer affect the body. Here is the true foundation of perpetual youth. This gives also an indication of what Christ meant when He said that we would be "like the angels." When what is sown in corruption rises in incorruption, then "God shall wipe away every tear from their eyes, and death shall be no more, neither shall mourning or wailing or pain be any more, because the first things are passed away" (Apocalypse 21:4).

Clarity indicates that the glory and beauty of the beatified soul shines through the body, as happened to Christ at the Transfiguration when the Apostles were unable to even look at Him so splendid was the sight. This is the fulfillment of the promise of Our Lord: "Then shall the just shine as the sun in the kingdom of their Father" (Matthew 13:43). The beauty of the soul that is in the state of grace must be taken on faith in this life. In the next world, we shall see what true beauty is, when it transfigures the bodies of the just in proportion to their possession of the life of God. "What is sown in dishonor, rises in glory."

Agility designates the manner in which the risen body overcomes the inertness that characterizes our bodies in this life. Theologians speculate that the body will be so perfectly attuned to the life of the soul that the glorified body will be able to pass to the uttermost ends of the universe with the speed of thought. "What is sown in weakness rises in power."

Subtlety is an elaboration of the final expression of St. Paul that what is sown a natural body will rise a spiritual body. We do not know just exactly what this means, but can gain some indication from the preternatural gifts of Adam. Just as God divinized the soul of man by grace which grants a share in divine life, so the preternatural gifts involved a spiritualizing of man's body to some extent, as we saw in the tract on Original Sin. Now that these gifts were lost, man's soul has a difficult time dominating the body in this life.

In the resurrection, God's plan for the more complete perfection of man's nature will be restored. This does not involve a suppression of man's body, but a greater domination of soul over body, so that the body becomes the perfect instrument of the soul, and not its antagonist as so often happens in this life. There will be no more concupiscence or insistence on the urges of the body. This will make for a deeper unity of human nature, a greater perfection of the total man as originally conceived by God in creation. In fact, man will be altogether better off in eternity than Adam was with his preternatural gifts in the Garden of Eden.

Thus is the perfect victory of the Risen Christ achieved. Once more, as St. Paul has beautifully expressed it: "for the trumpet shall sound, and the dead shall rise again incorruptible. And we shall be changed. For this corruptible (body) must put on incorruption, and this mortal (body) must put on immortality. And when this mortal (body) has put on immortality, then shall come to pass the saying that is written: Death is swallowed up in victory. O death, where is thy victory? O death, where is thy sting?" (I Corinthians 15:52–55). It is fitting that these words are chanted in the Liturgy for Holy Saturday when we commemorate the victory of Christ over sin and death, the cause and pledge of our own final victory in Christ. Such is the glory of the Christian faith and hope in the Resurrection of the body.

C. The Final or General Judgment

This is the third and final act in the great drama that is to bring all mankind together for a final reckoning at the end of time. It will be the climax of human history in which the hopes of the Old Testament and the achievements of the New Testament will be manifest to all men. We have already seen the stages of preparation that will herald the second coming of Christ, the central person of all history. The first time He came in humility as the Saviour of all mankind. This time, He will come in power and glory as the Judge of the living and the dead.

There will be a tremendous setting for the drama with a gathering of all the millions of people who have ever lived on earth. It will be the last time that all of them will be together, the last moment that the faithful will be misunderstood and the evil man condoned, for now, the rich pattern of God's plan for mankind will be manifest. The plan of God's providence, and mercy and wisdom will shine throughout the whole course of human ways. All will see the mystery of evil that seemingly went unpunished and good that was scorned and penalized. There will finally be an end to misunderstanding, a definitive victory over the mystery of iniquity.

While the whole scene is now shrouded in mystery, we can listen to the words of Christ and see the picture of what will happen. His revelation is twice recounted in the closing chapters of St. Matthew's Gospel: "Then shall appear the sign of the Son of Man in the heavens. And then shall all tribes of the earth mourn, and they shall see the Son of man, coming in the clouds of heaven with much power and majesty. And He shall send His angels with a trumpet and a great voice. And they shall gather together His elect from the four winds, from the farthest parts of the heavens to the utmost bounds of them" (24:30–31).

"And when the Son of man shall come in His majesty, and all the angels with Him, then shall He sit upon the seat of His majesty. And *all* nations shall be gathered together before Him, and He shall separate them one from another as the shepherd separates the sheep from the goats. And He shall set the sheep on His right hand but the goats on His left. Then shall the King say to them that shall be on His right hand, Come you blessed of my Father, possess the kingdom prepared for you from the foundation of the world. . . . Then He shall say to them also that shall be on His left hand: Depart from me, you cursed, into everlasting fire which was prepared for the devil and His angels" (Matthew 25:31–34 and 41).

This will be the counterpart of creation when by God's omnipotent power the world was begun and man began the long days of his history. Here at the end, God will write the final page and close the book of mankind's earthly strivings. Good and evil have been mixed together in the pages of that history. Here they will be separated for eternity. We do not know precisely when and where the judging will take place, but we do know that Christ Our Lord will do the judging. And we know that all the questions in the minds of men will be answered, and the light of God's wisdom will pervade every mind. There will be no loose ends, no room left for saying it should have been otherwise, for the story that will be told to everyone will be manifest in the words of divine wisdom and mercy and justice. Even the damned will have to admit that they had every chance and more. The blessed will never cease to praise the Providence of God that through many devious ways brought them to this final end of glory.

D. The End of the World

When all this has come to pass, the world as we know it shall have ended. The final words of St. Peter recorded in his last epistle may well serve as a conclusion to all we have said: "We look for new heavens and a new earth according to His promises, in which justice dwells . . . you therefore brethren, knowing these things before, take heed, lest being led aside by the error of the unwise, you fall from your own steadfastness. But grow in grace, and in the knowledge of Our Lord and Saviour Jesus Christ. To Him be glory both now and unto the day of eternity. Amen" (II Peter 13 and 17–18).

Index

in the teaching of the Church, 96
common to All Three Persons, 97
a divine action, 98
scope, 98
hierarchy, 99
exemplar, 100
time, 101, 114
and Providence, 103
mythical accounts, 104
days of, 107–110
scientific account, 112
and evolution, 112
beginning of time, 114
of souls, 120
Creed:
  Apostles', as an example of tradition, 24
  Nicene, 70, 71
  Apostles', on the Holy Trinity, 72
  Athanasian, on procession in Holy Trinity, 78
  Athanasian, on hell, 223
  Athanasian, on the resurrection of the body, 235
  Nicene, on the resurrection of the body, 235
CRONIN, A. J., 161
CYPRIAN, ST., on original sin, 175

DARWIN, 127
Days of Creation, 107–110
Death:
  reason for, 144
  in Old and New Testament, 144
  freedom from, in Adam, 144
  and immortality in Adam, 145
  natural to man, 145
  as consequence of sin, 204
DE BONALD, 31
de CHARDIN, S.J., P. TEILHARD, on evolution, 112, 113
DE LAMENNAIS, 31
DE LUBAC, S.J., H., on natural and supernatural, 135
DE VAUX, 123
DENZINGER, S.J., H., *Enchiridion Symbolorum*, 25
Devil:
  first temptation, 162
  cursed by God in Paradise, 165

Didache, The:
  as an example of tradition, 24
  trinitarian formula of baptism, 73
Divine Indwelling, of Holy Trinity, 85
Divine Life, shared by men, 151
Divine Missions, The, in Holy Trinity, 79
Dogma:
  in relation to other courses, 1
  as foundation of theology, 8
  definition, 10
  its development, 27, 129
Doppler Shift, 116
DOSTOEVSKI, FYODOR, 190
Doubt, as contrasted from difficulty, 15
Doxologies, Ancient, profess Holy Trinity, 73
du BAY, MICHAEL (BAIUS), on nature of man, 188

EA, 110, 111
Eastern churches, on Holy Trinity, 78
Ecclesiasticus, Book of:
  on the Holy Trinity, 64
  on knowledge of Adam and Eve, 147
ELIOT, T. S., on hell, 224
ELOHIM, 64
Elohistic tradition, 105
ENLIL OF NIPPUR, 106–108
Enuma Elish, 106
EPIPODIUS, 73
Eschatology, 203
ESHARRA, 108
Essence, meaning of term, 136
Eternal Life, 152
Eternity, definition, 43
Eternity of God, 42
Ethics, object, 136
EUPLUS, ST., 73
EVE:
  origin from Adam, 123
  punishment of, 166
Evil, the problem of, 54
Evolution:
  and creation, 112
  Humani Generis on, 113, 120, 121
  God as goal, 113, 129
  of matter, 113
  of life, 119
  of man, 119
  fossil evidence for, 119–121

GOD, Our knowledge of:
  its object, 32
  means, 32
  sources, 32
  mode, 32
GOLD, 114
Grace, a new life, 151
GREGORY, ST., on hell, 228

Heaven:
  mysterious character, 213
  degrees of happiness, 214
HEIDEL, 106
Hell:
  existence, 222
  teaching of Christ, 222
  pain of sense, 225
  pain of loss, 226
  degrees of suffering, 228
HEMINGWAY, ERNEST, 190
HOBBES, THOMAS, 189
Holy Eucharist and Holy Trinity, 86
Holy Saturday, liturgy, 193
HOLY SPIRIT, THE:
  appropriation in the Holy Trinity, 80
  meaning of name in the Holy Trinity, 80
Hominids, 119–125
Homo, genus, 124, 126, 127
Homo Neanderthalensis, 124, 126
Homo Sapiens, 120–128
Homoiousios, 62, 70
HOYLE, 114
Hubble's Constant, 116
Human evolution, 119
Human race, Unity of, 122, 129–132
Humani Generis; encyclical:
  on interpretation of Genesis, 104
  on evolution, 113, 120, 121
  on polygenism, 121
Humanism, Christian, 55
Humans not descended from Adam, 122
HUXLEY, ALDOUS, 190

Ice Age, 126
IGNATIUS OF ANTIOCH, ST., on hell, 222
IMMACULATE CONCEPTION, THE:
  image, 166
  definition, 196
  in the Fathers, 197

feast, 198
  in the scholastics, 198
  popular confusion, 199
  Lourdes, 200
  Sixth Council of Baltimore, 200
  liturgy, 201
Immensity of God, 40, 41
Immortality in Adam, 144
Immutability of God, 44
Incorporation into Christ, 157
Infinity of God, 39
Integrity:
  in Adam, 138
  argument of fittingness, 144
Intelligence, evolution of, 124
Intervention, Divine, in evolution, 120, 128

JAMES, ST., on the immutability of God, 45
Java, 125
JEROME, ST., 22
JESUS CHRIST:
  man's unity in, 129, 130, 131
  the second Adam, 172
JOHN, ST.:
  on Holy Trinity, 67
  on Christian life, 82
  on Holy Eucharist and Indwelling, 86
  on creation, 96
  on God as Alpha and Omega, 129
  on love, 131
  on grace as new life, 151
  on sharing life of God, 152
  on eternal life, 155
Judgment:
  particular, 207
  general, 239
  last judgment in Sacred Scripture, 239
JULIAN THE APOSTATE, 62

Kanjera Man, 126
KIERKEGAARD, SOREN, 190
KISHAR, 111
KNOX, RONALD, 22

LAHAMU, 111
LAHMU, 111
LAMARCK, 127
Last Day, The, teaching of Sacred Scripture, 230